T0313183

Development-Oriented Corporate Social Responsibility
Volume 1

Development-Oriented
Corporate Social
Responsibility

VOLUME 1
MULTINATIONAL CORPORATIONS
AND THE GLOBAL CONTEXT

**Edited by Dima Jamali, Charlotte Karam
and Michael Blowfield**

Routledge
Taylor & Francis Group

LONDON AND NEW YORK

First published 2015 by Greenleaf Publishing Limited

Published 2017 by Routledge
2 Park Square, Milton Park, Abingdon, Oxon OX14 4RN
711 Third Avenue, New York, NY 10017, USA

Routledge is an imprint of the Taylor & Francis Group, an informa business

British Library Cataloguing in Publication Data:
   A catalogue record for this book is available from the British Library.

ISBN-13: 9781783534760 [pbk]
ISBN-13: 9781783532452 [hbk]

Contents

Figures and tables

Acknowledgements

The idea for this book came about at the 2013 Academy of Management annual meeting where we organized a Professional Development Workshop to bring together researchers and practitioners to deliberate and debate the development-oriented potential of corporate social responsibility (CSR) within developing world contexts. In this workshop a vibrant discussion ensued which explored the role of the private sector in serving as a positive change agent in these developing countries. Sparked by this workshop and through the genuine interest and concerted efforts of the editors to gain a better understanding of the peculiar dynamics and expressions of development-oriented CSR in these countries, we embarked on this journey to compile key insights from scholars and practitioners from all around the world and from multiple disciplines. The result is this book.

The growing interest in this topic is evidenced by the outstanding number of submissions we received. Indeed, we were overwhelmed and pleasantly surprised by the positive vibe and enthusiasm that the book generated within a span of a short few months. As we embraced this enthusiasm, and selected key chapters from the submissions, we ended up with two volumes for our edited book rather than one! As CSR continues its ascendancy as a global trend, the compilation of papers spread over two volumes allows us to take stock of what is happening in the domain of CSR in contexts that fall outside the developed core. Such a focus on the developing periphery has, to date, received rather scant attention in the CSR literature. Ultimately, we embarked on this journey to jointly edit this book with the hope to gain an understanding and advance knowledge of the dynamics and peculiarities of CSR in developing countries.

To our readers, we hope that the two volumes provide a rounded and comprehensive understanding of the current practice of CSR in developing countries and the manifold opportunities and constraints. We feel confident, that in combination, the volumes reconcile breadth with depth and provide a solid overview of the CSR landscape across the developing world. In this regard, we wish to extend our most sincere thanks to the authors of the chapters, who have been generous with their time and effort, providing key insights in relation to an important topic, showing willingness to rewrite and fine tune their chapters as well as providing feedback to other authors. The commitment of the contributors made this process more meaningful and created enriched opportunities to share ideas and to further develop their own lines of inquiry relating to development-oriented CSR. We feel fortunate to have worked with each of you and hope that our collective effort contributes to advancing existing knowledge in this important area of research, and invite or entice more writings on this topic.

We also take the opportunity to extend our most sincere gratitude to the various graduate assistants whose help was instrumental in compiling this edited volume. Primary among these is Edwina Zoghbi, whose conscientious follow-up has helped to keep us on track. We also wish to extend sincere thanks to Nadine Mohanna, who, although she joined the team at a later stage, made an instrumental effort in filling final gaps and helping us bring the project to a successful completion. Finally, we wish to acknowledge the great support from the Greenleaf Publisher Team for the professional assistance and follow-up throughout the various phases of this project.

Dima Jamali, Charlotte Karam and Michael Blowfield

Abbreviations and acronyms

AEC	ASEAN Economic Community
AIDS	Acquired Immune Deficiency Syndrome
ALS	Area of Limited Statehood
AMSI	African Mineral Skills Initiative
ASEAN	Association of Southeast Asian Nations
AWCC	Afghan Wireless Communication Company
BAT	British American Tobacco
BBBEE	Broad Based Black Economic Empowerment
BCS	Business Corporatist State
BMWU	Botswana Mine Workers' Union
BOP	bottom of the pyramid
BSC	BHP Billiton Sustainable Communities
CARI	Chevron Aceh Recovery Initiative
CBA	cost–benefit analysis
CBFL	computer-based functional literacy
CC	corporate citizenship
CDA	critical discourse analysis
CDC	Commonwealth Development Corporation
CDP	Carbon Disclosure Project
CED	Committee for Economic Development
CEO	chief executive officer
CII	Confederation of Indian Industry
CIPD	Chartered Institute of Personnel and Development
CMB	Capital Market Boards
CME	Coordinated Market Economy
CONCOR	Container Corporation of India
COO	chief operating officer
CSO	civil society organization

CSR	corporate social responsibility
CSRI	Corporate Social Responsibility Initiative
DAC	OECD Development Assistance Committee
DDS	Dominant Developmental State
DFAT	Australian Government Department of Foreign Affairs and Trade
DFI	Development Finance Institution
DFID	UK Development for International Development
DHS	Demographic and Health Survey
DICA	Myanmar Directorate of Company Administration
DPE	Department of Public Enterprises
EEP	Entrepreneurship Education Programme
EITI	Extractive Industries Transparency Initiative
ESIA	Environmental and Social Impact Assessment
EU	European Union
FAO	Food and Agriculture Organization
FDI	foreign direct investment
FESR	GOM Framework for Economic and Social Reforms
FIMM	Macquarie Infrastructure Fund Mexico
FMCG	fast-moving consumer goods
FPIC	free, prior and informed consent
GDP	gross domestic product
GHBC	Ghana Business Code
GHEITI	Extractive Industries Transparency Initiative
GNI	gross national income
GOI	Government of India
GRI	Global Reporting Initiative
HDI	Human Development Index
HELP	Health, Education, Livelihoods and Public infrastructure
HIV	Human Immunodeficiency Virus
HP	Hewlett Packard
HR	human resources
ICD	Inland Container Depot
ICMM	International Council on Mining and Metals
IFBWW	International Federation of Building and Wood Workers
IFC	International Finance Corporation
IFI	international financial institution
ILO	International Labour Organization
IM	Itaú Microcrédito
IMF	International Monetary Fund
INGO	international non-governmental organization
IOM	International Organization for Migration
ISCT	Integrative Social Contracts Theory
ISKCON	International Society of Krishna Consciousness

ISO	International Organization for Standardization
LDC	least developed country
LME	liberal market economy
LPG	liquefied petroleum gas
LUMS	Lahore University of Management Sciences
MCIT	Ministry of Communication and Information Technology
MDA	Mineral Development Agreements
MDG	Millennium Development Goal
MENA	Middle-East and North Africa
MIC	Myanmar Investment Commission
MIDA	Migration for Development in Africa
MIDCO	Migrants Initiatives for Development of the Country of Origin
MLE	Maximum Likelihood Estimation
MNC	multinational corporation
MNCH	Maternal, Newborn and Child Health
MNE	multinational enterprise
Moroccan CISE	Moroccan Centre for Innovation and Social Entrepreneurship
MOU	memorandum of understanding
MSI	multistakeholder initiative
MSMEs	micro, small and medium-sized enterprises
NDDC	Niger Delta Development Commission
NEEEF	Namibia's New Equitable Economic Empowerment Framework
NGGL	Newmont Ghana Gold Ltd
NGO	non-governmental organization
NPO	not-for-profit organization
NTDA	Non-traditional Development Assistance
NVG	National Voluntary Guideline
ODA	Official Development Assistance
OECD	Organization for Economic Co-operation and Development
OHSAS	Occupational Health and Safety Advisory Services
PP	polypropylene polymer
PPP	public–private partnership
PRI	Principles for Responsible Investment
PSC	Production Sharing Contract
QDB	Qatar Development Bank
RMG	ready-made garment
SABIC	Saudi Basic Industries Corporation
SBLF	Sustainable Business Leadership Forum
SDG	Sustainable Development Goal
SE	social entrepreneurship

SEBI	Securities and Exchange Board of India
SEC	Securities and Exchange Commission
SLME	state-led market economy
SME	small or medium-sized enterprise
SP	Symbolic Politics
SPDC	Shell Petroleum Development Company
SRI	socially responsible investment
TCL	Tsumeb Corporation Ltd
TDA	Traditional Development Assistance
TERI	The Energy and Resources Institute
TNC	transnational corporation
UN	United Nations
UNCAC	UN Convention Against Corruption
UNDP	United Nations Development Programme
UNECA	United Nations Economic Commission for Africa
UNGP	United Nations Guiding Principle
UNICEF	United Nations Children Fund
UNIDO	United Nations Industrial Development Organization
UNGC	United Nations Global Compact
UNGEI	United Nations Girls Education Initiative
USAID	United States Agency for International Development
VPSHR	Voluntary Principles on Security and Human Rights
WBCSD	World Business Council for Sustainable Development
WEBS	World Bank Enterprise Surveys
WEF	World Economic Forum
WHO	World Health Organization
WTO	World Trade Organization

Introduction
Corporate social responsibility in developing countries: a development-oriented approach

Dima Jamali, Charlotte Karam and Michael Blowfield

Since the turn of the millennium, we have witnessed a surge of interest in the notion of corporate social responsibility (CSR) coupled with an explosion in the number of articles, books and chapters written on the topic. CSR is generally used as an umbrella term to describe the complex and multi-faceted relationships between business and society and to account for the economic, social and environmental impacts of business activity. The World Economic Forum (WEF) defines CSR as "the contributions a company makes to society through its core business activities, its social investment and philanthropy programs, and its engagement in public policy. The manner in which a company manages its economic, social and environmental relationships, as well as those with different stakeholders, in particular shareholders, employees, customers, business partners, governments and communities determines its impact" (WEF, 2002, p. 1). We would extend this definition because CSR is as much about what responsibilities companies have as members of society and how these are decided as it is about management practice.

Our concern as we embarked on editing two volumes that comprise this title was precisely not only with the expressions of development-oriented CSR, or the manner in which a company manages its economic, social and environmental relationships, but as importantly with the forms and type of impact that CSR activities have in contexts outside the developed core. While scholarship on CSR in developing countries has been increasing and developing countries today account for most of the searches for CSR using Google Trends as a proportion of total searches worldwide (Crane *et al.*, 2015), there has been very little research that attempts to systematically gauge the impact or outcomes of CSR activities in the developing world. The positive buzz of CSR has thus permeated the developing world, and the language of CSR is becoming more familiar and mainstream (Jamali, 2010; Jamali and Neville, 2011) but the preoccupation has been mostly with types of CSR programs and processes, rather than the more fundamental question of how CSR programs are yielding (or not) tangible developmental benefits in communities around the world. We hence requested our contributors to reflect on CSR in developing countries, with a particular focus on results, outcomes or impacts of CSR programs, and whether we can really speak of development-oriented CSR or business as an effective agent of change in these contexts.

Exploring how the business sector can serve as an effective agent of change in the developing world is important and timely, particularly as self-regulatory conceptions of CSR continue to prevail (Barkemeyer, 2009; Jamali, 2010). Blowfield and Dolan (2014, p. 5) noted a recent shift from business as an unintentional actor in development to business as a conscious agent in intentional development. They note that the current engagement of business in development has come under intense scrutiny in recent years leading an increasing number of companies to abandon their reactive approach to CSR, and to, instead, embrace more proactive and pre-emptive CSR strategies that make a real difference for a myriad of stakeholders in a developing world context. By tackling substantive development challenges ranging from climate change to hazardous waste, nuclear energy, ecological balance, social diversity, human rights and consumer protection, such proactive CSR strategies may hold real developmental promise (ibid.). Blowfield and Dolan (ibid.) further assert that, within the span of less than two decades, private sector actors are more cognizant that it is in their own interest to not only operate in developing countries, but to also help foster the actual development of these countries.

In this book, we further explore the developmental role of the private sector through development-oriented CSR. We invited authors from across the world to reflect critically on the question of business as a development tool as they present their findings and cases pertaining to CSR in developing countries. We were pleasantly surprized with the overwhelming enthusiasm and the wide and interesting coverage of cases and examples of CSR from across the developing world. Indeed, we received chapters exploring CSR and development issues from Sub-Saharan Africa, the Americas, Middle East and North Africa, South Asia, East Asia and Southeast Asia. Even more important were the varied reflections put forth by the authors on the question of business as a development tool and the nature of results or outcomes of CSR programs observed in these developing world contexts. Taken as a whole, the chapters included within this edited book present enriching findings and insights that will likely prove instrumental in advancing our most needed knowledge on the question of development-oriented CSR or business serving as an agent of change in areas of the world where development is most needed.

As revealed in the various chapters, the notion of business as a development agent, and variants of development-oriented CSR, are certainly gaining traction across the developing world. The growth in this regard is met with considerable variation in the actual CSR expressions, with differentiated outcomes and implications in each of the developing countries examined. The contributions to this edited volume make clear that a minority of companies today adhere to the view that the business of business is simply business where the corporation has no obligation to society beyond the creation of economic rents. Instead, it appears that the business–society interface is one imbued with various notions of responsibility. Despite this sense of responsibility, it is also apparent from the contributions that few companies lie at the other end of the continuum, rarely viewing themselves as instruments of public policy or true development agents. From this latter side of the continuum, development-oriented CSR would necessarily involve corporations seeking tangible development benefits or outcomes and acting on behalf of the marginalized, disadvantaged and the poor (Devinney, 2009; Blowfield and Dolan, 2014). Whether focused on the global context of MNC operations in the developing world or on the local context of indigenous business, the majority of companies and cases discussed in the chapters seem to lie somewhere in between.

Overall this edited book includes 26 chapters, 13 of which are more geared toward exploring development-oriented CSR in the global context. Here authors provide interesting insights derived largely from the outside-in, that is, from the global arena to the local developing country context. The remaining 13 chapters adopt a more insider-out perspective, with indigenous voices explored and discussed. The chapters included in both volumes attempt to suggest ways forward for CSR strategies in the developing world that lie closer to the side of instruments or agents of true development agents.

Volume 1

Volume 1 synthesizes a number of perspectives and cases intended to provide insights into the CSR activities of Multinational Corporations (MNCs) and other international and cross-national business entities in developing countries, and gauging their developmental effectiveness. In the age of economic globalization where expanded production networks transcend economic and political divides and where companies continuously search sources of cheap materials and labour, developing countries increasingly represent growth opportunities for MNCs. Providing cases and examples from across the developing world, this volume sheds light on various aspects of MNC CSR interventions in developing countries and salient opportunities and limitations. The contributions to Volume 1 highlight the potential for MNCs to diffuse CSR best practice in the developing world, complement the role of government, and to spearhead various capacity building efforts. However, serious limitations are also highlighted, largely stemming from isolated assessments, limited appreciation of the complexities of context, and the continued permeation of CSR agendas that take their priorities from headquarters largely based in the developed world thereby marginalizing local voices and concerns (Barkemeyer and Figge, 2014). Within the larger debate on the merits and evils of globalization, Volume 1 hence captures a mixed record concerning MNCs promotion of effective development through CSR initiatives in those parts of the world where it is most needed.

More specifically, in this volume there are various contributions that highlight the inherent development potential of CSR in theory and in practice and how it can be leveraged to create effective development tools. Windsor (Chapter 1) proposes a CSR calculus aimed at helping managers make better decisions with regard to having real impact according to the specific context. He outlines seven propositions that function as a decision heuristic for MNC managers in developing countries that take into consideration both global dialogue as well as local discourses. Windsor further suggests that managers can take these into consideration when thinking about responsibility in a specific context. Beyond this heuristic model, other authors provide concrete examples and success cases are highlighted that showcase how CSR can complement the role of governments in bridging governance gaps and spearheading various capacity building efforts across the developing world. For example, Adelopo *et al.* (Chapter 2) present ten case studies from across the Middle East, representing unique interactions between corporations and the state in addressing development challenges that would have normally fallen in the realm of state responsibility. The majority of companies have also realized the importance of CSR in integrating themselves into the fabric of local communities and building social capital and relationships including a positive image, brand equity, legitimacy, trust, and reputation in local markets. It is clear from this volume that for the vast majority of MNCs, CSR programs seem akin to strategic investments comparable to R&D and advertising in the sense that they help overcome nationalistic barriers and build local advantage as suggested by Gardberg and Fombrun (2006, p. 330).

Yet there is also evidence from across the two volumes that companies are prioritizing these instrumental considerations pertaining to reputation and social capital over considerations of meaningful and substantive interventions. Kemp *et al.* (Chapter 3), for example, note how the CSR program of a mining company in Southeast Asia prioritizes short-term land access and reputational gain and serves to buffer the company from community complaints and what its managers perceive as unmanageable demands. They warn of the danger of conducting isolated CSR interventions and assessments in the context of the complex and dynamic environments characteristic of the developing world. Similarly, Barkemeyer *et al.* (Chapter 4) note the prevalence of a strategic and centralized approach to CSR among MNCs in developing countries which marginalizes genuine development and reduces the opportunity to respond to the concerns of local communities. Along the same lines, Ramirez (Chapter 5) notes how MNCs seem to go about their business in developing countries and implement CSR programs without consultation with indigenous groups and other salient stakeholders. Similarly,

Bolzani and Marabello (Chapter 6) note how CSR initiatives in Ghana have been mostly identified and planned for in the Global North (Italy) without soliciting feedback from Ghanaian local counterparts.

This volume also presents some evidence associating business with developmentally detrimental outcomes across the developing world, including human and labour rights abuses and environmental degradation. For example, Littlewood and Russon (Chapter 7) note the considerable potential of MNCs to negotiate their development responsibilities, and the significant environmental liabilities and negative development impact of mining companies in Namibia. They warn that the weakness of legislation in developing countries, coupled with the government's pro-mining orientation, may seriously curtail corporate accountability. Similarly, Yap (Chapter 8) notes the virtual absence of countervailing policy and social forces across the developing world allowing private enterprises to define what development can and cannot mean. Various authors note the need for pressure groups and civil society organizations in developing countries to come together and exert a countervailing force to lobby companies to intervene in substantive development issues including poverty alleviation, employment creation, countervailing corruption, and boosting legislation and taxation compliance. Belal (Chapter 9) invokes the need for a surrogate (i.e. proxy) accountability as an alternative to the current corporate driven form of accountability, whereby corporations can be held to account by the civil sector on behalf of the victims of corporate activities in developing countries.

Finally, this volume also includes a detailing of specific cases of MNC CSR strategies and practices in specific developing countries. For example, Uyan-Atay and Tuncay-Celikel (Chapter 10) describe the publishing of CSR reports and compare MNCs to local Turkish conglomerates in the impact of their CSR activities. A second example comes from Husain and Lund-Thomsen (Chapter 11), who explore the limited provision of benefits that meet the needs of the sexual and reproductive health of female employees in the football manufacturing industry of Pakistan. Although the authors identify the CSR strategies of a single manufacturer that provides clear benefits, the overwhelming picture is of limited provision of these benefits to the employees of local suppliers. The final example comes from the chapter by Amini and Dal Bianco (Chapter 12), who detail the CSR initiatives of an immigrant-led transnational entity—Ghanacoop. The analysis of the CSR activities of this transnational agro-food cooperative based in Italy found that diaspora engagement in CSR does not necessarily guarantee local or Southern-driven CSR actions but rather that the CSR and development discourses were largely Northern-based and therefore lacked specificity in terms of a clear development agenda for local Ghanaian development.

After the review of these chapters, the promise of MNCs' development-oriented CSR as the way forward for positive development in these local contexts in unclear. The source of this lack of clarity lies at the doors of multiple stakeholders with competing and different interests grounded in a complex global–local contextual puzzle. Many of the authors, in acknowledging this complexity, call for a forward path toward developmental CSR that works to address the needs and issues of multiple stakeholders. Tackling this complexity requires an integration of these multiple stakeholders' perspectives into the design and implementation of CSR strategies. For example, Huber and Gilbert (Chapter 13) recommend that such integration should be facilitated by framing CSR as political and corporations as political actors. Such framing opens opportunities for greater engagements in multistakeholder initiatives (MSIs) and therefore greater engagement with a wider breadth of concerned people, groups and entities. These authors further assert that attention should be given to the role of civil society organizations (CSOs) as they can help to better embed corporations in public deliberations about development. Other recommendations for taking development-oriented CSR forward include the need for companies to enforce capacity-building measures that ensure a better integration and acknowledgment of non-salient stakeholders and reducing the resource dependency of Southern NGOs on their Northern counterparts (Barkemeyer *et al.*, Chapter 4); applying the principle of volunteering to guide CSR (Adelopo *et al.*, Chapter 2); embedding a development orientation into the values, structures, practices and decision-making of companies (Littlewood and Russon, Chapter 7); and strengthening and promoting non-corporate actors (e.g. civil society entities, trade unions) as accountability holders for corporations (Belal, Chapter 9) among others.

Volume 2

Volume 2 of our book provides more localized perspectives of CSR efforts spearheaded by local or indigenous actors from across the developing world. This volume collects insights and perspectives from countries that are at various stages of economic development, including Myanmar, Botswana, Russia, Afghanistan, China, Ghana, Kenya, Tanzania, India, Brazil and some nations within the Arab world. Through empirical examples, this volume highlights successful and less successful examples of locally led CSR efforts, and captures the complex paradoxes of CSR including the enigma of self-interested actors voluntarily providing social services and public goods in the context of weakened states and institutional environments. The heterogeneity in national institutional profiles across the developing world is hard to conceptualize in a singular model ever with multiple factors. Indeed, the chapters in this volume highlight a myriad of factors shaping CSR. Additionally, however, there are persistent and durable features that are commonly discussed in a number of the chapters (e.g. weak political and regulatory institutions) that often work to limit the developmental impact of CSR. Further, what comes across through this volume is the need to embrace partnership models that leverage the strengths of different actors (government, non-profit, international organizations) to promote effective development and tackle the complex challenges (e.g.

poverty, unemployment, corruption, weak legislation, taxation evasion) facing the developing world.

More specifically, in this volume there are various contributions that expand the field of consideration to include multiple stakeholders in the local context. In this regard, the chapters in this second volume provide insights into unique challenges and considerations that are only perceptible from the insider-out and not from the perspective of the global arena. From a local perspective Volume 2 brings context front and centre, thereby highlighting a myriad of salient factors that help to better paint a picture of the potentiality and limitations of development-oriented CSR. Generally speaking, key contextual factors explored by the authors include, for example: level of governance and corruption; level of statehood and strong and weak states; pressures from market anarchy; pressures from traditional communities; worker migration patterns and legal structures; rate of economic progress; socio-cultural institutional structures; national socio-political settings; relationships between state–civil society–business; levels of obstructionism; as well as local realities relating to poverty, legislation, economic opportunities, vested interest groups, incompetent government agencies, and the changing regulatory environment for CSR. These contextual factors are expansive and are likely to be relevant to many developing nations. Each chapter focuses on a sub-set of these and explores how these shape the possibilities for development-oriented CSR.

For example, Turkina *et al.* (Chapter 1) argue that the developmental type of CSR activity will depend, in fact, largely, on the institutional context of the specific developing country. Examining differences between mining companies in Russia versus Botswana, these authors illustrate the utility of theorizing context (e.g., corruption, employee–community relations) in shaping CSR programs in a specific developing national context. As a second example, Ahen (Chapter 2) explores the contextual dynamics of the Ghanaian pharmaceutical SMEs marred by vested interest groups, incompetent government agencies and other obstructionist factors using post-colonial theory. He asserts that in this context development-oriented CSR is based on strategic ethical leadership of individual businesspersons who create innovative channels to overcome the barriers of context and provide access to medicines.

Including contextual factors as part of the analytic lens through which CSR researchers explore and map local expressions of CSR in developing countries is a fundamental characteristic of this body of literature. The chapters in the volume certainly attest to the importance of this exploration and mapping. Expanding the analytic lens to include such heterogeneous and irregular contextual factors carries with it a burden of complexity often leading to the obscuring of the analytical frameworks commonly used in CSR literature. Across the board, the contributors to the second volume paint pictures of complex landscapes with inherent complex and problematic dynamics that are socio-politically, geo-economically and historically grounded. Such landscapes do not easily fit within the frameworks developed and used in CSR literature on developed nations.

It is perhaps this realization that explains the efforts of a number of chapters in this volume to propose analytic frameworks or typologies to make sense of and/or tease apart some of these contextual complexities. For example, Azizi (Chapter 3) highlights poverty and limits of statehood as two salient contextual factors triggering companies to engage in particular forms of CSR. He proposes a business–poverty analytic framework which includes three categories of (conditions of/responses to) business responses to developmental issues: for example, when businesses view themselves as victims of poverty versus as solutions to poverty. A separate chapter by Jain and Jamali (Chapter 4), similarly, proposes a CSR typology which considers CSR approaches in terms of their core business relatedness, the target of CSR activities, as well as the expected benefits and proposes three types of CSR: Philanthropy, CSR Integration, or CSR Innovation. These authors then apply the typology to tease out the CSR approaches of Indian versus Arab companies and note striking differences between the two.

Furthermore, Jeppesen and Azizi (Chapter 5) also propose an analytic frame-work. This is a two-pronged lens which includes either a governance approach which considers socio-political governance issues, the role of the state, and the relationship between state, civil society actors, industries and specific firms; or a responsible business approach which considers local values and norms and differentiating between strong and weak states. The authors argue that both avenues are important in understanding the possibility of development-oriented CSR in developing countries. Finally Mitra and Warshay (Chapter 6) explore through critical discourse analysis the 2013 India Companies Act vis-à-vis prevalent CSR practices in India. Their findings provide interesting insights about ways to think about and categorize CSR and tease out the discursive prac-tices surrounding CSR including: local/global, developmental/economic, and mandatory/obligatory.

Finally, similar to Volume 1, this volume also includes a detailing of specific cases of CSR strategies and practices but in this case those initiated by local businesses in specific developing countries. Examining specific cases of CSR practices, a number of authors provide concrete recommendations to help build a better road map to move forward. For example, Bisley and Coyne (Chapter 7) explore how development-oriented CSR initiatives differ from other more traditional development programming in Myanmar and note that differences exist along the drivers to undertake CSR activities; the development needs addressed; and the nature of the actors involved. In India Thakur *et al.* (Chapter 8) detail an interesting and informative case of the Indian company CONCOR and present it as a successful example of development-oriented CSR. Describing the particular CSR model devised by this firm, the implementation steps as well as the impact, the authors argue for the importance of creating an enabling environment. Also in India and in the context of new regulations mandating CSR, Ray (Chapter 9) embarks on a qualitative examination of two Indian mining companies and highlights the key role of partnerships in such instances. He further argues for the need for better partnership models that deliver the goal of business-funded inclusive development. Finally, Marconatto *et al.* (Chapter 10) also focus on a case-in-point by examining the Brazilian Bank Itaú. This chapter explores the interface between microfinance and strategic CSR and the potential to contribute to economic and social development in Brazil. Both sides of the argument are presented but the authors conclude that the bank fails to, for example, engage the bottom of the pyramid and to relieve poverty and therefore may raise important questions about the true developmental nature of the CSR–microfinance operations of the bank.

The last three chapters also focus explicitly on specific case examples, but provide insights into the lives of individual citizens. Hack-Polay and Qiu (Chapter 11), for example, bring to light the plight and significant importance of migrant workers to China's rapid development and the role that companies and state can, together and through CSR programming, play in better addressing the needs of these workers, hence changing the traditional socio-cultural institutional structures that perpetuate societal inequalities in China. A second example, giving individual citizens a face, is the chapter by Andrawes and McMurray (Chapter 12), who adopt a unique perspective on the possibilities for development-oriented CSR partnerships. The contributors explore what they refer to as a spiritual corporate awakening, and provide qualitative examples from Ghana, Kenya and Tanzania with regards to engaging in CSR activities conceived at the intersection of design thinking and international development.

The volume ends with a critical examination of the role of accounting education in facilitating more developmentally oriented CSR practices in India. The authors of this chapter, Tejura and Girardi (Chapter 13), suggest that corporate aspects of their cultural heritage should be integrated within the accounting syllabus, particularly those that help to cement the need for CSR. The authors point to the need to educate and equip future generations of accounting professionals in the developing world to think about local applications. They also caution against the blind adoption of Western accounting which inculcates in students the idea that CSR is optional and voluntary. Accounting systems, it is proposed, should from the outset teach students to measure the impact of corporations on the rest of society.

In closing, each of the chapters in this volume highlights key recommendations for taking development-oriented CSR forward. Some of these recommendations include: meeting the needs of migrant workers (Chapter 11); rethinking governance approaches and structures to trigger CSR (Chapter 5); recognition and development of responsible leaders (Chapter 2); addressing the specific and pressing needs of local communities such as water solutions, agricultural solutions and educational facilities (Chapter 8); building better partnerships between NGOs and businesses (Chapter 9); and designing better educational curricula that mainstream CSR as a significant consideration (Chapter 13).

Conclusions

Taken as a whole, the evidence emerging from our two volumes regarding development-oriented CSR or the ability of business to serve as development agent does not allow simplistic conclusions to be drawn, whether they be about the benevolence, barbarity or intentions of business. While there is growing appreciation of the importance of strategic philanthropy and how it can help build long-term advantages for companies by enhancing their local embeddedness, their legitimacy, and the institutional contexts in which they operate (Gardberg and Fombrun, 2006), the constraints facing development-oriented CSR are real as documented throughout the two volumes. Value creation continues to be defined using traditional criteria such as efficiency, productivity and the instrumental value of actions to business rather than the benefits for the poor or otherwise marginalized. There are few companies that have been successful at consciously creating a wider pool of value across the developing world. Furthermore, the compilation of evidence from the two volumes highlights the continued preoccupation of business with instrumental considerations, which can severely restrict their ability to serve as true development agents. According to Blowfield and Dolan (2014), the very ideas of the poor, poverty, beneficiary, and development-worthiness are being constructed around what is material, instrumental and comprehensible to business. This is a trend evident around the world, and some economists in particular would argue that developing countries are doing better in tackling poverty and marginalization than the post-industrial economies of the OECD. However, in terms of infrastructure, governance, incomes, balance of the economy, and national wealth, "developing country" remains a valid concept, even if not in the ways the pioneers of international development described in the 1960s and 1970s. For as long as this remains the case, and particularly as new "development-oriented" initiatives such as the Sustainable Development Goals become the focus of the international government and business community's attention, the notion of specific forms of CSR theory and practice shaped by the situation in developing countries remains valid. A key issue that this book brings to the surface is the importance of establishing a development ethos that is congruent with the aspirations of and recognizable to people in those countries, and not something that is considered legitimate simply because it sits comfortably with the norms, values and priorities of certain groups in the North or elsewhere.

What seems particularly challenging is the virtual absence of true evidence-based impact, documenting which CSR programs have yielded positive benefits, and especially which ones go beyond what Blowfield (2013) calls "pilot paralysis" to become scalable. In this respect, context seems important in discussions of development-oriented CSR. As suggested by Gardberg and Fombrun (2006, p. 336), context does matter and determines the appropriateness of CSR programs. Varying contexts present distinct institutional environments, and make different demands on companies, granting them varying levels of legitimacy and performance (ibid.). Institutions have persistent and durable features and hence enduring implications for CSR expressions. The characteristics of institutions work to amplify or constrain the developmental impact of CSR across the developing world. The contributions to this book invite us to think about the potential fundamental and latent precursors of CSR, especially at the country level, and the influence of historically grown national business systems and frameworks including economic, political and cultural institutions and institutional heritage (Jamali and Neville, 2011).

As a whole, the two volumes provide key insights into the opportunities and limitations for businesses to serve as development agents in developing countries. The chapters combined also accentuate the need for further comparative research on CSR that would enhance our understanding of how CSR can be better mobilized to address the endemic developmental challenges of the developing world. The contributions to this book also invite us to think more about the potential institutional determinants affecting CSR, especially at the national level, and whether CSR in either theory or practice is failing to live up to its promise in the developing world because of the paradox of self-interested actors or because of latent yet potent institutional heritage. In this respect, we agree to an extent with Devinney (2009) that CSR itself is not de facto good or bad, and that, like any organizational instrument, it is neutral depending on how it is used in a specific context by interested actors. However, what Devinney and some of our contributors are referring to is CSR defined as management practice. It is undeniably true that some of the practices undertaken in the name of CSR by local and multinational companies would have been difficult to imagine a few decades ago when business leaders and policy-makers alike would have been far more forthcoming than they are today that companies deliver development good when they do what business does best. Unfortunately, it has been evident since the 1980s that some of what business does in developing countries, such as hazardous working conditions, exploitative labour practices and environmental neglect, is not always what is good for local people or even itself.

This realization spurred a revitalized interest in CSR that has spread across the global economy. But an emphasis on CSR simply as management practice disguises the fact that CSR is not neutral: it is the manifestation of a set of ideas rooted in a moral project and this means that there is tension and dispute about what CSR means and ever can mean. CSR is situated within economic globalization which, although typically portrayed as an amoral and even a historical system, is ultimately a moral project that regards as universalizable particular ideas of good, utility, flourishing, prosperity and moral creditworthiness. Modern CSR is a battleground on which the rights and wrongs of that project are being fought over. The skirmishes, tactics and weapons of the battle are evident in many of the contributions to this book.

How long the moral project continues, given the array of interconnected mega-challenges such as climate change and population growth that threaten it, is open to debate, and perhaps the experiences of implementing CSR will inform the way companies tackle these challenges. But the authors in our two volumes are focused on the here and now, and their examples and arguments succeed in lifting the fog of CSR to provide evidence about what the moral project permits or prohibits in terms of development outcomes. Some of the contributors are angry about what they see, some are pleased, and some see it as a challenge to improve. But collectively by lifting the fog they reveal that, although there is much that is not permissible given the norms and values of modern capitalism, there is significant opportunity to extend its boundaries so that genuine development outcomes are achieved through the actions of business.

Bibliography

Barkemeyer, R. (2009). Beyond compliance: below expectations? Cross-border CSR, development and the UN Global Compact. *Business Ethics: A European Review*, 18(3), 273-289.

Barkemeyer, R., & Figge, F. (2014). CSR in multiple environments: the impact of headquartering. *Critical Perspectives on International Business*, 10(3), 124-151.

Blowfield, M. (2013). *Business and Sustainability*. Oxford, UK: Oxford University Press.

Blowfield, M., & Dolan, C. (2014). Business as a development agent: evidence of possibility and improbability. *Third World Quarterly*, 35(1), 22-42.

Crane, A., Henriques, I., Husted, B., & Matten, D. (2015). A new era for business & society. *Business & Society*, 54(1), 3-8.

Devinney, T.M. (2009). Is the socially responsible corporation a myth? The good, the bad, and the ugly of corporate social responsibility. *Academy of Management Perspectives*, 23(2), 44-56.

Gardberg, N., & Fombrun, C. (2006). Corporate citizenship: creating intangible assets across institutional environments. *Academy of Management Review*, 31(2), 329-346.

Jamali, D. (2010). The CSR of MNC subsidiaries in developing countries: global, local, substantive or diluted? *Journal of Business Ethics*, 93(2), 181-200.

Jamali, D., & Neville, B. (2011). Convergence versus divergence of CSR in developing countries: an embedded multi-layered institutional lens. *Journal of Business Ethics*, 102(4), 599-621.

WEF (World Economic Forum) (2002). Global corporate citizenship initiative. Retrieved from http://www.weforum.org/pdf/GCCI/GCCI_CEO_Questionnaire.pdf.

1

A corporate social responsibility calculus

Global dialogue and local discourses

Duane Windsor
Jones Graduate School of Business, USA

This study proposes the concept and application of a multi-dimensional corporate social responsibility calculus for use by managers. This responsibility calculus is a heuristic and not an algorithm. The purpose is to help managers think about responsibility more concretely in specific country and issue contexts than conveyed by the general ideas of corporate social responsibility or corporate citizenship. Assuming mandatory compliance with laws and ethics, the emphasis is on voluntary corporate citizenship beyond compliance. Voluntary assumption of responsibility is subject to definition of limits and to variation in local circumstances. A calculus suggests some kind of propositional inventory that aids a decision-maker, such as a manager, and is intended to be a more or less formal system separate from the specific applications. This study distinguishes between global dialogue about universal standards and local discourses about context-specific decisions. An illustration for Eastern Europe and examples from developing countries are discussed.

This study proposes the concept and illustrative application of a multi-dimensional corporate social "responsibility calculus" for use by managers. In the rest of the chapter, the shorter term responsibility calculus will be used for convenience. In this chapter, the notion of a "calculus" has the sense of a reasoning framework or approach drawing on logical propositions. The purpose is to help managers think about responsibility more concretely in specific country contexts than is conveyed by the general ideas of corporate social responsibility (CSR) or corporate citizenship (CC). The term "multidimensional" means that the analysis problem cannot be reduced to a single criterion such as profit maximization (Jensen, 2001) but rather unavoidably concerns two or more dimensions, which must be weighted in some way (Brenner, 1995; Martin, 2002), that cannot be formalized theoretically. The term "social" can mean a society (i.e., the public interest or some aggregation of constituency interests) or specific stakeholder groups within this society (e.g. communities, customers, employees, or suppliers). The application of the proposed calculus is thus intended to occur by country (whether home or host). How to aggregate customers (or any other stakeholder group) across two or more countries is a separate step or consideration. A single solution may serve, or there may be country-specific solutions.

In effect, the approach is intended to organize or structure responsibility assessments being made by managers. Such assessment may include predicted return (Martin, 2002), positive or negative, but will be broader than return. The reason is that a responsibility calculus will involve both tangible and intangible dimensions (Brent, 2006b), the weighting of which by managers (or others) will be difficult (Brent, 2006a) and thus require heuristic rather than algorithmic handling. Non-measureable intangibles require subjective evaluation, relative to more objective evaluation feasible with measurable tangibles, a matter long addressed in economic (or social) cost–benefit literature (Murphy and Simon, 2002). Cost–benefit analysis (CBA) with intangible dimensions may be a reasonable analogy to the proposed responsibility calculus. There are also indirect effects (or repercussions) to be considered in CBA (Rouwendal, 2012).

A calculus in the most general sense of the term suggests some kind of propositional inventory (which may be complex or rudimentary in content) that aids a decision-maker, such as a manager, and is intended to be a more or less formal system separate from specific applications. The proposed responsibility calculus is a heuristic rather than an algorithm. An algorithm, as the term is classically used in mathematics and computer science, is a step-by-step procedure for making calculations typically involving numbers. An illustration would be a discounted cash flow analysis or narrowly economic CBA, which involve calculations with numbers expressed in currency units. Estimating the return on investment of a CSR initiative would involve an algorithm of this kind. A heuristic is a decision-making aid that is substituted when an algorithm procedure is not feasible. In a broad sense, a pure heuristic is a short cut to a solution that draws on experience and/or trial-and-error experimentation. The development of a propositional inventory is intended to help position a responsibility calculus away from a pure heuristic of this kind and toward a somewhat more algorithmic approach. Manager judgment will nevertheless necessarily draw on experience and experimentation, as an illustration and some examples in Section 1.3 will suggest. The essence of a logical calculus is its validity (internal and external) and usefulness to a manager.

This study distinguishes between global dialogue about universal standards and local discourses about context-specific decisions. A global dialogue can occur in various international forums and through the development of international policy regimes (see Preston and Windsor, 1997). The term "discourses" means conversations between firms and local stakeholders, including governments, concerning CSR matters. These conversations may occur in various ways, including formal and informal bargaining. This distinction is partly, but only partly, about moral universalism and cross-cultural moral relativism (Demuijnck, 2014). In this chapter, the distinction permits variations in local contexts concerning expectations of firms and managers but only to the extent that such variations do not violate universal standards which are binding on those firms (domestic or multinational) and managers. For instance, corruption may be a widespread sociological phenomenon in particular countries and one might thus make an argument justifying such country-level variation in corruption as cross-cultural moral relativism. There is however, a UN Convention against Corruption (UNCAC, adopted December 2003 and effective December 2005) and the tenth principle of the UN Global Compact (added in 2004) is an anti-corruption position based on the UNCAC.

The distinction used in this chapter draws on Donaldson and Dunfee's (1999) integrative social contracts theory (ISCT). In the ISCT framework, local standards are acceptable so long as they do not violate global standards. By extension, local CSR requirements can exceed global standards. The European Union (EU) arguably frames higher expectations of domestic firms and multinational enterprises (MNEs) than global standards reflected in the UN Global Compact principles (EC, 2011). Donaldson and Dunfee view global standards as reflecting both rational consensus and historical evolution. A first step is to define global standards (bearing in mind ISO 26000 CSR guidance) through global dialogue; a second step is to investigate local variations exceeding or applying those standards in detail. The constraint imposed in this chapter is that local practices by managers cannot fall below global standards, although local practices can exceed global standards increasing CSR requirements for managers.

The rest of this chapter is organized as follows. The following section explains some basic considerations in CSR theorizing including key debates that may affect development of this proposed responsibility calculus. Section 1.2 focuses on exposition of the proposed multidimensional responsibility calculus through a set of propositions. Section 1.3 provides an illustration and some examples to help make the responsibility calculus concrete for the reader and managers. The final section gives the author's reflections on how the proposed responsibility calculus can contribute development-oriented CSR.

1.1 Key debates concerning CSR

The theoretical concept of CSR continues to be a topic of considerable controversy among scholars. The most negative view argues that voluntary CSR beyond minimalist legal and ethical standards is pure altruism constituting bad business practice adverse to proper roles of business and government in society. In a negative view, a key issue is how far minimalist standards, or the legal and ethical floor, can be reduced toward 19th century laissez faire conditions devoid of any legal and ethical standards under the guise of profit maximization. The most positive view argues that CSR, especially for MNEs operating in developing countries, is expansively "political"—meaning that corporations should be responsible for public goods provision where government lacks capacity and responsible for promoting internal and societal democracy in all countries (Morsing and Roepstorff, 2014; Scherer and Palazzo, 2011).

In practice, managers use the language of responsibility—as well as of citizenship and stakeholder dialogue—and position businesses along the continuum between the minimalist and expansive conceptions of CSR. Managers must also craft policies, make decisions, and allocate resources concerning social issues—in the case of MNEs across a wide array of countries at different levels of economic, political, and social development. Managers will also consider how to calculate return on CSR initiatives (Martin, 2002).

Three key questions concerning CSR are whether: (1) CSR is good or bad business practice?; (2) CSR has a global definition or involves local variations across countries?; and (3) MNEs, typically from advanced countries, have special and higher responsibilities when operating in developing countries?

This study addresses the second and third questions and argues that answers to those questions shape the answer to the first question. A negative view of CSR simply precludes any other questions. Literature addressing these three questions tends to do so at a high level of abstraction. One thinks that CSR is good or bad practice, is defined globally or locally, and is appropriately imposed disproportionately on MNEs relative to domestic firms or not. ISO 26000 is a guideline, not a certification standard (unlike other ISO standards), because of the difficulties in defining CSR.

A proposed multidimensional responsibility calculus draws on Donaldson and Dunfee's (1999) ISCT, as mentioned in the introduction. A first step is to define global standards (bearing in mind ISO 26000) through global dialogue; a second step is to investigate local variations exceeding or applying those standards in detail. Local standards are acceptable so long as they do not violate global standards. This argument implies that local CSR requirements can exceed global standards but cannot fall below. So, if the EU frames higher expectations of domestic firms and MNEs than global standards (reflected in UN Global Compact principles), such framing is plainly acceptable and arguably desirable.

Figure 1.1 facilitates consideration of logical possibilities for relationships between universal standards and local discourses. The horizontal axis is a continuum for

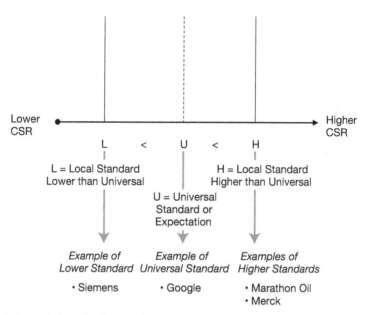

Figure 1.1 **Local standards in relationship to universal standards**

CSR standards or expectations ranging from lower CSR on the left to higher CSR on the right. The dashed vertical line at the centre of the CSR continuum reflects a proposed or recognized universal standard (U) on a specific matter. In this continuum, L is lower than U which is lower than H. A specific country may have a local standard L that is below the universal standard U. In the figure, this lower local standard is shown to the left of the universal standard. A specific country may have a local standard H that is above the universal standard U. In the figure, this higher local standard is shown to the right of the universal standard. Each country can have a different L or H located along the horizontal axis. Both universal standards and absence of universal standards can be depicted as follows.

In a depiction in which U exists, a firm must locate either at U or at H; the firm cannot properly locate at L. The purpose of any international policy regime development (Preston and Windsor, 1997) on a specific issue is to encourage L countries to move toward U in accordance with the Donaldson and Dunfee expectation.

The basic alternative to this depiction is that there is no universal standard (or such a standard is widely disputed): then U effectively disappears from Figure 1.1 and all local discourses default to an L or H positioned relative to one another. A firm can locate at L or at H by country as a function of choice shaped by internal firm values and firm strategic considerations. The firm can also choose to adopt the highest H everywhere.

For purposes of a multidimensional responsibility calculus, U can vary by dimension. The anti-corruption standard is universal: no firm can properly locate at corruption discourse L. But, within both the UN Global Compact and the UN human rights regime, the relationship between firm responsibility and local standards concerning human rights is still being worked out. Thus U is not well developed as yet. The final report of the special representative on human rights, John Ruggie (UN Human Rights Council, 2011), is a "Respect, Protect, and Remedy" framework. The first guiding principle for this framework assigns to governments (or states) the "existing obligations to respect, protect and fulfil human rights and fundamental freedoms." The second guiding principle is that businesses are "organs of society" that must comply with laws and respect human rights. The third guiding principle concerns remedies when rights and obligations are violated—by governments or businesses. The framework does not itself create new international law with respect to human rights definition and protection. A firm can locate at L in one country and H in another country—by choice.

The company examples below the figure should be read vertically. Siemens is an instance of violation of a universal standard. Google is an instance of a universal standard. Marathon and Merck are instances of CSR activities that are higher than a universal standard.

The Siemens bribery scandal illustrates an example in which a firm violates a universal standard U, which also happens to be a local legal standard everywhere, and does so because sociologically corruption varies greatly by country and the firm can take advantage of this variation. In terms of Figure 1.1, as depicted, Siemens located itself at L because there were various countries that tolerated L, in violation of universal standards expressed in the UNCAC. US and German authorities determined that Siemens had operated by systematic corruption in various countries, often through agents or middlemen (Baron, 2008; Schubert and Miller, 2008). Siemens ultimately paid US$1.6 billion in fines to US and German authorities, to which one must add substantial internal investigation and reform costs. One study using data for about 20 countries reports that robust legal enforcement can have a deterrent effect on the propensity of firms based in those countries to engage in bribery (Sanyal and Samanta, 2011). The authors conclude that international cooperation can result in a successful prosecution of such bribery.

A different situation is illustrated by Google in China. In this instance, Google is located at U with respect to internet access and privacy of communication as an asserted value which is, however, arguably not a universal standard U. China, a one-party state located at L relative to Google, interferes markedly with internet access and privacy of communication. The situation might be viewed as a cross-cultural ethical conflict (Hamilton *et al.*, 2009). The Google stance is an instance of civil disobedience, a special case in which there is a responsibility not to comply fully with local standards set by government—the disobedience must be based on an asserted U. Both the motives and actions of Google might be criticized on various grounds. But Google acts basically to protect Chinese citizens from coercion by their government. Fundamentally the Chinese government is a self-perpetuating authoritarian regime or collective dictatorship although not a strong-man dictatorship in the classic sense of a dictator, and Google asserts a claim to be at the leading edge of social media freedom (Google, nd).

1.2 Developing a multidimensional responsibility calculus

Firms are mobile and thus can avoid local but not global standards by shifting location. In Figure 1.1, the dashed line marked U disappears if there is no universal standard. Then a mobile firm can choose between L and H without violating U. A recent illustration is the April 2014 decision of the board of Weatherford International Limited, an oil field services company trading on the New York Stock Exchange, to recommend to their shareholders moving the corporate headquarters from Switzerland (Geneva) to Ireland. The board acted following a decision by the Swiss Federal Council in November 2013 to permit shareholders to make binding votes on compensation of executives and board directors while prohibiting severance payments to departing executives. Weatherford had moved to Geneva five years previously, while keeping the operational office in Houston, Texas. In June 2014, the shareholders approved a decision to merge into a new subsidiary Weatherford Ireland which would become the publicly traded parent company (Cain, 2014; Eaton, 2014). Movement to Ireland did not violate a recognized universal standard and the move was legal if approved by shareholders and Ireland. However, in November 2013, Weatherford International and three subsidiaries pleaded guilty to US anti-bribery and export controls violations and agreed to more than US$252 million in fines and penalties (US Department of Justice, 2013).

There has been increasing criticism of corporate practices that involve avoidance of taxes in one country by shifting profits to other countries. In April 2014, the US Senate investigations subcommittee released a report that Caterpillar had avoided paying US$2.4 billion in US taxes since 2000 through shifting profits to a wholly controlled affiliate in Switzerland (AP, 2014). Such tax avoidance is legal. While Senator Carl Levin (Democrat, Michigan), chair of the subcommittee, criticized such avoidance (as at other companies being examined), Senator Rand Paul (Republican, Kentucky) argued that Caterpillar has a responsibility to shareholders to minimize corporate taxes legally. There is no universal standard concerning tax avoidance practices, and the shift is legal if acceptable under US and Swiss laws. The point of the Levin criticism is that US tax policy should be changed (Desai and Dharmapala, 2009; Keightley and Sherlock, 2014).

Application of a responsibility calculus as explicated here involves consideration of the differences between advanced and developing countries. The reason is that the condition of developing countries arguably imposes greater responsibilities on MNEs in particular (Scherer and Palazzo, 2011). Table 1.1 lists seven verifiable logical propositions. More propositions may be identified in time (for instance, one might develop a set of propositions focused on advanced countries—see Proposition 1).

Each proposition is stated *ceteris paribus* (i.e., holding all other propositions constant). A responsibility calculus considers all dimensions simultaneously to identify the specific responsibilities of specific MNEs in particular countries. Proposition 7 on political CSR is arguably the broadest and most controversial, but the proposition reflects a growing body of scholarship concerning responsible business–government relations. Governments in developing countries may lack effective capacity and resources (as illustrated by the 2014 Ebola crisis in West Africa). These governments are also often riddled with corruption. Such widespread corruption is a serious problem for firms. At a minimum, firms should practice responsible lobbying in advanced countries and avoid engaging in the corruption of government and political officials in developing countries. Google in China is difficult to interpret without invoking some level of Proposition 7 (see Figure 1.1).

Table 1.1 **List of seven proposed propositions and their implications**

	Proposition	Implications
1	Overall need for economic and social development is more acute in developing countries.	Proposition 1 implies that MNEs should prioritize CSR activities in relationship to need. Rawls's (1999) principle of assisting the disadvantaged is relevant on a cross-country basis. Acute needs can be found within advanced countries as well: Porter's work on the Initiative for a Competitive Inner City (ICIC) in US cities illustrates that such acute needs exist in US inner cities (Porter, 2011). The assertion of Proposition 1 is that overall need is more acute in developing countries.
2	MNEs headquartered outside host countries play a critical role in meeting development needs through investment and operation.	Proposition 2 implies that MNEs from advanced countries are an essential source of development resources through both investment and operation. This proposition does not restrict MNEs simply to business activities because Proposition 2 is subordinate to Proposition 1. Developing countries typically cannot generate sufficient resources domestically.
3	MNEs and domestic firms are subject to a capability or competence requirement. The greater a firm's capability or competence to address local needs, the greater is its responsibility to do so.	Proposition 3 implies that CSR is limited by capability or competence. Responsibility cannot simply be imposed, internally or externally, without regard for capacity to act effectively. Responsibility rises with capability or competence.
4	MNEs and domestic firms are subject to a resources requirement. The greater a firm's resources, the greater is its responsibility to address local needs.	Analogously to Proposition 3, Proposition 4 implies that CSR is limited by resources. Responsibility cannot simply be imposed, internally or externally, without regard for resources to deploy. Responsibility rises with resources.
5	The greater the relative bargaining power of the developing host country government, the lower the MNE's voluntary responsibility (and vice versa).	Proposition 5 addresses bargaining theory as a dynamically changing process (see Eden et al., 2005). The proposition implies that a stronger developing host country government can shift toward imposing mandatory CSR, the imposition of which tends correspondingly to reduce the MNE's voluntary responsibility under Propositions 1 through 4.

| 6 | The greater the negative impact of an MNE on a country, the greater the responsibility. Greater positive impact of an MNE on a country may not however reduce responsibility. | Proposition 6 implies that MNEs should minimize negative impacts on a country and that, where there are negative impacts, CSR rises accordingly. However, positive impact may not reduce CSR correspondingly, or offset negative impacts. |
| 7 | Firms have a responsibility to promote constitutional democracy across societies; this responsibility translates into responsible lobbying in advanced countries and democracy promotion in developing countries. | Proposition 7 addresses the argument of Scherer and Palazzo (2011) concerning political CSR. The proposition implies that MNEs have a responsibility to promote appropriate business–government relations for future country prosperity. Promotion might be interpreted as implying at a minimum not undermining constitutional democracy, as illustrated by the implication that firms should practice responsible lobbying. Actively promoting democracy in developing countries may be a much more difficult task. |

MNEs must allocate capital across countries, meeting both profitability and responsibility standards. It may not be possible to meet all needs with the available resources as needs are likely to exceed resources under the best possible scenario; a responsibility calculus helps with prioritization. A responsibility calculus helps with global dialogue concerning minimum standards for CSR across countries. The calculus reaches different findings between advanced and developing countries, and across developing countries. Specific industries, such as pharmaceuticals and minerals extraction, arguably have special and higher responsibilities.

1.3 An illustration and some examples

An approach to explicating the logic of a proposed responsibility calculus is to construct a hypothetical illustration for a developing country. It is useful to separate developing countries into three broad categories: (1) resource-rich countries arguably including Russia (e.g. possessing oil and other valuable minerals); (2) other countries not geographically adjacent to developed countries (e.g. much of Africa, Latin America, and South and Southeast Asia); and (3) countries geographically adjacent to developed countries (e.g. Eastern Europe). Each category is effectively a logical subset of the proposed responsibility calculus. Resources attract foreign investment; the resulting relationship is governed by bargaining (Eden *et al.*, 2005).

The illustration focuses on Eastern Europe—a transitional region lying between advanced and developing country status. The countries (whether labelled as developing or emerging) in this region are in the process of joining the EU (and Euro zone), to which they will be increasingly bound economically (Blazejewski and Dorow, 2003). MNEs operating in the region are frequently EU-based and the

European Commission promotes CSR (EC, 2011). A baseline study of CSR practices in various but not all of the countries in Central and Eastern Europe was published by the EU and the United Nations Development Programme (UNDP) (Line and Braun, 2007).

A large team of researchers surveyed 3,064 managers and business students in eight European countries—both Western Europe and Central and Eastern Europe (Furrer *et al.*, 2010). The authors report significant differences between the two areas of Europe concerning social, economic and environmental corporate responsibilities. These three responsibilities comprise what is typically termed "triple bottom line" (see Elkington, 1997). Respondents in both areas viewed environmental responsibility as the most important dimension. Western European respondents viewed social responsibility as more important than economic responsibility, while Central and Eastern European respondents viewed economic responsibility as more important than social responsibility. However, attitudes in the Central and Eastern Europe area were not homogenous, as the Czech Republic in particular is closer to Western European attitudes. The authors also reported on differences between managers and business students and also generational differences. Interestingly, managers reported more importance to social responsibility and business students more importance to environmental responsibility.

Given these variations, the same company from the EU (Germany or the UK, for instance) or elsewhere in Western Europe (Switzerland or Austria, for instance) would reach different choices across countries of Eastern Europe. The baseline study (Line and Braun, 2007) includes (listed geographically from north to south) Lithuania, Poland, Slovakia, Hungary, Croatia, Bosnia Herzegovina, Bulgaria, Macedonia and Turkey. The Czech Republic, not included, is already more like the EU in reported CSR attitudes as noted above (Furrer *et al.*, 2010).

Following the order of the propositions, some countries are more developed than others in Eastern Europe (Proposition 1), which is adjacent to the EU rather than resource rich or distant. Much of the investment and operations are coming from Western Europe (Proposition 2). MNEs from Western Europe do have reasonable capability and resources to address local needs (Propositions 3 and 4). Some countries (the Czech Republic, Hungary, and Poland) have greater bargaining power, while other countries have less bargaining power (Proposition 5). Generally, MNE operations in Eastern Europe are likely to impose less negative impacts than they do in mineral-rich developing countries such as Nigeria or Papua New Guinea (Proposition 6). Governmental and political functioning is arguably uneven across the area, with reasonable constitutional democracy in the Czech Republic, Hungary, Lithuania, Poland and Slovakia and more problematic government in Bulgaria, Romania and some former constituent republics of the disintegrated Yugoslavia. Belarus is effectively a dictatorship. Russia forcibly annexed the Crimea from Ukraine in March 2014. MNEs have a stronger political responsibility the weaker the democratic and judicial institutions of a specific country (Proposition 7).

The idea of a multidimensional responsibility calculus is abstract, even enhanced by testable logical propositions and hypothetical illustrations. A next step is to translate the idea into practical take-aways for both researchers and practitioners. In theory, weights must be assigned to each dimension (Brenner, 1995). In practice, managers judge trade-offs rather than assigning formal weights.

In a positive view, a key issue is how to determine upper limits to responsibility (Windsor, 2013). Whether responsibility shows an immediate or longer-term return (or advantage), and whether in cash flow and market valuation terms (Mackey *et al.*, 2007), managers will be concerned with the upper limits. CSR investments are unlikely not to show diminishing returns. This issue (see Figure 1.1) concerns the situation marked as H. The firm operates to the right of U as the result of a management judgement. The rationales might be political advantage, moral commitment or expectation of future return in some form. Two examples concerning the relationship between MNEs and health issues in developing countries (Windsor, 2009) reveal how firms might elect H above U and above local expectations. The case of Marathon Oil illustrates special responsibilities in resource extraction industries. The case of Merck illustrates special responsibilities in pharmaceutical industries.

Marathon Oil and other MNEs operate in Equatorial Guinea, reportedly the most prosperous country in Africa because of its energy resources (Frynas, 2004; Shah, 2013). High prosperity does not mean automatically acceptable distribution of prosperity within the population. Malaria is endemic, as in various other parts of Africa (Corporate Alliance on Malaria in Africa, 2010). Marathon and partners began a malaria control campaign on Bioko Island, the site of the nation's capital (Chaouch, 2009). Marathon estimated that for every dollar spent, there was about four dollars in economic return to the community (Chaouch, 2009). In 2007, the campaign was continued onto continental Equatorial Guinea with reportedly less success (Rehman *et al.*, 2013). Most of the cost of the continental campaign was donated by the Global Fund for Aids, TB and Malaria. Marathon is a member of the Global Business Coalition supporting these kinds of health campaigns. Malaria is a key cause of poverty; campaigns to eradicate it in tropical countries have typically not succeeded (Gallup and Sachs, 2001). With partners and donors, the cost of the program has been moderate relative to company revenues, employee motivation and social benefits. Both economic motivation and humanitarian motivation are required (Spielman, 2006).

There are many diseases and parasites in tropical countries, which are mostly poor countries distant from the developed countries. In 2010, the Bill and Melinda Gates Foundation pledged to donate an additional US$10 billion over the next decade (in addition to the US$4.5 billion already donated previously) to help research new vaccines and support immunization in the poorest countries (AP, 2010). River blindness (onchocerciasis) occurs near rivers in tropical countries spread by the black fly. The nematode worm is a filarial parasitic worm from the same family elephantiasis. River blindness is endemic in some 34 countries, mostly in Africa but also in the Arabian Peninsula and some countries of Latin America. River blindness causes intense itching and ultimately blindness (Rea *et al.*, 2010). The World Health Organization (WHO) estimates about 123 million at risk of infection, of whom at least 25 million are infected, 300,000 blind and 800,000 visually impaired (CDC, 2014). Most of the individuals at risk and infected live in Africa (Rea *et al.*, 2010, p. 295). Intervention against transmission has stopped in Colombia (2008), Ecuador (2010), Guatemala (2012) and Mexico (2012) due to progress, with risk in Latin America now restricted to one area of Brazil and one area of Venezuela (CDC, 2014). The pharmaceutical firm Merck developed ivermectin (from a microbe) for veterinary purposes. Then a Merck scientist reported that ivermectin might have human applications. Merck Research Laboratories supported development of what became Mectizan for use against river blindness (Collins, 2004; Vagelos and Galambos, 2004). An annual dose is needed in pill form. Even at US$1 per dose, most of the afflicted victims could not afford the cost (Rea *et al.*, 2010, p. 298). Merck concluded that no profit could be earned on Mectizan. Governmental, intergovernmental and private organizations failed to provide any financial support. Merck therefore decided to fund the Mectizan Donation Program, still operating past its 25th anniversary in 2012, to provide free treatment for as long as necessary. The program eventually attracted partners and became regarded as a model program (Peters and Phillips, 2004). The veterinary sales provided funding, while still generating a net profit for Merck. As with malaria control, parasite control yields strong economic benefits for local communities relative to costs (Waters *et al.*, 2004). Wider applications, as to elephantiasis, may be possible and the program has stimulated other approaches (Hopkins, 2012).

1.4 Reflections on development-oriented CSR

A key concern of this book is what businesses contribute toward the development of countries that are not advanced economically. These countries are located primarily, but not exclusively, in Africa, Latin America, and South and Southeast Asia. This chapter separates developing countries into the three broad categories of resource-rich countries, other countries not geographically adjacent to developed countries, and countries geographically adjacent to developed countries. This chapter uses as an example the countries of Eastern Europe where the MNEs are quite often from the EU which is geographically adjacent to Eastern Europe. The example facilitates variations in governmental conditions (from democracy to dictatorship), as well as transition from communism and Soviet domination and issues in development CSR.

One theme in the book is a distinction between two categories of companies. One category contributes to development simply through contributing investment and operations in developing countries where the companies simply avoid being bad to the extent possible. The other category identifies an overt development agenda and undertake development-oriented CSR activities. In Figure 1.1, Siemens is an instance of what was a bad company practising corruption as a global strategy. Google is an instance of a good company attempting to promote a universal standard concerning freedom of speech and information—in effect, engaged in civil disobedience in China. Marathon and Merck are examples of companies with more of an overt development agenda illustrating the second category identified in this book.

The seven propositions explained in Table 1.1 function as a decision heuristic for MNE managers in developing countries. The set of propositions qualifies as development-oriented CSR. The propositions favour a development agenda, while recognizing practical considerations of implementation in specific country conditions. A corporate development agenda should have some structure based on judgement rather than being something like a random collection of activities by country and issue. Proposition 1 implies that MNEs will find considerable need for a corporate development agenda including CSR activities. Proposition 2 implies that MNE responsibility is not fulfilled simply by being in the first category of companies that provide investment and operations and avoid doing wrong. Propositions 3, 4, 5 and 6 imply that MNE responsibility is limited by capability, resources, relative bargaining power (i.e., governmental capability and resources), and negative impact on the host country. Proposition 7 implies a broader responsibility for promoting, or at least not undermining, constitutional democracy in both advanced and developing countries. In advanced countries (including some countries in Eastern Europe), this proposition implies responsible lobbying. In developing countries (including some countries in Eastern Europe), there is pervasive corruption and weak judicial institutions. Siemens took advantage of this circumstance in practising a global corruption strategy. The propositions are intended to help managers think through the conditions and options which vary by country. Since resources are limited, managers have to determine priorities concerning development agenda and CSR-oriented activities by country. This determination involves judgement (aided by a logical calculus) rather than a formal calculation of benefits and costs of specific initiatives.

The significance of this proposed responsibility calculus approach is to advance theorization and practice of CSR beyond the abstract level of bad versus good practice occurring as a global dialogue and specific concrete instances of bad versus practice occurring as local discourses which can reflect external bargaining and internal lobbying. The approach does so by formalizing the logical calculus of multidimensional CSR decisions.

Such a responsibility calculus has limitations for both CSR and country development efforts. For CSR theorizing and practice, the approach is effectively a framework or engine for reasoning. The approach does not provide specific answers: the approach marshals more careful analysis and judgement. For country development efforts, the approach is about managerial judgements in specific contexts about concrete decisions. The approach presumes significant discretion concerning what managers should do locally, beyond strict compliance with minimalist universal standards.

Bibliography

AP (Associated Press) (2010, January 30). Gates makes $10 billion vaccines pledge. *Houston Chronicle*, p. A2.

AP (Associated Press) (2014, April 2). Caterpillar: Firm's tax-avoiding wins Paul's praise. *Houston Chronicle*, D10 (Business).

Baron, D.P. (2008). Siemens: Anatomy of Bribery. Stanford Graduate School of Business, Case P68.

Blazejewski, S., & Dorow, W. (2003). Managing organizational politics for radical change: the case of Beiersdorf-Lechia S.A., Poznan. *Journal of World Business*, 38(3), 204-223.

Brenner, S.N. (1995). Stakeholder theory of the firm: its consistency with current management techniques. In J. Näsi (Ed.), *Understanding Stakeholder Thinking* (pp. 75-96). Helsinki, Finland: LSR-Publications.

Brent, R.J. (2006a). Distribution weights. In R.J. Brent, *Applied Cost–Benefit Analysis* (2nd edition) (pp. 323-358). Cheltenham, UK and Northampton, MA: Edward Elgar.

Brent, R.J. (2006b). Measurement of intangibles. In R.J. Brent, *Applied Cost–Benefit Analysis* (2nd edition) (pp. 248-281). Cheltenham, UK and Northampton, MA: Edward Elgar.

Cain, J. (2014). Weatherford shareholders approve HQ move. *Houston Business Journal* (June 17, 2014). Retrieved from http://www.bizjournals.com/houston/morning_call/2014/06/weatherford-shareholders-ok-move-hq-move.html, last accessed 14 October 2014.

CDC (Center for Disease Control and Prevention) (2014). Parasites—Onchocerciasis (also known as River Blindness). Retrieved from http://www.cdc.gov/parasites/onchocercia-sis/epi.html, last accessed 14 October 2014.

Chaouch, A. (2009). Combating malaria: How an oil company is helping to tackle the problem. Retrieved from http://knowledge.insead.edu/healthcare/combating-malaria-how-an-oil-company-is-helping-to-tackle-the-problem-1750.

Collins, K.L. (2004). Profitable gifts: a history of the Merck Mectizan donation program and its implications for international health. *Perspectives in Biology and Medicine*, 47(1), 100-109.

Corporate Alliance on Malaria in Africa, Global Business Coalition on HIV/AIDS, Tuberculosis and Malaria, and World Economic Forum (2010). Business engagement on malaria in Africa. Retrieved from http://www.weforum.org/pdf/GHI/MalariaMapping.pdf.

Demuijnck, G. (2014). Universal values and virtues in management versus cross-cultural moral relativism: an educational strategy to clear the ground for business ethics. *Journal of Business Ethics* (February 2014). Retrieved from http://link.springer.com/article/10.1007/s10551-014-2065-3.

Desai, M., & Dharmapala, D. (2009). Corporate tax avoidance and firm value. *The Review of Economics and Statistics*, 91(3), 537-546.

Donaldson, T., & Dunfee, T.W. (1999). *Ties That Bind: A Social Contracts Approach to Business Ethics*. Boston, MA: Harvard Business Press.

Eaton, C. (2014, April 3). Pay issue spurs Weatherford's move to Ireland. *Houston Chronicle*, p. D3 (Business).

EC (European Commission) (2011). Communication from the Commission to the European Parliament, the Council, the European Economics and Social Committee and the Committee of the Regions: A renewed EU strategy 2011-14 for Corporate Social Responsibility. Brussels, Belgium: 25.10.2011 COM(2011) 681 final; http://ec.europa.eu/enterprise/policies/sustainable-business/files/csr/new-csr/act_en.pdf.

Eden, L., Lenway, S., & Schuler, D.A. (2005). From the obsolescing bargain to the political bargaining model. In R. Grosse (Ed.), *International Business and Government Relations in the 21st Century* (pp. 251-272). Cambridge, UK: Cambridge University Press.

Elkington, J. (1997). *Cannibals with Forks: The Triple Bottom Line of 21st Century Business.* Oxford, UK: Capstone Publishing.

Frynas, J.G. (2004). The oil boom in Equatorial Guinea. *African Affairs* 103.413 (2004), 527-40.

Furrer, O., Egri, C.P., Ralston, D.A., Danis, W.M., Reynaud, E., Naoumova, I. *et al.* (2010). Attitudes toward corporate responsibilities in western Europe and in central and east Europe. *Management International Review*, 50(2), 379-398.

Gallup, J.L., & Sachs, J.D. (2001). The economic burden of malaria. *American Journal of Tropical Medicine and Hygiene*, 64(1), Supplement, 85-96.

Google (nd). Ten things we know to be true. Retrieved from http://www.google.com/intl/US-en/about/company/philosophy/, last accessed 19 April 2014.

Hamilton, J.B., Knouse, S.B., & Hill, V. (2009). Google in China: a manager-friendly heuristic model for resolving cross-cultural ethical conflicts. *Journal of Business Ethics*, 86(2), 143-157.

Hopkins, A. (2012). Beyond providing drugs: the Mectizan® donation stimulates new strategies in service delivery and in strengthening health systems. *Current Pharmaceutical Biotechnology*, 13(6), 1110-1119.

Jensen, M.C. (2001). Value maximization, stakeholder theory, and the corporate objective function. *Journal of Applied Corporate Finance*, 14(3), 8-21.

Keightley, M.P., & Sherlock, M.F. (2014). The Corporate Income Tax System: Overview and Options for Reform. Washington, DC: U.S. Congressional Research Service, February 14, 2014, 7-5700, R42726, http://www.fas.org/sgp/crs/misc/R42726.pdf.

Line, M., & Braun, R. (2007). Baseline Study on CSR Practices in the New EU Member States and Candidate Countries. European Union and United Nations Development Programme, http://europeandcis.undp.org/uploads/public1/files/BASELINE_STUDY_ON.pdf.

Mackey, A., Mackey, T.B., & Barney, J.B. (2007). Corporate social responsibility and firm performance: investor preferences and corporate strategies. *Academy of Management Review*, 32(3), 817-835.

Martin, R.L. (2002). The virtue matrix: calculating the return on corporate responsibility. *Harvard Business Review*, 80(3), 5-11.

Morsing, M., & Roepstorff, A. (2014). CSR as corporate political activity: Observations on IKEA's CSR identity–image dynamics. *Journal of Business Ethics*, March. doi:10.1007/s10551-014-2091-1.

Murphy, K.E., & Simon, S.J. (2002). Intangible benefits valuation in ERP projects. *Information Systems Journal*, 12(4), 301-320.

Peters, D.H., & Phillips, T. (2004). Mectizan donation program: evaluation of a public–private partnership. *Tropical Medicine & International Health*, 9(4), A4-A15.

Porter, M.E. (2011). Rebuilding America's inner cities: interview by Scott Olster. Retrieved from http://money.cnn.com/2011/05/12/smallbusiness/michael_porter_rebuilding_inner_city_america.fortune/.

Preston, L.E., & Windsor, D. (1997). *The Rules of the Game in the Global Economy: Policy Regimes for International Business* (2nd edition). Dordrecht, Netherlands: Kluwer Academic Publishers.

Rawls, J. (1999). *The Law of Peoples.* Cambridge, MA: Harvard University Press.

Rea, P.A., Zhang, V., & Baras, Y.S. (2010). Ivermectin and river blindness: science and philanthropy put an end to blindly following the next generation. *American Scientist*, 98(4), 294-303.

Rehman, A.M., Mann, A.G., Schwabe, C., Reddy, M.R., Gomes, I.R., Slotman M.A. *et al.* (2013). Five years of malaria control in the continental region, Equatorial Guinea. *Malaria Journal*, 12, 154. doi:10.1186/1475-2875-12-154.

Rouwendal, J. (2012). Indirect effects in cost–benefit analysis. *Journal of Benefit-Cost Analysis*, 3(1), 1-25.

Sanyal, R., & Samanta, S. (2011). Trends in international bribe-giving: do anti-bribery laws matter? *Journal of International Trade Law and Policy*, 10(2), 151-164.

Scherer, A.G., & Palazzo, G. (2011). The new political role of business in a globalized world: a review of a new perspective on CSR and its implications for the firm, governance, and democracy. *Journal of Management Studies*, 48(4), 899-931.

Schubert S., & Miller, T.C. (2008, December 20). At Siemens, bribery was just a line item. *The New York Times*. Retrieved from http://www.nytimes.com/2008/12/21/business/worldbusiness/21siemens.html?pagewanted=all&_r=0, last accessed 19 April 2014.

Shah, N.K. (2013). Corporate philanthropy and conflicts of interest in public health: ExxonMobil, Equatorial Guinea, and Malaria. *Journal of Public Health Policy*, 34(1), 121-136.

Spielman, A. (2006). Ethical dilemmas in malaria control. *Journal of Vector Ecology*, 31(1), 1-8.

UN Human Rights Council (2011). Report of the Special Representative of the Secretary-General on the issue of human rights and transnational corporations and other business enterprises. John Ruggie: Guiding Principles on Business and Human Rights: Implementing the United Nations "Protect, Respect and Remedy" Framework. Retrieved from http://www.ohchr.org/Documents/Issues/Business/A-HRC-17-31_AEV.pdf.

U.S. Department of Justice, Office of Public Affairs (2013). Three Subsidiaries of Weatherford International Limited Agree to Plead Guilty to FCPA and Export Control Violations: Weatherford International and Subsidiaries Agree to Pay $252 million in Penalties and Fines. Retrieved from http://www.justice.gov/opa/pr/2013/November/13-crm-1260.html.

Vagelos, P.R., & Galambos, L. (2004). *Medicine, Science and Merck*. Cambridge, UK: Cambridge University Press.

Waters, H.R., Rehwinkel, J.A., & Burnham, G. (2004). Economic evaluation of Mectizan distribution. *Tropical Medicine & International Health*, 9(4), A16-A25.

Windsor, D. (2009). Multinational corporations and basic health services. In J. Friedland (Ed.), *Doing Well and Good: The Human Face of the New Capitalism* (pp. 187-214). Charlotte, NC: IAP—Information Age Publishing.

Windsor, D. (2013). Corporate social responsibility and irresponsibility: a positive theory approach. *Journal of Business Research*, 66(10), 1937-1944.

2

Bridging the governance gap with political CSR

Ismail Adelopo
Bristol Business School, UK

Kemi Yekini
Leicester Business School, UK

Lukman Raimi
Centre for Entrepreneurship Development (CED), Nigeria

Corporate social responsibility (CSR) has attracted varied applications in management. This chapter provides evidence of a political CSR where multinational corporations (MNCs) are complementing governments' roles in bridging the governance gap. The governance gap thesis and political costs hypothesis provide grounding for the discussions in this chapter. Data from case studies across Middle-Eastern countries were critically analysed and justify the political and developmental undercurrents of CSR initiatives. The key argument is that governance is crucial for development, and where there is a governance gap, it is in the interest of corporations to bridge the gap with their CSR initiatives to stimulate development. Pressure groups and civil society organizations in developing countries could leverage the political dimension of CSR to lobby corporations to intervene in socio-economic issues, especially poverty alleviation, through entrepreneurship development in their operating environment for mutual benefits.

Corporate social responsibility (CSR), although an old concept, has taken on a new dimension in recent times (Broomhill, 2007). It has emerged as a topical issue in management and international business literature (van Tulder and van der Zwart, 2006). In the globalized world, the term CSR attracts numerous definitions and synonyms, namely: corporate conscience, corporate citizenship, social performance, sustainable responsible business, responsible business (Amaeshi *et al.*, 2006; Wood, 1991) and the triple bottom line (Haskins, 2009). The domain of CSR encompasses social philanthropy (Carroll, 1999; Smith, 2011) and extends to curtailing the impact of industrial effluents on the environment, sustainability, biodiversity, trust, and legitimacy of corporate behaviour (Crowther and Rayman-Bacchus, 2004; Hart, 2012; Tombs, 2005). CSR has also been viewed as corporate altruism (Lantos, 2001) and social responsible investment (George *et al.*, 2012; Scholtens, 2014). With regard to compliance with international standards and best practice, Valmohammadi (2011) includes within the scope of CSR seven core elements of ISO 26000 standards, that is to say, organizational governance, human rights, labour practices, the environment, fair operating practices, consumer issues, community involvement and development.

Viewing CSR as an umbrella term allows for its innovative reinvention and application. In developing nations with infrastructural deficit, there is an upsurge in corporations' involvement in the well-being of their host communities; the MNCs flag nuances such as community engagement (Yekini and Jallow, 2012), social entrepreneurship and corporate social entrepreneurship (Austin and Reficco, 2009; Covin and Miles, 1999), corporate citizens (Amaeshi *et al.*, 2006) or responsible investors/responsible investment (Scholtens, 2014) as evidence of their commitments to business–society relationships. Notable corporations like General Electric, IBM, Google, eBay, Johnson & Johnson, Grameen Bank & Grameen Foundation, KaBOOM, DonorsChoose, Intel, Nestlé, Unilever and Walmart are using CSR as a worthwhile tool for sustainable development of their host nations without losing their economic objective (Akhuemonkhan *et al.*, 2012; Haskins, 2009; Kerr, 2007; Porter and Kramer, 2011).

In pursuit of the intent, the reviewed literature focused more on the relationship between CSR and financial performance metrics like improved profitability, enhanced customer patronage, positive stock-market rating, reputation building, ease of access to bank loans and other economic measurements of performance (Sweeney, 2009; Waddock and Graves, 1997; Walsh *et al.*, 2003). However, very modest attention is given to the reinvention of CSR as a developmental and political tool to complement roles of the state, especially in developing countries where poverty, lack of inclusiveness, corruption, crime, unemployment, bad governance and underdevelopment have become endemic (Akhuemonkhan *et al.*, 2012; Amaeshi *et al.*, 2006; Frynas, 2005; Idemudia, 2011; Sharp, 2006; World Bank, 2003).

Pioneering studies on political CSR can be traced back to the work of Baumann and Scherer (2010); Scherer and Palazzo (2007, 2008, 2011); Matten (2003) and Matten and Crane (2005). In a unique style, Matten (2003) described the newly emerging political roles of corporations as symbolic politics (SP) because several corporations were political actors in the design and implementation of environmental regulation in their host communities/countries after globalisation had ascribed increasing responsibility to them. The implication of this development is the erosion of traditional roles and powers of national governments. Similarly, Matten and Crane (2005) alluded to the political role of corporations within the corporate citizenship discourse in another novel work.

This chapter, therefore, fills the knowledge gap on political CSR and development-oriented CSR by reviewing pioneering works on the subject matter with evidence from selected corporations that have deployed their CSR investments for political developmental purposes.

2.1 Literature review

2.1.1 Conceptual issues

Political CSR is defined by leading proponents as a theory and practice whereby corporations and civil society groups take on the roles traditionally assigned, ascribed and assumed by governments in a democratic milieu (Scherer and Palazzo, 2008). Edward and Willmott (2008) explained that a political CSR perspective merely extended the understanding of the role of corporations in the political processes of their host countries beyond the conventional explanation of corporate citizenship. According to Scherer and Palazzo (2007), the conventional understanding of CSR in business–society research could be classified into two schools, namely, *positivist* and *post-positivist CSR*. The positivist perspective of CSR is considered weak because it views CSR in theory and practice as an instrumental and normative concept, while the post-positivist perspective of CSR suffered the same criticism because of its relativism, foundationalism, and utopianism. Political CSR is a new way of theorizing to explain the interventionist roles of corporations in contemporary times with a view to strengthening the existing perspectives of CSR (Scherer and Palazzo, 2007, 2008, 2011). In other words, the "insertion of 'political' into corporate social responsibility (CSR) is intended to replace an implicit compliance with assumed societal norms and expectations with an explicit participation in public processes of political will formation" (Edward and Willmott, 2008, p. 771).

Political CSR emerged for several reasons: (a) globalization pressure, (b) a need for inclusiveness in governance, (c) socio-political risk management and (d) pervasive infrastructural deficits in developing nations. Globalization is an unstoppable wave that necessitated a political CSR in a changing world and its influence has been used by corporations beyond the domain of business for "transformation of private attitudes, morals, practices, and institutions" in regions where MNCs have influence and control (Donaldson, 2010, p. 728). The globalization wave aided MNCs like KFC, McDonald's, Coca-Cola, Johnson & Johnson, Nike, Sony, Unilever and

Figure 2.1 **The three key actors**

Nestlé to establish their presence and influence across the globe. In the Middle-East and North Africa (MENA) countries, the same wave spurred corporations like Western Zagros Limited, HSBC, Al Muhaidib Group and SEDCO Holding to refocus their CSR programs on economic growth and redevelopment of the local communities (Booz and Company, 2013).

The need for inclusiveness in governance became expedient because of the changing role of governance which allows for role-sharing among three key actors (the state, civil society and corporation) in the face of increasing challenges of government and dwindling resources (Akhuemonkhan *et al.*, 2012). With regard to the politics of inclusiveness, the private sector actors argued that politics or governance is a cumulative process that involves consultations, disagreement and consensus building among state actors and non-state actors; it is not an exclusive activity reserved for, or confined to agencies or institutions of the states (Scherer and Palazzo, 2008, 2011). Within the political CSR framework, the three actors that emerged have complementary roles in governance (see Figure 2.1). The role of the state is essentially to provide an enabling environment for capitalism (Porter and Kramer, 2011). The role of the civil society group is to serve as a watchdog in order to apply pressure to corporations when needed. The civil society group includes private, independent organizations including NGOs, social movement organizations, institutional investors, and the press (Campbell, 2007, p. 958). The role of corporations is to complement government by contributing to economic growth and development in different ways (Akhuemonkhan *et al.*, 2012; Gond and Matten, 2007).

A political CSR emerged because of the need to mitigate the social and political risk posed by the industrial activities of corporations in some host communities (Kytle and Ruggie, 2005; Nwadialor and Igwe, 2013). Social involvement in such environments becomes political in order to reconcile and demonstrate empathetic concerns for their well-being as well as curbing social and environmental degradation arising from the industrial activities of corporations (George *et al.*, 2012;

Raimi and Adeleke, 2010). For instance, there are unending oil spillages, pollutions, chemical diffusion and emissions of carbon monoxides as well as abuse of the eco-system linked to MNCs like Shell, Chevron and Exxon Mobil (Friends of the Earth, 2004). A political CSR is therefore favoured because of the prospect of creating a "business of peace" (BOP) in hostile communities (Nelson, 2000). Putting it differ-ently, it represents a compensatory mode of CSR (Mordi *et al.*, 2012).

Another reason that brought political CSR into the limelight was the need to bridge infrastructural deficits in host communities with failed public governance. According to Boyle and Boguslaw (2007), corporations have become active in tack-ling poverty issues in their operational domains through CSR involvements. Also, Natufe (2011) confirms that Adidas, Nike, IBM, BP and several MNCs have pas-sionately adopted CSR as a tool for impacting on the business environment where they all operate. Furthermore, some studies provide justification for political CSR as a tool for tackling problems of poverty, unemployment, crime, conflict and infrastructural neglect in Nigeria and Tanzania (Raimi and Adeleke, 2010; Ufadhili *et al.*, 2005).

Related to the instances listed above, Charitoudi *et al.*, (2011) note that corpora-tions have pro-actively used CSR as a tool for national economic recovery in peri-ods of financial crisis, by catering for the welfare needs of the poorer members of society. In essence, political CSR represents a tool for helping the suffering citizens out from under the "bottom of the pyramid" (Boyle and Boguslaw, 2007, p. 103). On the strength of the viewpoints above, the distinctions between conventional CSR (which is instrumental) and political CSR are as shown in Table 2.1.

The political CSR that underpins this chapter is CSR entrepreneurship synergy, a form of developmental CSR. This type of CSR finds relevance in developing countries where small and medium enterprises (SMEs) are hindered by governance constraints especially infrastructural deficiencies and unfriendly business environments (Newberry, 2006; Oyelola *et al.*, 2013). The aforementioned governance constraints, which are global, have engendered weak SMEs that cannot create jobs, add value to national GDPs or, are able to improve the quality of the lives of their citizens.

2.1.2 Approaches for reinventing CSR as a political tool

Corporate social involvement, historically, has social and political undercurrents. As a social concept, CSR at a formative stage was used as palliatives for support-ing the society. At present the role of CSR has expanded as corporations used their CSR as a political tool to further imperialistic and exploitative goals in developing nations. In other words, corporations, especially MNCs, are empowered to pursue political agenda, while at the same time doing business in developing nations. CSR is a political weapon deployed by MNCs to cushion the ripple effect of market failures and other negative externalities they engender while doing business. Pratap (2011), however, argues that CSR is a farce and a political tool of neoliberals designed as "relief measures [intentionally to save]… the reputation, credibility and

Table 2.1 **Characteristics of the instrumental and new political approach to CSR**

Characteristics	Instrumental CSR	Political CSR
Governance model		
• Main political actor	State	State, civil society, and corporations
• Locus of governance	National governance	Global and multilevel governance
• Mode of governance	Hierarchy	Heterarchy
• Role of economic rationality	Dominance of economic rationality	Domestication of economic rationality
• Separation of political and economic spheres	High	Low
Role of law		
• Mode of regulation	Governmental regulation	Self-regulation
• Dominant rules	Formal rules and "hard law"	Informal rules and "soft law"
• Level of obligation	High (enforcement)	Low (voluntary action)
• Precision of rules	High	Low
• Delegation to third parties	Seldom	Often
Responsibility		
• Direction	Retrospective (guilt)	Prospective (solution)
• Reason for critique	Direct action	Social connectedness (complicity)
• Sphere of influence	Narrow/local	Broad/global
Legitimacy		
• Pragmatic legitimacy	High (legitimacy of capitalist institutions via contribution to public good)	Medium–low (capitalist institutions under pressure, market failure and state failure)
• Cognitive legitimacy	High (coherent set of morals that are taken for granted)	Medium–low (individualism, pluralism of morals)
• Moral legitimacy	Low	High–low (depending on level of discursive engagement)
• Mode of corporate engagement	Reactive (response to pressure)	Proactive (engagement in democratic politics)
Democracy		
• Model of democracy	Liberal democracy	Deliberative democracy
• Concept of politics	Power politics	Discursive politics
• Democratic control and legitimacy of corporations	Derived from political system, corporations are de-politicized	Corporate activities subject to democratic control
• Mode of corporate governance	Shareholder oriented	Democratic corporate governance

Source: Scherer & Palazzo (2011).

Figure 2.2 **Motives for CSR**

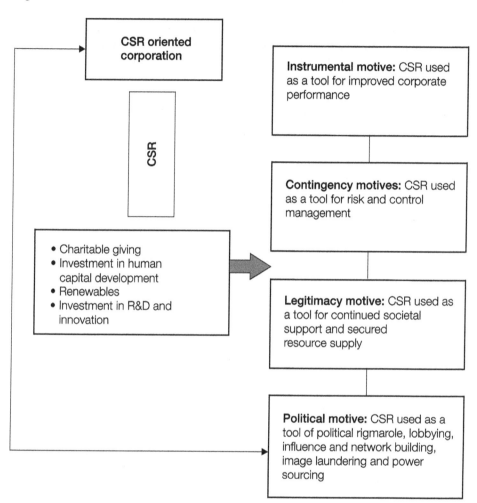

acceptability of the market god, corporate priests and the whole neoliberal religion. It is in this context that the role of corporate social responsibility (CSR) has been created. It has been propagated that the 'externalities', the term neoliberals give to poverty, unemployment and environmental disasters, that result from 'market failures', should be taken care of by voluntary corporate initiatives" Pratap (2011, p. 1).

From the foregoing discussion, the application of CSR by corporations have four motives (instrumental, contingent, legitimacy and political). The scope of involvement in socio-economic wellness of the society by corporations determines which motive to be given preference. With regard to the practical application of a political CSR, Scherer and Palazzo (2011, p. 918) contend that "corporations thereby become politicized in two ways: they operate with an enlarged understanding of responsibility and help to solve political problems in cooperation with state actors and civil society actors."

Figure 2.2 provides a visual explanation of the various motives for corporate social involvement by corporations. Whilst the first three are well documented in the literature, political motive for CSR is emerging. There are several cases of enlarged politically motivated interventions across the globe. For instance, a political CSR has often been used for lobbying and reconciling "conflicts (obvious or perceived) between public and private interests" in hostile communities (Fooks *et al.*, 2013, p. 283). In the Niger Delta region in Nigeria, an example of CSR as a conflict resolution tool is the partnership between the Shell Petroleum Development Company (SPDC) and the government-owned Niger Delta Development Commission (NDDC) where the aim is to build infrastructural facilities for the host communities, as well as empowering victims of any environmental degradation caused by SPDC (Ite, 2005, 2007). Another instance is British American Tobacco (BAT), which utilized its CSR programs as a lobby for neutralizing the negative impact of its products and for gaining political support and thereby avert harsh tobacco regulation and control (Fooks *et al.*, 2013). Also, under the guise of political CSR, several MNCs provide support through exports of military hardware to oppressive governments and give bribes to politicians as well in developing nations (Fooks *et al.*, 2013; Leigh and Evans 2009). The next section looks at the theoretical foundation of political CSR.

2.2 Theoretical underpinning

2.2.1 Theoretical foundation

Scherer and Palazzo (2007) hinged the political CSR on Jürgen Habermas's theory of democracy. The theory simply explains the emerging political roles of multinational corporations in their host countries in conjunction with two other players—governments and civil society groups. Habermas's theory of democracy is a new way of thinking and the conception is called deliberative democracy which advocates a hybrid democracy from two dominant political traditions, namely: (a) the public autonomy of republican political theory which emphasizes the general will and popular sovereignty and (b) the private autonomy of liberal political theory which gives prominence to private interests and individual freedoms. The Habermas's deliberative model incorporates and integrates two political theories (republican and liberal political theories) to form a distinct political concept (Lubenow, 2012).

Within the present discourse, the two theories that provide further explanations for the political roles of corporations in the Habermas deliberative democracy are: (a) governance gap thesis and (b) political cost hypothesis. The two theories reinforce the Habermas theory of democracy in the sense that they explain the rationale for the political roles of corporations in modern governance. The term governance has attracted varied definitions in the literature across multidisciplinary fields in the present millennium (Blatter, 2012; Center for International Private Enterprise and Global Integrity, 2012; Coyle, 2003). The World Bank (2003) admits that governance is a complex concept that lack distinct definition and measurement. In other words, governance touches on how the affairs of politics are run and how the well-being of the society is overseen by managers.

Besides, Vrajlal and Kandarp, (2010) define governance as an organized system employed by the private sector, public sector and not-for-profit sector for managing the affairs of their organizations. Governance (irrespective of levels) covers issues relating to organizational objectives, power-sharing and obligations as well as challenges of actors. Governance in practice could be dichotomized as shown in Figure 2.3 below into good governance and bad governance (Rizk, 2012; Young, 1999). Good governance allows for efficient markets and provides effective government service delivery for citizens. Government within a good governance system creates a public sector that is responsive and accountable as opposed to bad governance which creates a predatory and corrupt public sector (Center for International Private Enterprise and Global Integrity, 2012).

However, the crisis of ineffective service delivery to citizens as a result of market failure and other factors is what theorists have described as "governance gap". The term "governance gap" refers to a lack of integration in government's planning processes and a failure of public authorities to meet the expectations of the citizens in terms of provision of public goods. Similarly, it entails the inability of government at all levels to effectively communicate and deliver services to the public (Bates, 2011). With regards to the MENA, the World Bank (2003) report observed worsening performance linked to two dimensions of the governance gap, namely: (a) poor quality of administration in the public sector and (b) weak public accountability. Both dimensions indicate that the MENA has low tolerance for "the efficiency of the bureaucracy, the rule of law, the protection of property rights, the level of corruption, the quality of regulations, and the mechanisms of internal accountability [as well as poor attitudes to] openness of political institutions and participation, respect of civil liberties, transparency of government, and freedom of the press" (World Bank,2003, pp. 6-7).

To close the governance gap in the MENA and other parts of the Asian continent, and to allow for effective service delivery of quality public goods, there is a need for collaboration and responsibility-sharing among governments, private sector, and civil society (Center for International Private Enterprise and Global Integrity, 2012). The collaboration of MNCs in for role-sharing is necessary to complement government efforts at improving the well-being of their people (Visser, 2008). The governance gap thesis is applicable to all parts of the globe where there is "widespread poverty, corruption, inadequate resources, poorly trained labour supplies, wars and other forms of civil strife such as ethnic cleansing, pandemic diseases such as HIV/AIDS and malaria, tribal tensions, and ruinous economic policies have led to problems of such scope and dimension that it is only governments, African and international, that can mobilize the necessary capital to begin to make headway on these enormous issues" (Roy, 2010, p. 49).

Figure 2.3 **Divergence between good and bad governance**

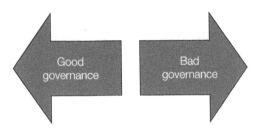

The solution to these ills caused by governance gap is for government to involve the private-sector corporations because they "have a creative role in defining possibly new ways of addressing these problems"(2010, p. 49). To forestall endemic poverty, the corporate businesses and multinationals need to appreciate the bitter truth that "poverty is a drain on resources that affects the business sector" when it is not tackled with an intervention tool like CSR (Boyle and Boguslaw, 2007).

2.2.2 Political cost theory

Political cost theory provides an explanation as to why corporations wilfully bear certain social costs in their quest for economic survival through social disclosures and other income-reducing accounting methods designed to protect managerial interests (Watts and Zimmerman, 1990). The theory (otherwise called political cost hypothesis or positive accounting cost) explains that social costs are borne by flourishing corporations in order to respond to pressures from politicians and civil society groups on social disclosures or social responsibility programs (Milne, 2001). Another viewpoint argued that corporations incur huge costs in the political process of their communities to forestall the impact of external pressure on their operations (Watts and Zimmerman, 1978).

Political costs refer to social costs required by corporations for continuing operations and businesses in line with regulatory requirements prevailing in a particular environment (Emadzadeh *et al.*, 2012). The political costs often incurred by corporations take the form of environmental rehabilitation costs, financial support for ruling or preferred political parties, sports sponsorship, costs for seminar/capacity-building workshops, insurance premiums, donations to parties during elections, monetary and non-monetary gifts and donations with political undertones (Tehrani *et al.*, 2009) as well as lobbying costs, costs for securing government contract and cost of avoiding government punitive regulations (Watts and Zimmerman, 1990; Emadzadeh *et al.*, 2012).

The MENA countries are behind several other nations on the governance index; they have a weak public sector because of poor openness, lack of transparency, weak reward system, dysfunctional institutional structures, widespread political corruption, poor policy implementation and inappropriateness of the policies and programs (World Bank, 2003). For these nations to grow and catch up with their developed counterparts, there is an the urgent need for a paradigm shift from cosmetic and palliative CSR to a viable political CSR that would help tackle hydra-headed poverty, unemployment, illiteracy, chronic diseases, maternal mortality, infant mortality, conflict, terrorism and insurgency, while at the same time, promoting the growth of SMEs, wealth creation, enhanced value reorientation, preserving the ecosystem from abuse and in the final analysis achieve sustainable economic development (Akhuemonkhan *et al.*, 2012; Kauffmann, 2005; Sagnia, 2005).

Besides, the proponents of political cost hypothesis state that the larger the corporation and its scope of operation, the larger should be the spending on political costs (Gray *et al.*, 1995; Milne, 2001; Watts and Zimmerman, 1978). An attempt to investigate the applicability of the theory in Tehran using econometric analysis revealed that "there is a correlation between political costs and company's size. It means that by increasing company's size the political costs increase too and by decreasing a company's size, political costs decrease too" (Tehrani *et al.*, 2009, p. 339). In theory and practice, it could be concluded that political cost is just management behaviour to project the corporation as socially responsible by defraying their profit through income-reducing social involvements (Emadzadeh *et al.*, 2012).

2.2.3 Criticisms against political CSR

The use of CSR for politically motivated social involvements within a capitalist free market system attracts criticisms. According to Brønn and Vrioni (2001), the debates on CSR have been confined to the domains of the free market proponents and socially oriented proponents. The protagonists of a CSR with political coloration believe that emerging social problems like poverty, recession, environmental degradation and unemployment aggravated by the state's "inability to cater for critical welfare needs of the citizens provide justification for a political CSR" (Charitoudi *et al.*, 2011; Porter and Kramer, 2011; Tausif, 2012). From a conflict mitigation perspective, a political CSR is believed to complement a government's efforts in boosting human capital development and thereby helping to stem the tide of conflict and youth restiveness in the Middle-East and Asian continent. In its report, UNESCO-UNEVOC (2012) lends credence to the statement above that developing human capital is a major prospect for tackling poverty, enhancing employability through skills acquisition and boosting sustainable development in Asia and especially Arab states where youth restiveness has resulted in violent protests and endemic demonstrations (e.g. Arab Spring). Raimi and Akhuemonkhan (2013, p. 131) notes that in the Asia and Pacific regions, TVET (technical and vocational education and training) has become a tool for enhancing social protection for the excluded and disadvantaged members of society as well as a catalyst for economic development.

The antagonists argue that in a genuine capitalist economy, the primary responsibility of corporations is profit maximization and that imperfection in the market economy and social problems are weak defence for corporate social involvements (Kakabadse *et al.*, 2005). Secondly, social involvement is flawed from governance and legal viewpoints because involvement by managers violates the terms of their engagements under the agency theory of corporate governance because participation is a violation of legitimate claims of shareholders to a return on investment. In other words, all forms of CSR are conceptually and practically incoherent with business thinking within the capitalist domain, because social welfare services are counterproductive to the owners' human rights (Sternberg, 2009).

2.3 Methods and analysis

The qualitative research method was adopted in this chapter because of its exploratory nature, while relying on documentary sources for data collection. In the quest to obtain relevant cases to justify a political CSR, a search on Google scholar for academic publications provided 25 citations on political roles of corporations in different parts of the world. The generated publications were systematically previewed to elicit relevant cases of political CSR with developmental undercurrents in the MENA countries and Asia. At the end of this, a sample of ten cases provided evidence of political CSR activities in MENA and Asia. The ten cases were subjected to discourse analysis on the basis of which CSR programs in the regions were described as either political or developmental and are shown in Table 2.2.

CSR initiatives become political when corporations take over the role of government or complement efforts of government (Matten, 2003; Scherer and Palazzo, 2008, 2011), while the developmental side of CSR addresses national issues like poverty, unemployment, diseases, infrastructural needs (Frynas, 2005, 2008; Idemudia, 2011; Sharp, 2006). The ten cases presented in Table 2.2 qualify as political and developmental CSR. Each of the cases represents a unique example of the interaction between corporations and the state in solving what would have been purely state responsibility. In our view, these instances of corporate involvement are beyond what some may simply see as philanthropic initiatives. For example, in case 1, the Aramex and Injaz corporations took over the governmental role for unemployment reduction and attendant consequences like poverty, youth disaffection and hopelessness. This form of CSR initiative is developmental because it is channelled towards entrepreneurship development. The MENA countries have one of the most youthful populations in the world with about 65% of the population aged under 25. This represents close to 300 million people and is in a region where youth unemployment stands at 25%, which is far above the global average of 14% One striking feature of this partnership is its long-term perspective, which means that both parties can develop trust and a closer working relationship on the understanding that a durable developmental infrastructure is being built for the future.

Case 2 is a political CSR like the former because Chevron desires to fill the governance gap and elicit legitimacy in its host country by building the capacity of small local businesses and cooperatives in Indonesia through an entrepreneurship training scheme and provision of financial support to the beneficiaries. Case 3 qualifies as a political CSR because Zain, as one of the leading telecommunication corporations in Bahrain, focused community development especially on the delivery of public goods for the citizens. Zain's CSR initiative is developmental because the issues targeted are environmental issues, educational support, youth engagement, funding of research and development, empowerment of women and children-oriented support programs, which are aimed at stimulating sustainable growth and development in the host country.

Table 2.2 **Political CSR initiatives in the MENA and Asia**

Description of case of PCSR	Country
Case 1: Creating the Culture of Entrepreneurship by Aramex and Injaz corporations. The CSR initiatives of the Aramex and Injaz corporations were designed to solve rising youth unemployment and constraints facing the SMEs in the Middle-East and Southeast Asia. The above-mentioned corporations initiated an entrepreneurship education program (EEP) in 2007 to motivate youth to create jobs (Murphy, 2010).	Middle East and Southeast Asia
Case 2: Building Skills and Capacity for Entrepreneurship by Chevron In Indonesia, Chevron established a CSR initiative tagged Chevron Pacific Indonesia (CPI) to support small and micro-enterprises (SMEs). The scheme trained over 4,000 small local businesses and cooperatives. The model provided financial support to the tune of $1.3 million in 2001 to small businesses and more than $114 million in 2009 (Murphy, 2010).	Indonesia
Case 3: Partner in community development by Zain Bahrain Zain Bahrain provides community support services directed at environmental issues, education, youth engagements, empowering of women, empowering and children-oriented philanthropy and research and development on technological progress. An internship program called GenNext was developed at Future University Network to provide students with a hands-on experience of work in the company (Zain Bahrain, 2013).	Bahrain
Case 4: Technical and Vocational Development in Host Community by Chevron Chevron established Chevron Aceh Recovery Initiative (CARI) to empower the local community through social investments in vocational and technical skill-acquisition programs in order to improve job prospects and the launching of new enterprises. Chevron's project intends to empower 1,200 SMEs, which would create an additional 6,000 jobs for Indonesians (Murphy, 2010).	Indonesia
Case 5: Embedding Sustainable Development in Local Areas by Western Zagros Western Zagros Limited. A Canadian-owned company integrates the wellbeing of the local communities into its business operations for long-term benefits. Its CSR programs cover community redevelopment, employment for locals, educational support, health and water supply (WesternZagros Annual Report, 2012).	Iraq

Description of case of PCSR	Country
Case 6: Entrepreneurship and Small Business Promotion by CISCO As part of CISCO's support for the host community, it initiated an entrepreneurship scheme aimed at inculcating "skills necessary to turn a business dream into reality" through global programs executed under the Global Education Initiative, the Cisco Networking Academy, and the Cisco Entrepreneurship Institute." (Murphy, 2010:12).	Egypt, Lebanon, Jordan, Saudi Arabia, Qatar
Case 7: Building Skills and Capacity of Students by CISCO For student empowerment, CISCO is funding education under public–private education partnerships in Jordan, Egypt and Qatar. It also partnered with the United States Department Middle East Initiative, to provide "internship opportunities for women from Lebanon, Jordan and Saudi Arabia on entrepreneurship and business courses at Emory and Duke Universities. Records indicated that CISCO "has nearly one million students in 165 countries." (Murphy, 2010).	Egypt, Lebanon, Jordan, Saudi Arabia, Qatar
Case 8: Business Linkages by National Beverage Company Coca-Cola/Cappy Coca-Cola/Cappy (National Beverage Company) utilized its CSR as a support mechanism for local entrepreneurs and SMEs in the Middle-East and West Bank. The CSR initiative is an inclusive business models created to help suppliers, distributors and retailers as well strengthening the local business system to protect its own markets (2010, p. 12).	Middle-East, West Bank
Case 9: Business Linkages in Singapore, Wales, Ireland, Vietnam and Thailand The CSR-oriented business linkages across the world provide logistical and financial support to SMEs through the private sector. Luetkenhors (2004) noted that the aim of the CSR-oriented business linkage is to enhance the capabilities and performance of SMEs as partners of MNCs. Selected CSR-oriented business linkage includes: Singapore's Local Industry Upgrading Programme, the Source Wales Programme, Ireland's National Linkage Programme and the programs of Unilever in Vietnam, Toyota in Thailand, Intel in Malaysia and Motorola in China.	Singapore, Wales, Ireland, Vietnam, Thailand Malaysia China
Case 10: CSR-Cluster Model in the Sialkot (India) and Jalandhar (Pakistan) The cluster model in India and Pakistan owned by Sialkot and Jalandhar, respectively, attracted support from the Soccer Industry Council of America, the International Labour Organization (ILO), UNICEF, Save the Children (UK) and the Sialkot Chamber of Commerce and Industry for being supportive of child/poor families in their host communities (UNIDO, 2009).	India and Pakistan

Case 4 like others discussed above is political and developmental. Chevron as a notable MNC desires to establish its presence in Indonesia. The country has a large market and economic potential by virtue of its large population. The CSR initiative of Chevron is development because the issue focused on is the development of technical and vocational education designed to enhance the skills of Indonesians thereby improving their job prospects and capacity to launch new enterprises. Case 5 is a political CSR initiative of Western Zagros Limited, a Canadian-owned company in Iraq. Being a turbulent region, the company initiated its CSR to complement the role of the Iraqi government by providing public goods and welfare support services to the poorer citizens. Secondly, intervention in welfare enhancement provides legitimacy for the corporation in the hostile Iraqi communities. Cases 6 and 7 have both political and developmental impacts. In a bid to elicit social licence, empowerment of women and stimulate small business development in Egypt, Lebanon, Jordan, Saudi Arabia and Qatar, CISCO, a leading MNC, initiated an entrepreneurship schemes aimed at building the entrepreneurship capacities of the youth for self-employment and self-reliance. It is their hope that businesses established by the youth and women would reduce unemployment, poverty rate, social exclusion and other social ills that are pervasive in the MENA. For women empowerment, CISCO provided internship opportunities for women from the above-mentioned countries on entrepreneurship and business courses at Emory and Duke Universities. Case 8 is political because the National Beverage Company (Coca-Cola/Cappy) desires to entrench its business influence in the turbulent Middle-East region of the West Bank and Gaza in spite of the conflict in the region. The National Beverage Company's initiatives are developmental because the citizens of the benefiting countries are being economically empowered through business support linkages as described above. Case 9 is a developmental CSR with political undercurrent. In Vietnam, Thailand, Malaysia and China, notable MNCs like Unilever, Toyota, Intel and Motorola, respectively, have developed CSR-oriented business linkages to provide logistic and financial support to SMEs to enhance their capabilities and performance as partners within the value chains. This CSR model is carefully designed to gain recognition from the governments of host countries and public legitimacy as corporate citizens. Finally, Case 10 is political because the Sialkot and Jalandhar corporations through their CSR initiatives assisted the international community in embedding international protocols on child labour in India and Pakistan, respectively. It is developmental because the victims of child labour were sent to schools with the expenses borne by the two corporations.

2.4 Conclusion, implication and recommendations

MNCs invoked a political CSR with developmental impact to elicit legitimacy and socio-economic licences from the social licensors (public, regulatory agencies and politicians). The practical implication of this chapter is that in the MENA and Asia where there is a governance gap, it is in the interest of MNCs to bridge the gap with CSR initiatives. However, the involvement of MNCs in social issues should not encourage government to abdicate its core statutory responsibility of provision of public goods as well as effective service delivery. The conclusion of this chapter is that developing nations could leverage the political dimension of CSR, by demanding from corporations more involvement in community development for mutual benefits. Future studies could undertake an empirical investigation of a political CSR which policy-makers could explore for practical application of a political CSR to solving problems of poverty, unemployment and conflicts in MENA and Asia. The principle of voluntarism that drives the conventional CSR should guide the embedding of a political CSR. In other words, political CSR should strictly be pursed as a private-sector-driven model because there is preference for private-sector-led development initiatives. The role of the government with a political CSR mechanism should simply be limited to providing legitimacy and enablement for a smooth business–society relationship. Government could encourage participation, not coercion, of MNCs. Coercive CSR compliance would be akin to double taxation. Civil society groups should be vigilant with regard to political CSR that subverts democracy and national independence like the ploy of rogue corporations, which deployed CSR programs as a lobby to neutralize the negative impact of their products and gain support from politicians. Finally, social ills such as worsening poverty, governance deficit improving, political corruption, poor labour standards, environmental degradation, surging violence, industrial pollution as well as chronic diseases are problems that MNCs could help tackle sustainably through genuine political CSR.

Bibliography

Akhuemonkhan, I., Raimi, L., & Ogunjirin, O.D. (2012). Corporate Social Responsibility and Entrepreneurship (CSRE): Antidotes to Poverty, Insecurity and Underdevelopment in Nigeria. Paper delivered at international conference on Poverty, Insecurity and Development in Africa, Universiti de Lome, Republic of Togo, November 1–2.

Amaeshi, K.M., Adi, B.C., Ogbechie, C., & Amao, O.O. (2006). Corporate social responsibility in Nigeria: Western mimicry or indigenous influences? *Journal of Corporate Citizenship*, 24, 83-99.

Austin, J., & Reficco, E. (2009). Corporate Social Entrepreneurship. Harvard Business School, Working Paper Number 09-101, 1-8.

Bates, S. (2011). Bridging the Governance Gap: Strategies to Integrate Water and Land Use Planning. Center for Natural Resources and Environmental Policy, The University Of Montana. Policy Report No. 7.

Baumann, D., & Scherer, A.G. (2010). MNEs and the UN Global Compact: An Empirical Analysis of the Organizational Implementation of Corporate Citizenship. IOU Working Paper No. 114. Retrieved from http://ssrn.com/abstract=1705532.

Blatter, J. (2012). Forms of Political Governance – Theoretical Foundations and Ideal Types. Working Paper Series, Global Governance and Democracy, Universität Luzern, Germany. Retrieved from http://www.unilu.ch/files/wp7_forms-of-political-governance.pdf.

Booz and Company (2013). The Rise of Corporate Social Responsibility—A Tool for Sustainable Development in the Middle East. Retrieved from http://www.booz.com/media/file/BoozCo_The-Rise-of-Corporate-Social-Responsibility.pdf.

Boyle, M., & Boguslaw, J. (2007). Business, poverty and corporate citizenship naming the issues and framing solutions. *Journal of Corporate Citizenship*, Summer, 101-120.

Brønn, P.S., & Vrioni, A.B. (2001). Corporate social responsibility and cause related marketing: an overview. *International Journal of Advertising*, 20(2), 207-222.

Broomhill, R. (2007). Corporate Social Responsibility: Key Issues and Debates. Dunstan Paper No. 1, Don Dunstan Foundation. Retrieved from http://firgoa.usc.es/drupal/files/Ray_Broomhill.pdf.

Campbell, J.L. (2007). Why would corporations behave in socially responsible ways? An institutional theory of corporate social responsibility. *Academy of Management Review*, 32, 946-967.

Carroll, A. (1999).Corporate social responsibility—evolution of a definitional construct. *Business & Society*, 38(3), 268-295.

Center for International Private Enterprise and Global Integrity (2012). Improving Public Governance: Closing the Implementation Gap between Law and Practice. Retrieved from http://www.cipe.org/sites/default/files/publication-docs/GI%20CIPE_Implementation%20Gap_for%20web.pdf.

Charitoudi, G., Giannarakis, G., & Lazarides, T.G. (2011). Corporate social responsibility performance in periods of financial crisis. *European Journal of Scientific Research*, 63(3), 447-455.

Coyle, D. (2003). Corporate Governance, Public Governance and Global Governance: The Common Thread. Working Paper, Institute of Political and Economic Governance, University of Manchester, December.

Covin, J.G., & Miles, M.P. (1999). Corporate entrepreneurship and the pursuit of competitive advantage. *Entrepreneurship Theory and Practice*, 23(3), 47-63.

Crowther, D., & Rayman-Bacchus, L. (2004). *Perspectives on Corporate Social Responsibility*. Farnham: Ashgate Publishing.

Dartey-Baah, K., & Amponsah-Tawiah, K. (2011). Exploring the limits of Western corporate social responsibility theories in Africa. *International Journal of Business and Social Science*, 2(18), 126-137.

Donaldson, T. (2010). The values realignment in modern industrial society. *Business Ethics Quarterly*, 20(4), 728-729.

Edward, P., & Willmott, H. (2008). Corporate citizenship: rise or demise of a myth? *Academy of Management Review*, 33(3), 771-773.

Emadzadeh, M.K., Shahrestani, B.A., Safanoor, M., & Shahraki, K. (2012). The survey of relationship between size of firms and political costs. *Interdisciplinary Journal of Contemporary Research in Business*, 3(10), 355-356.

Fooks, G., Gilmore, A. Collin, J., Holden, C., & Lee, K. (2013). The limits of corporate social responsibility: techniques of neutralization, stakeholder management and political CSR. *Journal of Business Ethics*, 112(2), 283-299.

Friends of the Earth (2004). Media Briefing on Gas Flaring in Nigeria. London: Underwood. Retrieved from http://www.foe.co.uk/sites/default/files/downloads/gasflaringinnigeria.pdf.

Frynas, J.G. (2005). The false developmental promise of corporate social responsibility: evidence from multinational oil companies. *International Affairs*, 81(3), 581-598.

Frynas, J.G. (2008). Corporate social responsibility and international development: critical assessment. Corporate Governance: *An International Review*, 16(4), 274-81.

George, O.J., Kuye, O.L., & Onokala, U.C. (2012). Corporate social responsibility (CSR) a catalyst to the Niger Delta crisis: the case of Nigerian oil multinational companies versus the militants of Niger Delta region of Nigeria. *Journal of Management Research*, 4(2), 1-11.

Gond, J.P., & Matten, D. (2007). Rethinking the Business-Society Interface: Beyond the Functionalist Trap. ICCSR Research Paper Series, No. 47-2007.

Gray, R., Kouhy, R., & Lavers, S. (1995). Corporate social and environmental reporting: a review of the literature and a longitudinal study of UK disclosure. *Accounting, Auditing and Accountability*, 8(2), 47-77.

Hart, R. (2012). Green Mining or Green Washing? Corporate Social Responsibility and the Mining Sector in Canada. MiningWatch Canada, Mine Alerte, September. Retrieved from http://www.miningwatch.ca/sites/www.miningwatch.ca/files/Green%20Mining%20 or%20Green%20Washing.pdf.

Haskins, C. (2009). Using the Concept of Sustainable Development to Encourage Corporate Responsibility in Small Enterprises. Working paper of Norwegian University of Science and Technology, Department of Industrial Economics and Technology Management, Trondheim, Norway, 1-13.

Idemudia, U. (2011). Corporate social responsibility and developing countries: moving the critical CSR research agenda in Africa forward. *Progress in Development Studies*, 11(1), 1-18.

Ite, U.E. (2005). Poverty reduction in resource-rich developing countries: what have multinational corporations got to do with it?. *Journal of International Development*, 17, 913-929.

Ite, U.E. (2007). Partnering with the state for sustainable development: Shell's experience in the Niger Delta, Nigeria. *Sustainable Development*, 15, 216-228.

Kakabadse, N.K., Rozuel, C., & Lee-Davies, L. (2005). Corporate social responsibility and stakeholder approach: a conceptual review. *Int. J. Business Governance and Ethics*, 1(4), 277-302.

Kauffmann, C. (2005). Financing SMEs in Africa. Policy Insights No. 7, African Economic Outlook/African Development Bank/OECD Development Centre, 1-4.

Kerr, J.E. (2007). Sustainability Meets Profitability: The Convenient Truth of How the Business Judgment Rule Protects a Board's Decision to Engage in Social Entrepreneurship. Retrieved from http://ssrn.com/abstract=1296270 or http://dx.doi.org/10.2139/ssrn.1296270.

Kytle, B., & Ruggie, J.G. (2005). Corporate Social Responsibility as Risk Management—A Model for Multinationals. Corporate Social Responsibility Initiatives (CSRI) Working Paper No. 10. Cambridge, MA: John F. Kennedy School of Government, Harvard University.

Lantos, G.P. (2001). The boundaries of strategic corporate social responsibility. *Journal of consumer marketing*, 18(7), 595-632.

Leigh, D., & Evans, R. (2009, October 1). Fraud Office seeks BAE's prosecution over bribery. *The Guardian*.

Lubenow, J.A. (2012). Public sphere and deliberative democracy in Jürgen Habermas: theoretical model and critical discourses. *American Journal of Sociological Research*, 2(4), 58-71.

Luetkenhorst, W. (2004). Corporate social responsibility and the development agenda: the case for actively involving small and medium enterprises. *Intereconomics*, May/June, 157-166.

Matten, D. (2003). Symbolic politics in environmental regulation: corporate strategic responses. *Business Strategy and the Environment*, 12(4), 215-226.

Matten, D., & Crane, A. (2005). Corporate citizenship: toward an extended theoretical conceptualization. *Academy of Management Review*, 30(1), 166-179.

Milne, M.J. (2001). Positive Accounting Theory, Political Costs and Social Disclosure Analyses: A Critical Look. BAA Annual Conference at the University of Nottingham. Retrieved from http://citeseerx.ist.psu.edu/viewdoc/download?doi=10.1.1.199.7620&rep=rep1&type= pdf, last accessed 25 August 2013.

Mordi, C., Opeyemi, I.S., Tonbara, M., & Ojo, S. (2012). Corporate social responsibility and the legal regulation in Nigeria. *Economic Insights—Trends and Challenges*, LXIV(1), 1-8.

Murphy, S. (2010). Corporate Partnerships for Entrepreneurship: Building the Ecosystem in the Middle East and Southeast Asia. Corporate Social Responsibility Initiative Working Paper No. 62. Cambridge, MA: John F. Kennedy School of Government, Harvard University.

Natufe, O.I. (2011). Corporate social responsibility: value and strategic intent. *Social Responsibility Review*, (2), 14-25.

Nelson, J. (2000).The Business of Peace: Business as a Partner in Conflict Resolution.

Newberry, D. (2006). The Role of Small- and Medium-sized Enterprises in the Futures of Emerging Economies. World Resource Institute. Retrieved from http://earthtrends.wri.org/features/view_feature.php?fid=69&theme=5.

Nwadialor, E., & Igwe, N.N. (2013). Adapting corporate social responsibility programs to risk management: a model for multinational organizations in Nigeria. *European Journal of Business and Management*, 5(15), 17-24.

Oyelola, O.T., Ajiboshin, I.O., Raimi, L., Raheem, S., & Igwe, C.N. (2013). Entrepreneurship for sustainable economic growth in Nigeria. *Journal of Sustainable Development Studies*, 2(2), 197-215.

Porter, M.E., & Kramer. M.R. (2011). Creating Shared Value: How to reinvent capitalism—and unleash a wave of innovation and growth, Harvard Business Review (HBR), January/February, HBR:1-17.

Pratap, S. (2011). Corporate Social Responsibility and the Political Agenda of the Corporate. CSR Research Paper Series No. 3, Asia Monitor Resource Centre, 1-25. Retrieved from http://www.amrc.org.hk/system/files/CSR%20Research%20Paper%20Series%20No%203.pdf, last accessed 28 February 2014.

Raimi, L., & Akhuemonkhan, I. (2013). Has technical vocational education and training (TVET) impacted on employability and national development? *The Macrotheme Review*, 3(2), 129-146.

Rizk, R. (2012). Governance and its impact on poverty reduction: is there a role for knowledge management?. *International Journal of Innovation and Knowledge Management in Middle East & North Africa*, 1(1), 81-104.

Roy, D.A. (2010). Trends in global corporate social responsibility practices. The case of Sub-Saharan Africa. *International Journal of Civil Society Law*, Washington & Lee School, 8(3), 48-64.

Sagnia, B.K. (2005). Strengthening Local Creative Industries and Developing Cultural Capacity for Poverty Alleviation. Sixth Annual Conference Background Document, International Network for Cultural Diversity, November 17–20, Dakar, Senegal.

Scherer, A.G., & Palazzo, G. (2007). Toward a political conception of corporate responsibility: business and society seen from a Habermasian perspective. *Academy of Management Review*, 32(4), 1096-1120.

Scherer, A.G., & Palazzo, G. (2008). Globalization and corporate social responsibility. In A. Crane, A. McWilliams, D. Matten, J. Moon & D. Siegel (Eds.), *The Oxford Handbook of Corporate Social Responsibility* (pp. 413-431). Oxford: Oxford University Press.

Scherer, A.G., & Palazzo, G. (2011). The new political role of business in a globalized world: a review of a new perspective on CSR and its implications for the firm, governance, and democracy. *Journal of Management Studies*, 48(4), 899-931.

Scholtens, B. (2014). Indicators of responsible investing. *Ecological Indicators*, 36, 382-385.

Sharp, J. (2006). Corporate social responsibility and development: an anthropological perspective. Development Southern Africa, 23(2), 213-222.

Smith, R.E. (2011). Defining Corporate Social Responsibility: A Systems Approach for Socially Responsible Capitalism. Master of Philosophy Dissertation (unpublished), University of Pennsylvania, Philadelphia, Pennsylvania. Retrieved from http://repository.upenn.edu/cgi/viewcontent.cgi?article=1009&context=od_theses_mp

Sternberg, E. (2009). Corporate social responsibility and corporate governance. Economic Affairs, Social Science Electronic Publishing, Inc., 29(4), 5-10.

Sweeney, L. (2009). A Study of Current Practice of Corporate Social Responsibility (CSR) and an Examination of the Relationship between CSR and Financial Performance Using Structural Equation Modelling (SEM). Doctoral Thesis (unpublished), Dublin Institute of Technology, Dublin.

Tausif, M. (2012). Corporate social responsibility practices: an exploratory study. ABHINAV, *National Monthly Refereed Journal of Research in Commerce and Management*, 1(5), 36-41.

Tehrani, R., Salehi, M., Valipour, H., & Lashky, M.J. (2009). The survey of the political costs and firm size: case from Iran. *Business Intelligence Journal*, 2(2), 319-342.

Tombs, S. (2005). Regulating safety at work. Policy and practice. *Health and Safety*, 3(1), 5-16.

Ufadhili, M.K., Yambayamba, K., & Fox, T. (2005). How can Corporate Social Responsibility Deliver in Africa? Insights from Kenya and Zambia. Perspectives on Corporate Responsibility for Environment and Development, IIED, Number 3, July, 1-5.

UNESCO-UNEVOC (2012). Transforming TVET from idea to action. UNESCO-UNEVOC International Centre for Technical and Vocational Education and Training, UN Campus, Bonn, Germany.

Valmohammadi, C. (2011). Investigating corporate social responsibility practices in Iranian organizations: an ISO 26000 perspective. *Business Strategy Series*, 12(5), 257-263.

van Tulder, R., & van der Zwart, A. (2006). *International Business-Society Management*.

Visser, W. (2008). Corporate social responsibility in developing countries. In A. Crane, A. McWilliams, D. Matten, J. Moon & D. Siegel (Eds.), *The Oxford Handbook of Corporate Social Responsibility* (pp. 473-479). Oxford: Oxford University Press.

Vrajlal, K.S., & Kandarp, V.P. (2010). Corporate Governance & Public Governance. Lambert Academy Publishing GmbH & Co. KG.

Waddock, S.A., & Graves, S.B. (1997). The corporate social performance–financial performance link. *Strategic Management Journal*, 18, 303-319.

Walsh, J.P., Weber, K., & Margolis, J.D. (2003). Social issues and management: our lost cause found. *Journal of Management*, 29, 859-881.

Watts, R.L., & Zimmerman, J.L. (1978). Towards a positive theory of the determination of accounting standards. The Accounting Review, 53(1), 112-134.

Watts, R.L., & Zimmerman, J.L. (1990). Positive accounting theory: a ten year perspective. *The Accounting Review*, 65(1), 131-156.

Western Zagros Annual Report (2012). Corporate Social Responsibility. Retrieved from http://www.westernzagros.com/wp-content/uploads/2013/05/Western_Zagros_2012-AR.pdf.

Wood, D. (1991). Corporate social performance revisited. *The Academy of Management Review*, 16(4), 691-718.

World Bank (2003). Better Governance for Development in the Middle East and North Africa: Enhancing Inclusiveness and Accountability. Washington, DC: World Bank. Retrieved from http://go.worldbank.org/LGTT1USV00.

Yekini, K., & Jallow, K. (2012). Corporate community involvement disclosures in annual report: A measure of corporate community development or a signal of CSR observance? *Sustainability Accounting, Management and Policy Journal*, 3(1), 7-32.

Young, T. (1999). The state and politics in Africa. *Journal of Southern African Studies*, 25(1), 149-154.

Zain Bahrain, (2013). Zain Bahrain and the Community. Social/CSR Report. Retrieved from http://www.bh.zain.com/ZainPortal/ZainBahrain_CSR.jsp.

3

Operational intent and development impact in mining

Deanna Kemp and John R. Owen
Sustainable Minerals Institute, Australia

Vimala Dejvongsa
In Situ Development Consulting, Australia

This chapter focuses on contemporary debates about mining, corporate social responsibility (CSR) and development. The authors engage the question of how observers are to interpret the intentions and actions of a mining operation relative to its development impact. The authors draw on fieldwork data collected through a commissioned review of a community development program being implemented by a mid-tier mining company. By taking an "embedded" rather than an "isolated" reading of corporate contributions to community development, the authors conclude that the program represents a tactical move on the part of the company to pacify local stakeholders with developmental "gifts", while denying them legitimate access to meaningful influence over mining and associated activities. The program positions the interests of the community as secondary to the interests of mining and limits the company's ability to move towards a development-oriented approach to CSR.

John Lubbock, a nineteenth-century English banker, once quipped that "what we see depends mainly on what we look for". For social scientists, subjective interest and positionality are crucial elements in attempting to understand perspective and intent. In this chapter, the authors embrace Lubbock's remarks as a starting point for examining operational intent in relation to local-level "corporate community development" initiatives in the minerals sector. When operating in developing countries with weak or corrupt governance structures, mining companies often adopt a truncated view of their development contribution. This occurs in part because it serves to minimize corporate social responsibility (CSR) for areas that are perceived to fall within the domain of the state, and in part because some companies are either unable or unwilling to construct or negotiate a development proposition that takes account of the operating context. To support this line of observation, the authors draw on fieldwork data collected through a commissioned review of a discrete community development program being implemented by a mid-tier mining company operating in mainland Southeast Asia.

In undertaking the review, we took the community development program to be a practical reflection of the company's overall approach to development. A range of factors present in the operating context were taken into account, including community expectations, local-level impacts, and aspects of the state–company–community interface. Our premise is that the relationship between these factors provides a useful indicator of operational intent. Contemporary development scholars interested in mining and CSR suggest that "intentional" corporate community development cannot be viewed in isolation from the multifarious social, ecological and economic transformations wrought by mining (Banks *et al.*, 2013). In a similar vein, others argue that companies cannot offset harm by doing corporate "good deeds" elsewhere (Ruggie, 2008). The suggestion here is that "impact" and "contribution" cannot be viewed in isolation; either from each other, or the context in which they interact. Our case highlights the practical importance of ensuring that operational "impact" and development "contribution" are viewed as co-terminus relative rather than in isolation.

At its core, our analysis confirms that layered readings and multiple perspectives are required in order to understand corporate intent with respect to community development initiatives in mining and CSR, and its relationship with operating context, local impacts and organizational systems. A major constraint within the mining industry is its ability to identify the links between operational impacts and community development outcomes. Another constraint is in the industry's own understanding of the internal dimensions of community relations practice (Owen and Kemp, 2014). The industry is not adept at identifying the influence of its own interests over social processes, which means that companies often fail to read the social landscape and account for any more than the "business case" for contributing to community development. Some commentators reinforce this view by suggesting that "development contribution" and "business case" require compatibility (Harvey, 2014). A certain level of compatibility is certainly reasonable. Our findings suggest that when business priorities dominate all other dimensions, a transactional, "user-relationship" between company and community readily ensues (Kemp and Owen, 2013). In developing country contexts, this can lead to a situation where corporate community development can appear to serve local people, but is in fact configured to serve the interest of the business.

The structure of the chapter is as follows: The first section describes the programmatic context of the case study itself. It outlines the methodological approach used for the review, as well as a descriptive summary of the program. Section two presents a discussion of two leading themes from the fieldwork. The first examines the mining operation's rationale for engaging in community development. The second discussion follows the consequences of this rationalizing processes on internal and external relationships, and the effect that this has on the strategic direction and utility of the program. In the final section we conclude with a call for a more coherent approach to understanding community development that enables an "embedded" reading that accounts for the operating environment and the operation's full suite of organizational processes and systems and a set of final reflections.

3.1 Programmatic context

This chapter is limited by the need to maintain anonymity around the location of the project site. This limitation reflects two significant barriers to knowledge building and knowledge transfer on the social dimensions of mining. The first barrier is that researchers who are interested in learning about mining and social performance often struggle to gain access to or cooperation from mining companies. The second barrier is that professionals and academics who are able to gain access through commissioned work are typically bound by confidentiality clauses which prohibit the publication and public sharing of information about the company (Kemp and Owen, 2013). Of the options available to us, we have elected to present the findings on the basis of an anonymous case study.

Despite this limitation we are able to provide useful contextual and background detail that does not compromise the identity of the operation and the communities involved. The mine is owned and operated by a mid-tier company with the national government holding a minority share. The country context presents unique challenges in terms of legislation, governance and rights for both the company and affected communities. As one of two remaining single party states in mainland Southeast Asia, there are few contexts that allow for direct comparison, and given the deleterious effects of this style of governance on freedom of speech in particular, information on contentious issues and projects is often difficult to source or share. Transparency around national revenue and expenditure, policy development, together with the state's protection of human rights all remain active challenges for the government, lenders, developers, civil society and citizens.

The operation is located in a rural and remote part of the country, itself having a history of war and conflict as countries in the region sought independence from colonial rule. Poverty levels for communities in the areas adjacent to the mine are broadly commensurate with those in surrounding districts where large scale mining is not a factor. Small increases in human development indicators have been recorded, but these are largely attributed to employees of the mine, many of whom have migrated to the area in search of economic opportunity. The general poverty context has not improved in the 15 years since mining commenced, despite improvement in roads, water and access to electricity to a small number of surrounding villages. Agriculture remains the dominant form of livelihood, however mining and natural resource development are widely understood as having the largest impact on gross domestic product (GDP) and state revenue.

A major limitation to improved human development has been the incremental "land take" by the mine, which has impacted or excised areas that communities have historically used for crops, rearing livestock or foraging either for foodstuffs or other valuable materials. The company's pattern of "recompense" has been both inconsistent and minimalist, other than in circumstances where operational access was urgent, in which case, compensation rates were inflated, creating new local-level inequalities. Changes to land tenure, land availability, and an increasingly cash-based local economy have meant that affected communities have fewer natural resources by which to meet basic provisioning needs. Changes in the local economy have brought a system of progressive inflation. Communities in the local area remain vulnerable to food insecurity. Those without access to mining or other employment and who are reliant on subsistence farming increasingly find themselves in especially precarious circumstances.

3.2 Sample and methods

In undertaking the review of the mine's community development program, we examined background documents (e.g. project plans, communication materials, evaluation reports etc.) and conducted a range of interviews on two separate site visits. A total of 27 interviews with 58 people were undertaken for this review with representatives at the company's country office, and at the operation, including community development staff (see Table 3.1).

Women and men were evenly represented in the overall sample, although men were more prominent in higher-level discussions. Representatives from local government agencies were also interviewed, as were local community representatives, community and village groups in near-mine and exploration communities. Across the review, the research team visited a total of six villages that were actively participating in the project, several of which were ranked in the "poorest" category, according to defined government criteria.

A semi-structured interview protocol was applied, with individual and small group discussions conducted through interpretation in the national language and English. Table 3.2 provides a summary of the methods applied.

Table 3.1 **Description of sample**

Sample	Description
Size	58 individuals
	Approximate equal number of men and women
Interview participants	Senior managers at operational level [n=9]
	Company community development supervisors and staff [n=14]
	Senior local government officials [n=3]
	Community leaders and representatives [n=17]
	Other community members [n=15]

Table 3.2 **Description of methods**

Method	Description
Technique	Face-to-face, individual and group interviews and observations
Language	Official national language (with interpretation to-from English)
Instrument	Semi-structured interview protocol
Duration	45–90 minutes
Location	On-site at the mine, in villages, at local government offices
Recruitment	Voluntary, confidential
Data	Verbatim transcriptions
Analysis	Thematic coding for themes and sub-themes

3.3 The community development program

The community development program that was subject of the review is a small-scale program that supports village participation in managing a local grant scheme. The primary scope of participation is around needs identification, decision-making, planning and implementation of village development activities. The company funds a team of dedicated community development staff tasked with program coordination and ensuring that villages adhere to an agreed set of criteria. Criteria outline expectations relating to gender representation, processes for acquiring approval for program activities from local authorities, and a well-documented plan of implementation, monitoring and reporting. The team comprises three female and four male staff. Two of the male staff are members of an ethnic minority group from the local area. Other staff are from the national/dominant ethnic group and fly in from different (but urban) parts of the country.

At the time of the review the program was in its fifth year of activity. The program was established in 2007 in response to a collective request from six near-mine villages which had experienced the full weight of mining impacts. The local and regional government had excluded these villages from government-sponsored initiatives on the assumption that they were accruing direct economic benefits from the mine (e.g. preferential employment and local business contracts). The six villages requested that the mine address their exclusion through an assistance program where they received direct funds, and had decision-making power over allocation of grant monies. With approval from the local government, the mine agreed to establish the program with the six villages. One of the early objectives of the program was to build a program that provided an alternative to existing "top down" models of development and the dominant patron-client relationship between the company and community (or government and community). While the program has evolved in scope and size since inception, its emphasis on participation, community benefit and gender representation were described by most interviewees as a consistent feature of the program.

The geographic scope of the program has grown significantly since 2007. Additional villages have been added over time with each new round of grants, largely in response to requests from the local government. The company has also added villages in its exploration area, essentially as a pre-emptive relationship building exercise ahead of drilling activities. In the future, the company plans to add villages on the basis that they are ranked "poorest" against government poverty rankings. These villages are in the company's lease area but not all of them have immediate exploration potential. No villages from outside the permit area are included in the program. Land access for mining activities and geographic proximity to the mine are the primary criteria for inclusion.

The program comprises five per cent of the company's overall in-country development spend.[1] The village grants can be used for a defined range of projects, including: small-scale village infrastructure construction and/or renovation; livelihood development; training and skills development; access roads and tracks and/or water and sanitation projects. The mine's departmental budget, including for the program, is approved on an annual basis, so planning horizons are not long-term and there is no guarantee that the program will continue. Projects awarded under the scheme must be completed within the year. None of the original participating villages had been transitioned out of the program.

In summary, it is notable that compensation payments have increased exponentially in both quantum and frequency over the past decade. This is a reflection of the company's incremental approach to land acquisition and a community more prepared to "hold out" for higher rates. As the project has expanded, the company has systematically recorded impacts through a series of discrete studies that are required by regulators for project permitting. However, findings from these studies are not well aligned or integrated within organizational systems (e.g. impact

---

1   The remainder is comprised of regional and national level development initiatives much of which is spent away from the footprint area of the mine. The company also operates a donation program administered from the regional office.

management and mitigation planning, engagement, grievance handling or development initiatives). In this sense, impact studies make reference to development, but do not take the full suite of development impacts into account. As discussed below, the dominant discourse was that of social licence; a live and tacit discourse driving CSR and development strategy in mining. This approach privileges those villages, such as the original six, that are most vocal, and most able to influence, disrupt or affect land access or production goals.

3.4 Discussion

3.4.1 Different readings and surface analysis

In our introduction we casually referred to the English Banker John Lubbock, and his light remarks on the nature of human perspective. The point we are looking to emphasize here is that motive and intent are important drivers and need to be considered when constructing and (equally) deconstructing analysis. To understand organizational intent, we interviewed senior managers at the operation and at the regional office and asked each person what they perceived to be the objective/s of the program. What we found was that few participants were able to provide an empirically informed set of responses, and simply reflected a certain accepted wisdoms or assumptions about the community, its needs, and the role of the company as a private developer. The company's "surface" read looks stark against the backdrop of perspectives from other stakeholders, including the community, and the context within which the operation is located.

Managers who were involved in or familiar with the program referred to its origins as an "appeasement strategy" for the six near-mine villages. While the original intent of the program was to ease tension with immediate host communities, it was not configured as a remedy or redress mechanism but a "relational mechanism" with "development benefits" attached. In this sense, the program targets impacted communities without the intention of addressing impacts, but rather, of maintaining land access in exchange for development goods. The scheme is considered to be a capillary program that forms an extension of larger-scale contributions that have profile at the national level, but bear little relation to the aforementioned effects that the mine has had on the community.

What company representatives nominate as "effectiveness criteria" provides one indication of where corporate priorities may lie. Exactly what is considered to be effective was not always clear amongst those managers interviewed. One manager explained that while the expenditure is small, the program is effective as "micro-level" CSR initiative. Another manager explained that the program provided "reputational value" because villagers do not tend to recognize the company's other more financially significant contributions such as those made through the government Trust Fund, or as part of development partnerships at the national level. It was the direct nature of the donation from the company that was spent on visible village level infrastructure that was clearly important to the company. Most other managers simply explained the program as a vehicle that helped to "smooth the way" and to support the company's "social licence to operate".

To understand the logic and rationale of the program, we also asked managers to describe the main objectives of the fund. Most senior managers referred to the program as a "capacity building" or "empowerment" program. When prompted, none of the senior leadership team could provide further explanation regarding the status or effectiveness of the program. In the end, most said the program was a mechanism through which the company could provide a "donation", "gift", "grant" or, in one case, a "handout". One senior manager said that while it was not altogether clear what the program was about, his approach was to support the expenditure because it enabled the company to contain costs and restrict the operation's spend per village. The program clearly provides the company with a defined level of financial control. What the company tended not to define, however, were program aims or objectives. Nor were outcomes formally monitored via an agreed set of indicators. The process aspects were monitored by staff on an ongoing basis. Where monitoring proved to be less than rigorous was around demonstrating development impact.

In terms of aims and objectives, several managers claimed that there was an operational benefit to having a scantly defined strategy. They maintained that this absence provided the business with flexibility in terms of how it responded to requests from local government and meant that they could approve development expenditure "as required". At the same time, however, the absence of a formal strategy does leave the company open to what managers referred to as "demands for development" where stakeholders leverage benefits based on points of corporate vulnerability (e.g. time-frames for exploration, land access or mine infrastructure). During the review, it was clear that "leveraging" was fast becoming the dominant approach to securing resources for local development.

We asked other groups within the company about their understanding of the program, and motivations for being involved. Program staff said that, first and foremost, they were servicing the mine's agenda in terms of enabling land access to areas of interest, either for exploration or mining. In addition to enabling mining, a range of other priorities were mentioned including capacity building for local women and ethnic minority communities. Gaining the support of local government was also a nominated priority that the program itself targeted. Staff readily acknowledged that the program was not designed to prevent or mitigate impacts or serve as a redress mechanism. Nonetheless there was a strong sentiment that the program served as some kind of reparation for impacts to "address a sense of loss" in impacted communities, and "overcome negative feelings towards the mine". In this sense, staff believe that the project serves to demonstrate to villagers that the mine is at least trying, in some way, to repair the relationship, and make amends via development contributions.

When attempting to categorize the development program, interviewees from within the company tended to discuss the program in isolated terms, without reference to external context, or other company systems. In effect, the review team had to "patch together" an understanding of how the program related to other organizational processes and systems. This "isolated read" is indicative of how the company commissioned the review. The company was, in fact, interested in understanding the effectiveness of the program *in isolation* from its other activities, rather than understanding how the program related to the internal and external context in a broader sense. The next discussion considers the outcome of this kind of narrow reading and draws out how the program functions within the broader context.

3.4.2 Community development as a relational buffer

A major finding from the review is the effect of approaching development in primarily "relational" and "reputational" terms. In the main, villagers suggested that the program provided an important relational benefit. For managers outside of community relations, the attribution of a relational benefit was read with a measure of scepticism. Essentially, they took this as meaning that the team responsible had not adequately tracked or quantified the costs or benefits of the program. At the same time, casting the program as having relational outcomes also meant the mine management team could talk about the fund as contributing to its "social licence". The relational outcomes that village participants spoke of is referred to here as a "buffering" outcome—a term used by management theorists to describe a strategy that aims to seal a firm off from external disturbances and prevent the environment from influencing internal operations. "Bridging", by contrast, promotes interaction with the external context and adaptation to stakeholder expectations (Meznar and Nigh, 1995; van den Bosch and van Riel, 1998). Before considering the buffering effect in more detail, we describe the relational dimensions of the program from the perspective of program staff, local government representatives and program beneficiaries.

The task of "making amends" and improving the relationship with the six original villages was, according to program staff, achieved through personal interactions in each village as part of administering and implementing the program. In their view, this task has not been achieved through the provisioning of grants or the building of projects, which they observed as making only small improvements to people's lives. Rather, program staff attribute positive relationships to consistent personal interactions and the participatory methodology. Staff travel to each village, every week, to spend time talking to different groups within the community about the program and other matters that relate to everyday village life. Senior managers valued the "visible" aspects of the program, whereas program staff described the "process elements" as far more critical to securing social licence and any development impact, however small.

Local officials were complimentary of the program, indicating that the intent, participatory method and outcomes were a positive indication that the company was working to uphold its social responsibility to support local development. Local authorities indicated that the program had also helped them meet certain poverty alleviation criteria set by the Central Government, as they have no other funds to draw on to address those issues. Encouraging the inclusion of the poorest villages into the program is what local authorities were focused on at the time of the review. The company on the other hand was focused on adding exploration villages that aligned with its land access agenda. It was, nonetheless, becoming increasingly cognizant of the insistent nature of the government's requests to include poor villages, and there had been agreement that villages with high needs may be added in future rounds.

Clearly, different parties value the program for very different reasons. Senior managers prioritize a land access agenda and visible development, program staff emphasize the process and interactional elements, and local government supports the program as part of a poverty alleviation and peace keeping agenda. Participating communities also have a distinct perspective. Across the board, local villagers were complimentary of the project. They expressed gratitude that the mine offered a small grant program and appreciated the opportunity to interact with program staff. Nonetheless, near mine villages were necessarily more focused on impacts, land access claims and outstanding grievances. They explained that while relations with program staff were good, the program did not address mining-related impacts or help those in greatest need. The scheme does not, for example, address the needs of families whose livelihoods are under greatest pressure from mining. In fact, the program is designed *not* to privilege a particular group but provide a "whole of community" benefit. While frustrations amongst the most impacted communities were high, communities still indicated that their relationship with program staff was positive; in fact at times they said it was the only positive point of connection with the company. They also expressed frustration that program staff did not represent their issues internally or have any influence over the mine itself. The connection that staff have with villages is not utilized for anything other than the program. One advantage of this is that workers have been able to focus on village-level engagement, rather than their work being dominated by company-related priorities. The program's relative autonomy and small size also means that it has been unaffected by cost-cutting demands placed on other parts of the business. However, the lack of internal integration with other parts of the business is a lost opportunity given the depth of knowledge that the program staff have about village context, local change and the effect that the mine has had on livelihoods. Better utilization of this knowledge provides an opportunity to enhance social risk management and minimize/offset grievances early in the conflict cycle.

It is at this point then, that we ask what outcomes the program actually achieves. The scenario mentioned above infers a "buffering" outcome. Buffering occurs when the community is kept at arm's length, thereby protecting the company from unmanageable demands and insulating them from community complaints of impacts and exclusion from mining benefits. In this case, buffering works to prevent the second (potential) outcome—that of bridging. Bridging relationships would occur where the content of engagement serves to prompt change to operational-level decisions or actions based on community feedback, concerns, needs or development aspirations (Meznar and Nigh, 1995; van den Bosch and van Riel, 1998). During the review, there was no evidence that the knowledge or relationships built through the program were used to inform or influence operational-level strategies, whether for engagement, impact management, risk analysis, grievance handling or development planning. The program is used to build the capacity of local villagers to manage small infrastructure grants. It is not used to build the capacity of the organization to understand community perspectives, or adjust organizational processes so that they are more community-oriented, and less impactful. In fact, the program has become so "successful" that other community engagement activities have diminished and the program has become the default form of local-level engagement.

This relational construct may feel like a "bridge" to beneficiaries but for all intents and purposes it is merely serving as a "buffer" for the company. In terms of what the program actually achieves, we read the relational buffering effect as a tactical move on the part of the company to pacify local stakeholders with developmental "gifts", while denying them legitimate access to meaningful input or influence over mining and associated activities. This clearly positions the interests of the community as secondary to the interests of mining. It also throws new light on the interaction between buffering and bridging tactics of mining operations in the context of CSR and development.

3.5 Conclusion

There is an urgent call for the minerals sector to respond with greater consideration and sophistication to the social issues posed by resource extraction. The development component of this call is inextricably linked to questions about impact and benefit sharing, good governance and sustainability, participation and inclusive economic growth. Confusion over the role of development in the resources industry is not confined to companies, but the problem of all stakeholders who seek to clarify the responsibilities of project proponents. What is clear, however, is the role of "interest" and "intent" in determining which variant of "development" is applied and to whose benefit. Given the range of uses, and the many combinations that can be constructed, the question of how a development effort will support company and community interests should be treated as a priority.

The case example depicted in this chapter illustrates the importance of identifying the various interests attached to development programs and the implications these interests have across a number of fronts. Understanding which parties have which stake in a given development initiative is critical for understanding the approach to CSR and development. The formulation and roll out of an operational strategy is almost entirely dependent upon whose interests are in frame. The future direction of debates about the function of development in mining (and vice versa) will only have legitimacy if the substance of those debates is grounded in an honest appraisal of who is in control of and driving the agenda.

It is only possible to understand the outcomes and implications of the program through an embedded account of its nature. From this perspective, the program was understood as entrenched within a corporate system that prioritizes short term land access and reputational gain over other considerations. Without taking an embedded account of the program, the review itself would have provided a surface reading that aligns with the corporate view, which would have been limited to: (1) identifying the proactive nature of company-community relationships, (2) describing the program as an encouraging example of participatory development and (3) noting the provision of small but positive development outcomes. This reading has, at best, a tenuous and superficial relationship with corporate motivations, actions and intentions, and at worst, represents a complete misread of the context and the nature of a program that provides a relational buffer and prevents beneficiaries from having meaningful influence over the mine and its activities. Our analysis confirms that corporate community development in mining cannot be read in isolation. Any program review must demonstrate a grasp of the external context and hold the structure, process, effectiveness, value and consequences of community development in relation to other activities, impacts and systems attached to the mining operation.

3.6 Reflections on development-oriented CSR

This case highlights an incongruence that often exists between "development" and "CSR". Mining operations are themselves a function of a global push by developing nations to mobilize their natural resource base in order to fund national development. The activity, the impact and the benefits that flow from that activity can all rightfully be regarded as "development". The key question that must be asked is: What kind of development do we want to see driving the CSR agenda of companies in developing countries? In answering this question, we must be mindful that CSR consists of internal tensions. For instance, in order to deliver the revenue that supports national development, mining companies see themselves as needing to maximize production while minimizing cost. At the same time, both consumers and shareholders send companies strong signals about their expectations. To be a responsible corporate actor under these conditions requires high levels of reflection and awareness; not simply about the immediate pragmatics associated with their business activities, but the broader implications that come with "development".

These questions do not sit neatly within the conventional reading of either development or CSR. They do however, reflect a need for companies to understand and analyse the world in which they operate. Within that process of analysis, one would expect mining companies to arrive at a clear statement of purpose about how they contribute beyond production and profit and generate benefit for project-affected people. In our case, we found this basic level of awareness to be largely absent. There was virtually no awareness of the link between operational activity, social impact and program objectives. The mining company could readily displace local communities, have significant negative impacts on local livelihoods and food security, and yet claim a "positive CSR contribution" through the program, while using it as a buffer to maintain the status quo. The relationship between a company's interests, its perceived obligations and its development contribution (however defined) was unclear to almost every person we spoke with. A lack of strategy does not automatically preclude the possibility of companies generating social good. It does, however, mean that the allocation, implementation or effect of these social goods will almost certainly appear in the form of "uneven development".

Bibliography

Banks, G., Kuir-Ayius, D., Kombako, D., & Sagir, B. (2013). Conceptualizing mining impacts, livelihoods and corporate community development in Melanesia. *Community Development Journal*, 48(3), 484-500.

Harvey, B. (2014). Social development will not deliver social licence to operate for the extractive sector. *Extractive Industries and Society*, 1(1), 7-11.

Kemp, D., & Owen, J.R. (2013). Community relations and mining: core to business but not "core business". *Resources Policy*, 38(4), 523-531.

Meznar, M., & Nigh, D. (1995). Buffer or bridge? Environmental and organizational determinants of public affairs activities in American firms. *The Academy of Management Journal*, 38(4), 975-996.

Owen, J., & Kemp, D. (2014). Mining and community relations: mapping the internal dimensions of practice. *Extractive Industries and Society*, 1(1), 12-19.

Ruggie, J. (2008). Protect, respect, remedy: a framework for business and human rights. Human Rights Council of the United Nations, A/HRC/8/5.

van den Bosch, F.A.J., & van Riel, C.B.M. (1998). Buffering and bridging as environmental strategies of firms. *Business Strategy and the Environment*, 7, 24-31.

4

The headquartering effect in international CSR

Ralf Barkemeyer and Frank Figge
Kedge Business School, France

Lutz Preuss
Royal Holloway, University of London, UK

The increasing professionalization of corporate social responsibility (CSR) has led to a more strategic approach and a more centralized mode of CSR-related decision-making. However, we argue that these developments limit the ability of multinational companies (MNCs) to respond to the needs of less salient stakeholders, particularly of local stakeholders in countries where subsidiaries, rather than corporate headquarters, are located. A more strategic orientation of CSR reduces slack for MNC subsidiaries but it also leaves less opportunity to engage with the concerns of local stakeholders. We provide empirical evidence of such a headquartering effect in international CSR based on a survey of UN Global Compact participants. This effect appears to be particularly pronounced for CSR activities that are global in scope, address the socio-economic dimension of sustainability and are based on a strong ethical motivation. Consequently, there is a risk that a more strategic and more centralized approach to CSR marginalizes genuine development.

One of the key challenges in CSR concerns the contributions of MNCs to international development, particularly to developing countries (Hopkins, 2007; Jamali, 2010). On the one hand, MNCs and their subsidiaries can make important contributions to human development in developing countries (Jenkins 2005; Kolk and Van Tulder, 2006) as they build hospitals and schools, finance the fight against AIDS or support cultural projects (Schepers, 2006; Valente and Crane, 2010). On the other hand, such engagement is frequently criticized as reflecting a northern bias, that is, it prioritizes the interests of northern developed countries at the expense of southern developing countries (e.g. Blowfield, 2003; Fox, 2004; Utting, 2001). The question whether CSR can serve as an effective development tool thus seems to be predicated on the question to what extent MNCs can engage with the social and environmental priorities of their stakeholders in the local (developing country) contexts they operate in.

In investigating this challenge, scholars have repeatedly borrowed from the international management literature, where dealing with cultural differences and complex environments has a long-standing tradition. In particular, Prahalad and Doz's (1987) integration-responsiveness framework and Bartlett and Ghoshal's (1989, 2000) resultant typology of international business approaches have become popular theoretical lenses through which the international CSR activities of MNCs have been analysed (Arthaud-Day, 2005; Barin-Cruz and Pedrozo, 2009; Husted and Allen, 2006; Logsdon and Wood, 2002; Muller, 2006). In short, MNCs should integrate their CSR activities globally in order to make the provision of CSR cost-effective and to adequately respond to global social problems; at the same time, they should be locally responsive to their various stakeholder groups in the particular contexts they operate in. Such a *transnational* (Bartlett and Ghoshal, 1989; Bartlett and Ghoshal, 2000; Husted and Allen, 2006) or *global* (Chaudhri, 2006; Post, 2000) approach to CSR should thus ameliorate the imbalance between the global north and south, and allow MNCs to effectively address the most relevant and pressing international development challenges.

Conceptually, a number of arguments have since been presented explaining why a transnational approach to CSR may not be too likely to emerge (Barkemeyer and Figge, 2014). The increasing professionalization of CSR has led to the creation of specialized departments, but these are usually located in corporate headquarters. More strategic approaches to CSR (Porter and Kramer, 2006) or instrumental stakeholder management (Donaldson and Preston, 1995) not only oversimplify the relationship between economic and social goals (Crane *et al.*, 2014) but may further augment the emphasis on the requirements of northern stakeholders as these usually are more salient than southern ones (Frynas, 2005). These developments may have led to a headquartering effect in international CSR, according to which strategic decision-making on CSR is increasingly confined to MNC headquarters rather than their subsidiaries (Barkemeyer and Figge, 2014).

This chapter investigates this headquartering effect empirically. To shed light on this issue, we conducted a survey of UN Global Compact signatories into decision-making on CSR projects. The responses generally confirm the existence of a headquartering effect in CSR-related decision-making. This effect appears to be particularly pronounced in CSR activities that are global rather than local in scope that address the socio-economic rather than the environmental dimension of sustainability and that are driven by a strong ethical motivation.

The remainder of this chapter is structured as follows. The next section briefly reviews the international CSR literature using Prahalad and Doz's (1987) integration-responsiveness framework and Bartlett and Ghoshal's (1989, 2000) typology of international business approaches as a starting-point. The following section explains the headquartering effect in international CSR. Subsequently, the research design is presented and justified. Next, we present the results of the empirical analysis. Before concluding, our discussion focuses on the implications of the headquartering effect for corporate practice and policy-makers as well as limitations stemming from the empirical analysis.

4.1 International CSR, global integration and local responsiveness

The international management literature, with its emphasis on operating across cultural differences and complex environments, has provided ample inspiration for the international CSR literature. In particular, Prahalad and Doz's (1987) integration-responsiveness framework and Bartlett and Ghoshal's (1989, 2000) resultant typology of international business approaches have repeatedly been applied to the domain of international CSR (Arthaud-Day, 2005; Barin-Cruz and Pedrozo, 2009; Husted and Allen, 2006; Logsdon and Wood, 2002; Muller, 2006). Prahalad and Doz distinguish between two generic types of pressures MNCs need to respond to throughout their international operations. Pressures for global integration result from cost pressures, stemming not least from the activities of multinational competitors. Pressures for local responsiveness arise from national differences in customer needs, distribution channels or host government demands. MNCs need to find answers in terms of their organizational structure, strategy and decision-making to both of these sets of pressures.

Building on the integration-responsiveness grid, Bartlett and Ghoshal have identified distinct types of organizational models that an MNC can apply in order to respond to these pressures: the *international* model (low degree of global integration/low degree of local responsiveness), the *global* model (high integration/low responsiveness), the *multinational* model (low integration/high responsiveness) and the *transnational* model (high integration/high responsiveness) (Bartlett and Ghoshal, 1989, 2000). As the *international* model is today seen as rather outdated, MNCs tend to adopt either a *global*, *multinational* or *transnational* model, depending on the external environments they face (e.g. Harzing, 2000). Bartlett and Ghoshal give strong preference to the *transnational* model as the complexity and diversity of global markets create the simultaneous need "to become more responsive to local needs while retaining [...] global efficiency" (Bartlett and Ghoshal 2000, p. 13). The *transnational* approach aims to take advantage of both high local responsiveness and global integration. Its organizational structure is characterized by a high level of interdependencies between different parts of the company, and also by a high level of specialization between subsidiaries (Bartlett and Ghoshal, 1989; Harzing, 2000).

Prahalad and Doz's integration-responsiveness framework as well as Bartlett and Ghoshal's resultant typology of organizational models have become popular lenses for the analysis of the international CSR strategies of MNCs. Logsdon and Wood (2002) reframe the two fundamental dimensions of the Integration-Responsiveness framework as the "universal ethical principles perspective" and the "communitarian view", respectively. Along these lines, Husted and Allen distinguish between global and local CSR strategies. Drivers for the adoption of a *global* CSR approach are "integration pressures [that] stem from multinational stakeholders and NGOs, global social problems, and the need to economize in the provision of CSR"; by contrast, drivers for the adoption of a local CSR approach are pressures that respond to "local issues stem[ming] from differences in stakeholders as well as market structure and the demands of host governments" (Husted and Allen 2006, p. 841). Mirroring the *transnational* model, MNCs hence ought to simultaneously respond to local norms and values whilst at the same time conforming to a minimum set of globally applicable values (Arthaud-Day, 2005; Chaudhri, 2006; De George, 2005; Logsdon and Wood, 2002; Husted and Allen, 2006; Muller, 2006; Post, 2000).

However, empirical studies have not found much evidence among MNCs of the *transnational* CSR model. For example, analysing MNC codes of conduct with regard to child labour, Kolk and Van Tulder (2004) conclude that a *multinational* approach seems to be the dominant strategy to deal with this issue. In an earlier study, Baron (1997) suggests more generally that non-market strategy formulation tends to be *multinational* rather than *transnational*. Examining the responses of oil and gas MNCs to climate change, Levy and Kolk (2002) found that company responses to the issue changed once the discourse on climate change had matured, and progressed from a *multinational* towards an increasingly globally integrated response. This overview points thus to an intriguing situation: there seem to be good reasons why companies should adopt a transnational approach to CSR—just as there are good reasons to adopt a transnational business strategy—yet empirical studies struggle to find companies that actually apply the transnational CSR model.

4.2 The headquartering effect in international CSR

A number of arguments have been presented to explain why the emergence of a transnational approach to CSR may not be too likely (Barkemeyer and Figge, 2014).

First, the increasing professionalization of CSR has led to the creation of special-ized departments, which are usually located in corporate headquarters. However, this choice of location moves decision-making away from host countries and requires local managers to follow the rules set by the headquarters. For exam-ple, budgets for CSR are often allocated relative to the economic importance of the market, and this process may disadvantage developing country subsidiaries (Jamali, 2010). Second, the growing scale of CSR activities has led to calls for a more strategic approach to CSR (Kanter, 1999; Kotler and Lee, 2005; Lantos, 2001; Porter and Kramer, 2006). However, a more strategic integration of CSR activities into the company's operations is also likely to lead to a more instrumental view on stakeholder relationships (Barkemeyer and Figge, 2014). As stakeholders in the MNC's home country are likely to have greater salience than local stakeholders in the various countries of its operation (Frynas, 2005), such a strategic approach to CSR could actually undermine attention to local CSR issues. Third, in the context of mainstreaming CSR, the argument is often presented that the credibility and proper functioning of CSR activities require the backing or active involvement of senior management, not least the CEO (Chen *et al.*, 2009; Mascarenhas, 2009). Taken together, these developments have led to a headquartering effect in inter-national CSR, "with strategic decision-making increasingly confined to the com-panies' headquarters, whilst the scope of action within the subsidiaries and the supply chain of MNCs becomes increasingly restricted over time" (Barkemeyer and Figge, 2014, p. 125).

To illustrate the headquartering effect, consider the workings of some of the major CSR tools, guidelines or initiatives. Some of these tools reinforce the headquartering of international CSR by design, that is the application of this tool requires a centralized management approach. This is the case for the sustain-ability balanced scorecard or socially responsible investment (SRI). To this day, the overwhelming majority of SRI assets are managed in northern countries (GSIA, 2013). Unsurprisingly, the SRI agenda remains relatively narrow and uniform rather than covering the entire spectrum of CSR issues (Barkemeyer *et al.*, 2014a).

For other tools or initiatives, the involvement of top-level management is an explicit requirement. This applies to mainstream initiatives such as the UN Global Compact. Senior management involvement plays a critical role in the Global Compact; only the CEO can sign up to the initiative and a range of governance ele-ments, such as the UN Global Compact Leaders Summit, the UN Global Compact CEO Survey or the CEO Water Mandate, are explicitly targeted at the top level man-agement of the participating companies (Fussler *et al.*, 2004; United Nations Global Compact, 2007). Finally, a number of tools and guidelines are commonly inter-preted in a way that presents senior management involvement as pivotal to the functioning and credibility of these approaches. These tools and guidelines include The Natural Step, the ISO 14001 series or ISO 26000. In the following we empiri-cally test the headquartering effect. First, however, the next section of the chapter describes the material and methods we used.

4.3 Material and methods

We conducted an online survey on decision-making in CSR projects among corporate UN Global Compact signatories. The sample consists of companies that have posted best practice examples (so-called UN Global Compact "case stories") on the UN Global Compact website. These best practice examples are intended to illustrate the various activities companies engage in as part of their participation in the UN Global Compact, and can focus on any (or any combination) of the ten UN Global Compact principles (Barkemeyer, 2009). Our survey was directed at company representatives who were specified as contact points on the UN Global Compact website for each of these best practice examples. The units of analysis were the individual best practice examples. In cases where one contact point was specified for more than one best practice example, respondents were asked to select one specific case. As our study is concerned with international CSR, companies only operating in one location were excluded from the sample.

A total of 421 company representatives were contacted and we received 102 usable responses, constituting a moderate but acceptable response rate of 24.2%. Responses covered companies from 28 sectors, with finance and insurance (15.2% of responses) and food and drink (6.7%) being the largest sector subsamples. In terms of geographic distribution, 80 respondents were based in OECD countries and 22 in non-OECD countries. Figure 4.1 shows the UN Global Compact principles addressed by the best practice examples represented in the sample. Of the 102 projects, 43 were based in developed countries and 38 were based in developing countries. A further 21 companies reported on projects that covered the companies' global operations.

Across the sample, projects addressing environmental sustainability (UN Global Compact Principles 7–9) were most prevalent, in particular with regard to projects based in developed countries (49%) and those that are global in scope (57%). By contrast, case studies reporting on activities based in developing countries most frequently addressed human rights (UN Global Compact Principle 1; 45%). In general, projects based in developing countries show a slightly stronger emphasis of the socio-economic dimension of sustainability. Across the three categories, freedom of association (Principle 3), forced labour (Principle 4) and in particular anti-corruption (Principle 10) are least represented, with less than 20 per cent of the case studies addressing these principles.

There was also a clear bias towards large companies. According to the categorization of participants on the UN Global Compact website, the sample included 36 respondents from FT Global 500 companies and 54 respondents from "large companies", whereas only 11 respondents were based in SMEs. Almost half of the respondents have a CSR-related position, such as CSR manager, sustainability specialist, or head of CSR/corporate responsibility. Approximately 25%

Figure 4.1 **UN Global compact principles addressed by best practice examples (*n*=102)**

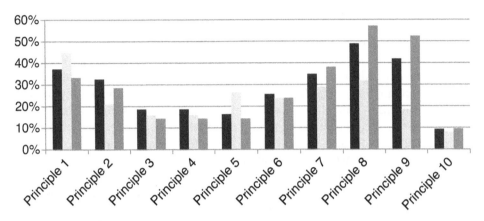

■ Developed country context   Developing country context ■ Global context

of respondents have middle- or top-management positions that are not directly related to CSR. No significant differences in mean responses were identified between these groups.

Respondents were asked to rate their approval/disapproval of two sets of statements: (a) four statements regarding the selection of and decision-making on the specific CSR activities their company published as best practice example; and (b) four statements regarding the nature of the CSR activity. Each of the statements was rated on a 7-point Likert scale. In addition, respondents were asked to rate the influence of 11 different drivers, such as ethical considerations, potential cost savings or employee motivation, on their decision to carry out the CSR activity.

The survey instrument was piloted with six corporate practitioners and expert academics who were asked to comment on the content and clarity of the survey. Their feedback resulted in minor modifications. The online survey was administered through Survey Monkey. Each respondent was contacted by email and sent an electronic copy of the survey together with a cover letter that explained the purpose of the research. In order to enhance the response rate, respondents also had the opportunity to respond via return post and could request a hard copy of the survey. Follow-up emails and phone calls were made to improve the response rate. Independent sample t-tests were conducted to test for statistical differences of means between the first three quarters and the final quartile of respondents (Armstrong and Overton, 1977; Lambert and Harrington, 1990). These suggest that there is no significant non-response bias.

4.4 Results

A range of underlying motivations acted as drivers for the selection of the specific CSR activities. Of these, risk management as well as innovation and learning appeared to be most influential, whereas market position, access to capital or cost savings received clearly lower average scores. One pattern that emerges from Table 4.1 is that respondents who reported on CSR activities in developing countries gave higher-than-average scores for all 11 drivers. For example, clear differences can be identified with regard to risk management, ethical considerations, strengthened supplier relationships and cost savings. Nevertheless, the set of CSR activities seem to have been triggered by a wide range of drivers.

Table 4.2 outlines the responses regarding the companies' decision to engage in the specific CSR activities they report on. Respondents are grouped into three generic categories, based on the information on the geographical scope of the CSR activities that is provided in the UN Global Compact case story database: (a) CSR activities that are located in developed countries; (b) CSR activities that are located in developing countries; and (c) CSR activities that are global in scope. Across these three, a relatively uniform pattern emerges. Kruskal-Wallis tests show significant differences of means for only one out of the eight statements

Table 4.1 **Drivers for carrying out CSR activities (n=102)**

	Total	Developed country contexts	Developing country contexts	Global activities
	(*n*=102)	(*n*=43)	(*n*=38)	(*n*=21)
Risk management or risk reduction	5.73	5.65	6.24	4.95
Innovation or learning	5.40	5.37	5.79	4.76
Reputation or brand image	5.01	5.21	5.18	4.29
Economic considerations	4.86	5.05	4.95	4.33
Ethical considerations	4.34	4.05	4.74	4.24
Employee motivation	4.23	4.28	4.26	4.05
Strengthened supplier relationships	4.10	3.95	4.58	3.52
Improved relationship with governmental authorities	4.07	3.95	4.50	3.52
Cost saving	3.76	3.72	4.34	2.81
Access to capital or increased shareholder value	3.14	3.16	3.37	2.67
Market position (market share) improvement	3.08	2.19	3.26	3.10

regarding content selection and decision-making procedures (statement B3: *activity selected according to the needs of local communities*), with activities based in developing country contexts receiving a higher score. Other than this, a very stable pattern emerges, in particular with regard to the questions where in the company reported activities have been initiated (statements A1 and A2) and where the final decision was made (A3 and A4).

Wilcoxon matched-pairs tests confirm that in each of the three subsamples, statements referring to central initiation and final decision-making receive significantly higher scores, with medium to high effect sizes in each case. This applies both to statements A1 and A2 (*initiated centrally/locally* developed countries: $z = -3.244$, $p < 0.01$, $r = -0.49$; developing countries: $z = -3.207$, $p < 0.01$, $r = -0.49$; global activities: $z = -3.481$, $p < 0.001$, $r = -0.76$) and statements A3 and A4 (*final decision in HQ/subsidiary* developed countries: $z = -3.513$, $p < 0.001$, $r = -0.54$; developing countries: $z = -3.284$, $p < 0.01$, $r = -0.53$; global activities: $z = 3.610$, $p < 0.001$, $r = -0.79$).

Tables 4.3 and 4.4 show that these general patterns are largely replicated irrespective of the nature of the CSR activities and the underlying drivers stated by the respondents. However, activities that are seen as reflecting the company's global CSR strategy are more likely to be initiated centrally (Table 4.1). Likewise, group-wise comparisons between respondents who have given a high score (6 or 7 on a 7-point Likert scale) for any of the five most influential drivers and the rest of the sample show a largely homogeneous pattern. However, where CSR activities are driven by strong ethical considerations, headquarters are more likely to initiate activities unilaterally, with significantly less involvement of local subsidiaries or affiliates (Table 4.3). At the same time, projects linked to innovation and learning are more likely to integrate local subsidiaries or affiliates into the final decision-making. Finally, headquarter involvement appeared to be significantly higher in the case of activities focusing on socio-economic sustainability (UN Global Compact Principles 1–6, 10) than for activities focusing on environmental sustainability (UN Global Compact Principles 7–9) (Table 4.1).

4.5 Discussion and implications

The above empirical analysis provides evidence for the existence of a headquartering effect within the sample. A uniform pattern emerged from the survey responses, largely irrespective of the nature, scope and geographical setting of the CSR activities as well as company characteristics, such as sector affiliation, size or country of origin. This headquartering effect appeared to be particularly pronounced for activities that focus on socio-economic challenges, that are linked to strong ethical motives and that are global in scope. The third category does not come as a surprise as a higher degree of centralization can be expected for activities that are rolled out across a company's global operations. Likewise, one could expect that those activities that are linked to strong ethical motives by the respondents—who were

Table 4.2 **Approval of statements regarding selection process and decision-making ($n=102$, categorized by geographical scope)**

	Total ($n=102$)		Developed country setting ($n=43$)		Developing country setting ($n=38$)		Global activities ($n=21$)		Kruskal-Wallis tests		
	Mean	s	Mean	s	Mean	s	Mean	s	H	df	Monte Carlo Sig.
A1. Headquarters involvement in initiation of CSR activity	5.59	1.90	5.40	2.06	5.53	1.55	6.10	1.90	2.239	2	0.326
A2. Local (subsidiary or affiliate) involvement in initiation of CSR activity	3.21	2.39	3.28	2.27	3.37	1.92	2.76	2.25	0.773	2	0.679
A3. Headquarters involvement in final decision to select CSR activity	5.76	1.88	5.49	1.75	5.84	1.60	6.19	1.78	3.556	2	0.169
A4. Local (subsidiary or affiliate) involvement in final decision to select CSR activity	3.21	2.27	3.02	2.23	3.74	1.91	2.62	2.21	3.980	2	0.137
B1. CSR activity is one part of a portfolio of very different CSR activities	5.71	1.63	5.63	1.55	5.84	1.72	5.64	1.61	0.496	2	0.780
B2. CSR activity reflects company's core business competencies	5.26	1.83	5.12	1.70	5.53	2.05	5.06	1.82	1.157	2	0.561
B3. CSR activity selected according to the needs of local communities	5.06	1.93	4.19	1.49	6.00	1.99	5.14	1.92	**16.613**	2	**0.000**
B4. CSR activity reflects company's global CSR strategy	5.99	1.44	5.81	1.27	6.11	1.15	6.14	1.32	1.054	2	0.590

Note: $^*p < 0.05$; $^{**}p < 0.01$; $^{***}p < 0.001$

Table 4.3 **Approval of statements regarding project initiation (n=102)**

	n		HQ involvement (initiation)				Local involvement (initiation)			
	High	Low	Δ Mean	u	z	l	Δ Mean	u	z	l
CSR activity is one part of a portfolio of very different CSR activities	67	35	0.11	1,080.5	−0.70	−0.07	−0.25	1060.5	−0.81	−0.08
CSR activity reflects company's core business competencies	55	47	0.38	1,226.5	−0.48	−0.05	0.18	1263.5	−0.20	−0.02
CSR activity selected according to the needs of local communities	63	49	−0.05	1,232.5	−0.48	−0.05	0.28	1253.5	−0.31	−0.03
CSR activity reflects company's global CSR strategy	69	33	1.50	650.5	−3.76	**−0.37***	−1.04	811.0	−2.42	**−0.24***
Risk management or risk reduction	70	32	−0.01	1,112.0	−0.06	−0.01	0.21	1083.0	−0.28	−0.03
Innovation or learning	52	50	−0.45	1,202.0	−0.71	−0.07	0.64	1099.0	−1.39	−0.14
Reputation or brand image	47	55	−0.18	1,234.5	−0.42	−0.04	0.37	1202.0	−0.63	−0.06
Economic considerations	44	58	0.04	1,243.0	−0.24	−0.02	−0.08	1265.5	−0.07	−0.01
Ethical considerations	36	66	0.59	963.0	−2.40	**−0.24***	−0.28	1265.5	−1.69	**−0.17***
Environmental versus social projects (High=green, Low=social)	36	66	−0.44	1,054.0	−1.01	−0.10	0.11	1141.5	−0.34	−0.03

Note: *p < 0.05; p <0.01; ***p <0.001

Table 4.4 **Approval of statements regarding project initiation (*n*=102)**

	n		HQ involvement (selection)				Local involvement (selection)			
	High	Low	Δ Mean	u	z	r	Δ Mean	u	z	r
CSR activity is one part of a portfolio of very different CSR activities	67	35	0.29	914.0	−1.99	**−0.20***	−0.34	1,045.0	−0.93	−0.09
CSR activity reflects company's core business competencies	55	47	0.43	1169.5	−0.90	−0.09	0.18	1,251.0	−0.29	−0.03
CSR activity selected according to the needs of local communities	53	49	0.02	1259.0	−0.29	−0.03	0.79	1,093.5	−1.42	−0.14
CSR activity reflects company's global CSR strategy	69	33	0.86	867.5	−2.12	**−0.21***	−0.50	972.0	−1.23	−0.12
Risk management or risk reduction	70	32	0.29	1013.5	−0.84	−0.08	0.21	1,103.5	−0.12	−0.01
Innovation or learning	52	50	0.01	1271.0	−0.21	−0.02	1.35	882.0	−2.88	**−0.29****
Reputation or brand image	47	55	0.24	1179.0	−0.83	−0.08	0.05	1,287.0	−0.04	0.00
Economic considerations	44	58	−0.11	1272.5	−0.03	0.00	0.48	1,090.5	−1.29	−0.13
Ethical considerations	36	66	0.15	1285.0	−0.08	−0.01	0.24	1,289.0	−0.05	0.00
Environmental versus social projects (High=green, Low=social)	36	66	−0.92	839.5	−2.67	**−0.26****	0.45	1,028.5	−1.15	−0.11

typically based in the corporate headquarters—would show a particularly strong headquarters involvement.

With regard to projects addressing socioeconomic challenges, one could argue that the integration of local subsidiaries and affiliates would be most crucial for activities focusing on issues such as human rights, labour rights or anti-corruption. Nevertheless, the headquartering effect appeared more pronounced here when compared to environmental projects. Equally surprising is the finding that CSR projects that, according to our respondents, were selected to specifically address the needs of local communities did not show significantly higher levels of involvement of local subsidiaries or affiliates. On the other hand, activities that are seen as being linked to innovation and learning were more likely to integrate the views of local subsidiaries and affiliates.

No clear differences emerged between projects that are based in developed or developing countries. As such, the headquartering of international CSR appears to exist irrespective of the geographical context the activity is carried out in. Nevertheless, it is likely to reinforce a northern CSR agenda given the stakeholder salience differential between global north and south. Whenever a more strategic orientation of CSR reduces slack at the level of MNC subsidiaries and suppliers, there will also be less opportunity to respond to the concerns of local stakeholders. Consequently, there is a risk that the headquartering effect in international CSR marginalizes genuine development. This bias may become ameliorated as emerging economy MNCs become more prominent, yet this would not remove the headquartering effect as international CSR would still reflect the priorities of an admittedly somewhat larger number of headquarters.

It should be noted that the headquartering of CSR is by no means *per se* a negative development. Whenever there is a match between the interests between headquarters and non-salient stakeholders, the resulting CSR activities will be beneficial for these non-salient stakeholders. Likewise, from the perspective of corporate citizenship (Matten and Crane, 2005) or political CSR (Scherer and Palazzo, 2011) it has been argued that certain activities necessitate the intervention of corporate headquarters in order to bring about change in the first place. However, as the debates over CSR and development (Frynas, 2005; Jenkins, 2005) and over the perceived northern bias of corporate normative guidelines (RING Alliance 2003; Barkemeyer *et al.*, 2014b) show, there is ample evidence for a mismatch of CSR-related priorities between north and south. Closely related to this point is the fact that the CSR activities of a multinational company will—to varying degrees—inevitably be geared towards its most salient stakeholders. Instead, addressing the claims of non-salient stakeholders is typically beyond a company's capacity or interest even if they conflict with corporate objectives and/or the claims of the company's primary stakeholders.

From a policy perspective, it is therefore advisable to put measures in place that ensure a better integration and acknowledgement of non-salient (developing country) stakeholders. Whilst this might not ameliorate potential trade-offs between the interests of different (salient and non-salient) stakeholder groups, it might at least help the company to take an informed decision on these trade-offs (Hahn *et al.*, 2015). Capacity-building measures should both strengthen existing institutions as well as allow for the creation of new institutions representing currently marginalized stakeholders. They should furthermore reduce the resource dependency of southern NGOs on their northern counterparts (Schepers, 2006). In a related fashion, CSR tools and initiatives need to be redesigned. From a corporate perspective, enhanced feedback loops and a stronger integration of local subsidiaries and affiliates may result in activities that are perceived as relevant locally while at the same time increasing the effectiveness of the company's CSR activities. Nevertheless, it should be noted that from a corporate perspective, a highly centralized CSR approach can be a perfectly rational choice given the need to prioritize primary stakeholders—even though from a societal perspective, this might be counter-productive as it might crowd out the interests of non-salient stakeholders.

We are aware of several limitations to our study. First, there is a bias within the sample towards best practice activities of very large companies, although this bias exists in large parts of the CSR literature. Furthermore, CSR-related decision-making may depend on the industry as some CSR tools and practices (e.g. environmental management) are closer to the competencies of some industries, such as manufacturing firms, than others, like banking (Molina-Azorín *et al.*, 2009). Another limitation may result from the use of an English language questionnaire for a cross-country sample (Harzing 2004). However, the sample consists of designated company contacts for the UN Global Compact, which is a networking and learning platform that predominantly uses English as it operating language.

Most importantly, survey respondents were typically based in corporate headquarters and thus were asked to respond to questions regarding their own levels of involvement. However, very clear and stable patterns emerged with regard to the headquartering effect and these seem to suggest that the impact of this potential bias is likely to have been small. Future research should employ a wider sample that investigates headquarters as well as subsidiary perspectives. In addition, research that collects case study data as opposed to a survey instrument could help to shed further light on this phenomenon.

4.6 Conclusion

Our study explored the headquartering effect in international CSR based on a survey of corporate UN Global Compact participants. In summary, decisions on both the initiation and the execution of international CSR projects appear to be mainly confined to the companies' headquarters, while only limited control rests with the companies' subsidiaries or local affiliates. A largely homogeneous decision-making pattern emerged from the analysis, providing empirical evidence for the existence of a headquartering effect. Moreover, this headquartering effect appeared to be most pronounced in the case of CSR activities that addressed socio-economic challenges, CSR activities that arose from strong ethical considerations, and CSR activities that were global in scope.

The headquartering effect, together with a dominance of MNCs in the global economy and a salience of stakeholders who are based in industrialized nations, is likely to reinforce a northern bias in the selection and execution of CSR initiatives. It is somewhat ironic that, just as CSR is becoming embedded in MNCs in a professional and structured manner, there should be less—rather than more—scope for addressing the needs of local stakeholders through actions in the subsidiaries of MNCs rather than their headquarters.

4.6.1 Reflections on development-oriented CSR

The existence of a headquartering effect has profound implications for development-oriented CSR. The increasing centralization of CSR decision-making at corporate headquarters makes it less likely that MNCs act as development agents in the developing countries they operate in. Although companies may continue to actively address development issues, such as absolute poverty, inequality or health in the host countries they operate in, these activities are increasingly driven by the MNCs' most salient (typically home country) stakeholders rather than the perceived beneficiaries of these activities based in the host countries. Given the existing concerns about a northern bias in international CSR (Blowfield, 2003; Fox, 2004; Utting, 2001), there is a risk that the headquartering effect reinforces this process. As a result, it might push development issues that are perceived as relevant by host country stakeholders—but less so by home country stakeholders—further down the international CSR agenda.

Bibliography

Armstrong, J.S., & Overton, T.S. (1977). Estimating nonresponse bias in mail surveys. *Journal of Marketing Research*, 18(3), 396-402.

Arthaud-Day, M.L. (2005). Transnational corporate social responsibility: a tri-dimensional approach to international CSR research. *Business Ethics Quarterly*, 15(1), 1-22.

Barin-Cruz, L., & Pedrozo, E.A. (2009). Corporate social responsibility and green management: relation between headquarters and subsidiary in multinational corporations. *Management Decision*, 47(7), 1174-1199.

Barkemeyer, R. (2009). Beyond compliance—below expectations? CSR in the context of international development. *Business Ethics: European Review*, 18(3), 273-289.

Barkemeyer, R., & Figge, F. (2014). Corporate social responsibility in the context of multiple environments: the impact of headquartering. *Critical Perspectives on International Business*, 10(3), 124-151.

Barkemeyer, R., Figge, F., Hahn, T., Hoepner, A., Liesen A., & Neher, A.L. (2014a). Operationalizing socially responsible investment: a non-financial fiduciary duty problem. In J.P. Hawley, A. Hoepner, K.L. Johnson, J. Sandberg, & E.J. Waitzer (Eds.), *Handbook of Institutional Investment and Fiduciary Duty* (pp. 364-377). Cambridge: Cambridge University Press.

Barkemeyer, R., Holt, D., Preuss, L., & Tsang, S. (2014b). What happened to the "development" in sustainable development? Business guidelines two decades after Brundtland. *Sustainable Development*, 22(1), 15-32.

Baron, D.P. (1997). Integrated strategy, trade policy, and global competition. *California Management Review*, 39(2), 145-169.

Bartlett, C.A., & Ghoshal, S. (1989). Managing Across Borders: *The Transnational Solution*. Boston: Harvard Business School Press.

Bartlett, C.A., & Ghoshal, S. (2000). *Transnational Management*. Chicago: McGraw-Hill.

Blowfield, M. (2003). Ethical supply chains in the cocoa, coffee and tea industries. *Greener Management International*, 43, 15-24.

Chaudhri, V.A. (2006). Organising global CSR. A case study of Hewlett-Packard's e-inclusion initiative. *Journal of Corporate Citizenship*, 23, 39-51.

Chen, D., Newburry, W., & Park, S.H. (2009). Improving sustainability: an international evolutionary framework. *Journal of International Management*, 15(3), 317-327.

Crane, A., Palazzo, G., Spence, L.J., & Matten, D. (2014). Contesting the value of "creating shared value". *California Management Review*, 56(2), 130-149.

De George, R.T. (2005). *Business Ethics*. Upper Saddle River, NJ: Pearson/Prentice Hall.

Donaldson, T., & Preston, L.E. (1995). The stakeholder theory of the corporation: concepts, evidence, and implications. *Academy of Management Review*, 20(1), 65-91.

Fox, T. (2004). Corporate social responsibility and development: in quest of an agenda. *Development*, 47(3), 29-36.

Frynas, J.G. (2005). The false developmental promise of corporate social responsibility: evidence from multinational oil companies. *International Affairs*, 81(3), 581-598.

Fussler, C., Cramer, A., & van der Vegt, S. (2004). *Raising the Bar. Creating Value with the UN Global Compact*. Sheffield: Greenleaf Publishing.

GSIA (2013). 2012 Global Sustainable Investment Review, Global Sustainable Investment Analysis.

Hahn, T., Pinkse, J., Preuss, L., & Figge, F. (2015). Tensions in corporate sustainability: towards an integrative framework. *Journal of Business Ethics*, 127(2), 297-316.

Harzing, A.W. (2000). An empirical analysis and extension of the Bartlett and Ghoshal typology of multinational companies. *Journal of International Business Studies*, 31(1), 101-119.

Harzing, A.W. (2004). Does the use of English-language questionnaires in cross-national research obscure national differences? *International Journal of Cross-Cultural Management*, 5(2), 213-224.

Hopkins, M. (2007). *Corporate Social Responsibility and International Development. Is Business the Solution?* London: Earthscan.

Husted, B.W., & Allen, D.B. (2006). Corporate social responsibility in the multinational enterprise: strategic and institutional approaches. *Journal of International Business Studies*, 37, 838-849.

Jamali, D. (2010). The CSR of MNC subsidiaries in developing countries: global, local, substantive or diluted?. *Journal of Business Ethics*, 93(Supplement 2), 181-200.

Jenkins, R. (2005). Globalization, corporate social responsibility and poverty. *International Affairs*, 81(3), 525-540.

Kanter, R.M. (1999). From spare change to real change: the social sector as beta site for business innovation. *Harvard Business Review*, 77(3), 122-133.

Kolk, A., & Van Tulder, R. (2004). Ethics in international business: multinational approaches to child labor. *Journal of World Business*, 39(1), 49-60.

Kolk, A., & Van Tulder, R. (2006). Poverty alleviation as business strategy? Evaluating commitments of frontrunner multinational corporations. *World Development*, 34(5), 789-801.

Kotler, P., & Lee, N. (2005). *Corporate Social Responsibility: Doing the Most Good for Your Company and Your Cause*. Hoboken, NJ: John Wiley & Sons.

Lambert, D.M., & Harrington, T.C. (1990). Measuring non-response bias in customer service mail surveys. *Journal of Business Logistics*, 11(2), 5-25.

Lantos, G.P. (2001). The boundaries of strategic corporate social responsibility. *Journal of Consumer Marketing*, 18(7), 595-632.

Levy, D., & Kolk, A. (2002). Strategic responses to global climate change: conflicting pressures on multinationals in the oil industry. *Business and Politics*, 4(3), 275-300.

Logsdon, J.M., & Wood, D.J. (2002). Business citizenship: from domestic to global level of analysis. *Business Ethics Quarterly*, 12(2), 155-187.

Mascarenhas, B. (2009). The emerging CEO agenda. *Journal of International Management*, 15(3), 245-250.

Matten, D., & Crane, A. (2005). Corporate citizenship: toward an extended theoretical conceptualization. *Academy of Management Review*, 30(1), 166-179.

Molina-Azorín, J.F., Tarí, J.J., Claver-Cortés, E., & López-Gamero, M.D. (2009). Quality management, environmental management and firm performance: a review of empirical studies and issues of integration. *International Journal of Management Reviews*, 11(2), 197-222.

Muller, A. (2006). Global versus local CSR strategies. *European Management Journal*, 24(2-3), 189-198.

Porter, M.E., & Kramer, M.R. (2006). Strategy and society: the link between competitive advantage and corporate social responsibility. *Harvard Business Review*, 84(12), 78-92.

Post, J.E. (2000). *Meeting the Challenge of Global Corporate Citizenship*. Boston: Boston College Center for Corporate Community Relations.

Prahalad, C.K., & Doz, Y.L. (1987). *The Multinational Mission: Balancing Local Demands and Global Vision*. New York: Free Press.

RING Alliance (2003). The Development Dimension of the UN Global Compact. Final Report, The Ring Alliance of Policy Research Institutions. Retrieved from http://ring-alliance.org/ring/documents/global_compact.pdf, last accessed 15 February 2009.

Schepers, D.H. (2006). The impact of NGO network conflict on the corporate social responsibility strategies of multinational corporations. *Business and Society*, 45(3), 282-299.

Scherer, A.G., & Palazzo, G. (2011). The new political role of business in a globalized world: a review of a new perspective on CSR and its implications for the firm, governance, and democracy. *Journal of Management Studies*, 48(4), 899-931.

United Nations Global Compact (2007). Annual Review. 2007 Leaders Summit. New York, NY: UN Global Compact Office.

Utting, P. (2001). Promoting Socially Responsible Business in Developing Countries. The Potential and Limits of Voluntary Initiatives. Report of the UNRISD Workshop, 23–24 October, 2000. Geneva, United Nations Research Institute for Social Development.

Valente, M., & Crane, A. (2010). Public responsibility and private enterprise in developing countries. *California Management Review*, 52(3), 52-78.

Indigenous communities and mega-projects

Corporate social responsibility (CSR) and consultation-consent principles

Jacobo Ramirez

Copenhagen Business School (CBS), Denmark

It is widely recognized that indigenous populations have become important actors as they have increasingly started to mobilize against the implementation of mega-projects. The importance of indigenous populations has moved beyond political dynamics into the related areas of development and corporate social responsibility (CSR) regarding mega-projects. This chapter employs CSR frameworks in relation to consultation and consent principles to discuss the conflicting political and economic elite groups' perspectives on the one hand and those of indigenous populations on the other in Mexico. This study examines an ecological and environmentally friendly mega-wind energy project that has led two multinational corporations (MNCs) into a conflict with indigenous people. The discussion will be framed on indigenous communities who are challenged by questionable institutional (legal systems) arrangements from political and economic elite groups. The Oaxaca saga provides fertile ground for

further developing new elements in studying development and CSR in Mexico and beyond.

Indigenous people appear to have become important political actors in several regions of the world (Sassen, 2004), including Latin America (Bowen, 2011). Indigenous peoples have shown their mobilization capacity to oppose and even shut down mega-projects involving the exploitation and commercialization of natural resources (e.g. Banerjee, 2000). Land dispute appears to be a recurrent concern across indigenous mobilizations (e.g., Colchester and Ferrari, 2007). The International Labour Organization's (ILO, 2009) Convention on Indigenous and Tribal Peoples in Independent Countries—169/1989 refers to the principle of free, prior and informed consent (FPIC) (Colchester and Ferrari, 2007, p. 1) in the context of relocation of indigenous peoples from their land (ILO, 2009), territories and natural resources. Mega-projects require "coordinated applications of capital and state power" (Gellert and Lynch, 2003, p. 15), where public consultation (Driscoll, 2006) and consent appears to be the cornerstone of mega-projects' development. The FPIC principle is expected to be reached through political freedom, freedom of speech and transparency between local communities and elite groups. In mega-projects, consultation and consent are prerequisites to change the use of the land, for example, from agricultural to industrial use, where local communities may be relocated.

From the point of view of sociological theory, elite groups are integrated by individuals who occupy formal positions of authority and control; these individuals can be found in governmental and private corporations sectors (Dye and Pickering, 1974; Porter, 1957). According to Porter (1957, p. 376), members of elite groups are "the effective decision-makers and coordinators of the social system", who promote and develop mega-projects. However, indigenous populations in Latin America have constructed an understanding of multinational corporations (MNCs), referred to in this chapter as economic elites that are rooted in imperialism and the history of European colonial power. European colonial power was characterized by "all forms of labour, production and exploitation" (Quijano, 2000, p. 216). Nevertheless, today's economic elite groups are expected to be self-regulated and proactively comply and even surpass national and international laws in relation to the social, environmental, political and economic consequences of their business activities. Elite groups (MNCs) are expected not only to contribute to the development of local communities, such as job creation, which is expected to reduce poverty but also to contribute as agent actors who are responsible for their actions to reach a defined development. This expected contribution of elite groups could be framed in relation to corporate social responsibility (CSR) (e.g. European Commission, 2011). To explore the conflicting perspectives between indigenous people and governmental and economic elite groups in relation to development and CSR, in this chapter, I examine an ecological and environmentally friendly wind energy project that led two MNCs, Vestas and Mareña Renovables, as well as investors into an international dispute in Mexico. The main question to discuss in this chapter is: What is the relation between consultation-consent and CSR?

The next section presents the theoretical background on CSR. It is followed by a description of the qualitative methodology employed in this chapter. The results and conclusions are then presented with the objective of raising awareness among students, academics, local communities, practitioners, and policy-makers regarding the importance of consultations with and consent from local communities when developing mega-projects. Such consultations may help to reconcile differences in stakeholders' approaches to the process of consultation and consent in mega-projects.

5.1 CSR

According to Matten and Moon (2008, p. 405), "the core of CSR is the idea that it reflects the social imperatives and the social consequences of business success". Bowen (1953) and Carroll, (1999, p. 270) argue for social responsibility that must guide business in the future. According to Carroll (1999, p. 289), "for CSR to be accepted by the conscientious business person, it should be framed in such a way that the entire range of business responsibilities is embraced". This suggests that, to ensure business success, businesses should proactively have "respect for applicable legislation, and for collective agreements between social partners, is a prerequisite for meeting that responsibility" (European Commission, 2011, p. 6). The emphasis of this chapter is placed on the social consequences of businesses' practices in their entire range of activities, in particular, in relation to firms' value chains. This is framed in the chapter to the United Nations Guiding Principles on Business and Human Rights (UNGPs):

> Principle 13: The responsibility to respect human rights requires that business enterprises: (a) Avoid causing or contributing to adverse human rights…, (b) Seek to prevent or mitigate adverse human rights impacts that are directly linked to their operations… (United Nations, 2011, p. 14).

Thus, in this chapter, CSR is understood to be how firms "should strive to make a profit, obey the law, be ethical, and be a good corporate citizen" (Carroll, 1991, p. 43). To implement the CSR strategy, firms may develop the "institutional capacity of the government, civil society" (Peinado-Vara, 2006, p. 62), which should be adapted according to the specific characteristics of the institutional context where the firm intends to operate. Firms' CSR could imply the creation of partnerships with governments and non-governmental organizations (NGOs), social societies and other firms, which directly and indirectly have links to firms' value chains.

The challenge for economic elite groups to operate in context with persistent institutional voids (Khanna and Palepu, 1999), such as corruption, rule of law and the presence of organized crime and violence, suggest that it is the economic elite groups' responsibility to build healthy institutional settings to create a legitimacy that may allow them to have a licence to operate (Porter and Kramer, 2006). The consequences of elite groups promoting and developing mega-projects in relation to CSR are presented in the following section.

5.2 Mega-projects: consultation and consent

According to Gellert and Lynch (2003, p. 15), "mega-projects broadly transform landscapes rapidly, intentionally, and profoundly in very visible ways, and require coordinated applications of capital and state power". Consultation mechanisms with local communities in relation to formal approval processes for land deals (Cotula and Vermeulen, 2011) appear to be one of the main problematic issues in mega-projects.

The FPIC principle (Colchester and Ferrari, 2007) is based on the ILO 169 Convention ratified by Mexico on September 5, 1990 and by Denmark on February 22, 1996. It is expected that the FPIC principle will lay the groundwork for fair compensation to local communities as part of the land transfer process in mega-projects.

The relation between the FPIC principle and CSR could be linked to the Committee for Economic Development's (CED) notion of business: "business functions by public consent and its basic purpose is to serve constructively the needs of society to the satisfaction of society" (CED, 1971, p. 11). It should be highlighted that a consultation process does not necessarily imply consent. To consult is to "seek information or advice" (Oxford Dictionaries, 2014). In this chapter, I argue that consultation should be the basis to seek inputs from local communities to then reach consent. Community consent "involves soliciting approval or permission" (Dickert and Sugarman, 2005, p. 1123-1124) to develop, for example, a mega-project that might necessitate the relocation of indigenous peoples from their lands.

As noted by Dickert and Sugarman (2005), consent may occur after a community consultation. Applying the FPIC principle implies consulting and reaching consent with the members of the communities that are legitimately part of such processes. Indigenous peoples' decision-making customs and systems (Colchester and Ferrari, 2007, p. 20), also referred to as practices and customs, should be integrated into the consultation and consent process.

To explore the relation between consultation-consent and CSR, the following section presents the context of this research, a wind park project in Oaxaca, Mexico. Next, it presents the methodology used in this chapter to explore and discuss the theoretical framework exposed in relation to consultation and consent.

5.3 Research context

5.3.1 The Isthmus of Tehuantepec, Oaxaca

The Isthmus of Tehuantepec is located in the state of Oaxaca, Mexico, one of the most important multicultural regions in Mexico. Indigenous inhabitants (Huaves, Zapotecas, Zoques and Chontales) have developed a strong regional culture. Huaves are also known as Mareños. Members of the community live near the coast of the Gulf of Tehuantepec, around the Laguna Superior lake, and in the cities of San Mateo del Mar, San Dionisio and Álvaro Obregon. Fishing and agriculture are the main activities in this region. Wind is closely associated with the Huave culture, as indicated by the name of one area in the region, La Ventosa, which means "The Windy."

Huave is a derogative term coined by the Zapotecas who mainly live in the city of Juchitán, 43.7 kilometres north of Álvaro Obregon. It means "people rotting in the humidity" (CDI, 2009). A Huave resident of San Mateo del Mar commented on this issue:

> We [Huaves] were the first residents in the area where Juchitán is located, but the Zapotecas expelled us, forcing us to move towards the sea [the Gulf of Tehuantepec]. We still have land disputes with the Zapotecas. This might be the reason why they call us Huaves ... (Have fisherman).

The Zapotecas and Huaves (or Ikoot) use the Isthmus of Tehuantepec for agriculture, to raise cattle, and to catch shrimp. According to the Mexican Association for Wind Energy (Asociación Mexicana de Energía Eólica, 2008), the La Ventosa area, which is plain coastal terrain, could harmoniously integrate the land activities of the Zapotecas and Huaves with the installation and operation of wind-power turbines (PROMÉXICO, 2013).

5.3.2 Land dispute

Land leases are commonly used in wind farm projects. Typically, a wind power plant uses less than 3% of the ground surface over which it is installed (AIDA, 2009) to ensure the owners can continue to use the remaining land. In addition, they receive payment in exchange for leasing the land for the wind power plant. However, in regard to communal lands (ejidos), developers must negotiate a land-lease payment that is fair and convenient for both parties. A difficulty in the negotiation process is preventing project development from speculating on land leases for wind farms. In 2014, there were 16 wind parks operating in the Isthmus of Tehuantepec region.

5.3.3 The Mareña wind-park project

Mareña is the name of a wind energy project started in 2004 by the Spanish renewable energy developer Preneal (McGovern, 2012). The Mareña project, or La Venta III, is the third phase of a wind-park project that was launched in Oaxaca in 1994 with the wind park La Venta I (Wind Power, 2013). This wind park was designed to test the region's wind-energy potential. The Mexican government selected Vestas, a Danish firm, to install seven wind turbines in La Venta I. In the second phase, known as La Venta II, Preneal (2009) handled the wind turbine installations. The third phase, La Venta III, is projected to be built by the Mareña project.

In February 2012, Preneal sold its affiliate in Oaxaca to the Mareña Renovables consortium. Mareña Renovables is owned by Mexican and international business groups including Fomento Económico Mexicano, S.A. (FEMSA), Macquarie Infrastructure Fund Mexico (FIMM), Macquarie Capital Society, the Mitsubishi Corporation, and the Dutch pension fund PGGM (Rojas, 2012; Preneal, 2011). Mareña Renovables became responsible for executing La Venta III (Mareña Renovables, 2013a). The power produced by the wind-power project would be purchased by the beer producer Cuauhtémoc Moctezuma, which was an operating company of Heineken NV and a subsidiary of FEMSA, under a 20-year power-purchasing agreement (CTBR, 2012).

On August 29, 2012, the IDB announced the approval of a loan of approximately US$75 million to fund the project (IDB, 2012). However, in the context of Latin America and, in particular, Mexico, there are no regulative laws and procedures to develop wind energy mega-projects that regulate the indigenous peoples' rights

Figure 5.1 **Timeline: Mareña project**

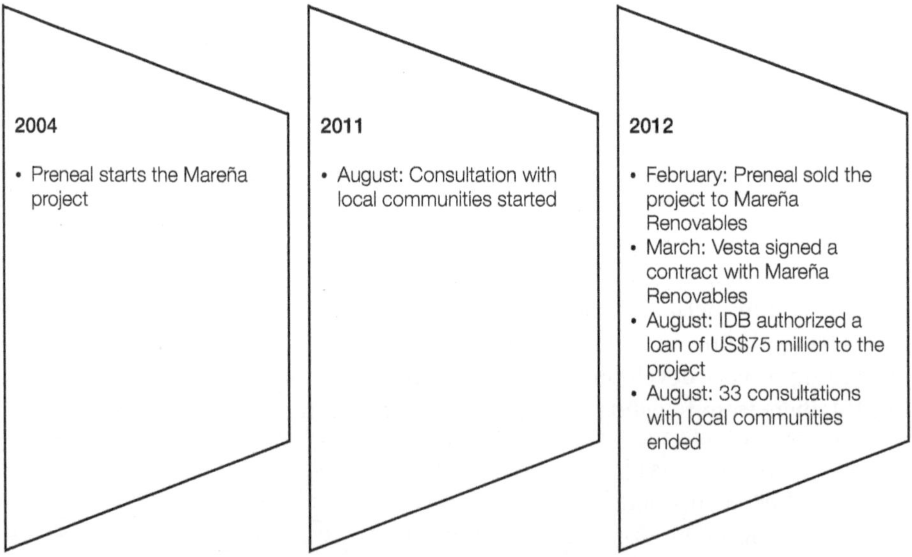

2004	2011	2012
• Preneal starts the Mareña project	• August: Consultation with local communities started	• February: Preneal sold the project to Mareña Renovables • March: Vesta signed a contract with Mareña Renovables • August: IDB authorized a loan of US$75 million to the project • August: 33 consultations with local communities ended

for self-determination according to their customs and systems of decision-making, known as "usos y costumbres".

In March 2012, Vestas announced that it had signed a contract with Mareñas Renovables to provide 132 V90-3.0 MW turbines for La Venta III. The deal encompassed a range of services associated with building a wind energy park, including: the provision of turbines; civil and electrical work; and the supply, installation, and commissioning of the turbines. Furthermore, the contract included a 10-year service and maintenance agreement (Vestas, 2012); refer to Figure 5.1 for a timeline that presents the sequence of events. The following section presents the methods designed to answer the main research question of this chapter.

5.4 Methods

This study was developed based on a sequential qualitative research strategy, which was divided into two phases.

Phase 1: The macro and meso levels of analysis were developed between June and September 2013 on the basis of secondary data sources. This phase relied on critical discourse analysis (CDA) (Fairclough, 2005) to develop an understanding of: 1) the Mexican government's strategy on wind-park projects "La Venta I, II, and III" in the Isthmus of Tehuantepec, Oaxaca, and 2) the private sector's strategy for wind energy in Mexico. Table 5.1 presents the documents consulted, which were read in full and imported into the qualitative software package, Nvivo 10. I grouped the CDA results by the type of actor: 1) Mexican government, 2) private firms, and 3) indigenous communities.

Phase 2: Data for the meso and micro analyses (social actors) were gathered between October 2013 and April 2014. The data were collected through semi-structured interviews, focus groups, and observations, as shown in Table 5.2 Notes were taken during all interviews. The observations, which covered a total of 65 hours, were conducted to understand the situation in the area in which the wind park was to be built. All interviews and notes were transcribed and imported into Nvivo 10. The following section presents the results.

5.5 Results

Results indicate that environmental issues were of concern to actors in this area. For example, a fisherman in San Mateo del Mar stated that the global warming phenomenon known as El Niño, which appears to be strengthened by global warming, had affected his activities. Furthermore, governmental officials and MNCs agreed that, while the installation of wind-power turbines in the park would not

Table 5.1 **Data sources**

Websites (17)	Firm websites: Vestas, Mareñas Renovables, FEMSA. Mexican government websites: Ministry of Energy, Proméxico, National Directorate for Liaison with Civil Society Organizations, Secretary of Indigenous Affairs of the State of Oaxaca, National Institute of Statistics and Geography. International and local organizations websites: United Nations (UN), Inter-American Development Bank (IDB), International Labour Organization (ILO), Amnesty International, Greenpeace, Mexican Wind Energy Association, Emerging Energy Research, Assembly of Indigenous People of the Isthmus in Defense of the Land and Territory.
Media articles	Sixty-two newspaper articles written in Danish, Spanish and English; published in Denmark, Mexico and the US, respectively
White papers	Thirty-eight official white papers (written in English and Spanish) retrieved from the 17 websites. They included firms' annual reports, ILO Convention 169, the United Nations Guiding Principles on Business and Human Rights: Implementing the United Nations Protect, Respect and Remedy Framework, Mexican Agrarian Law, the IDB's official reports on the Mareñas Renovables Wind Project (ME-L1107), and other documents.
Social media	Three videos in Spanish found on YouTube: 1) Somos Viento Somos viento—resistencia en el Istmo contra el proyecto eólico de Mareña. Retrieved from http://www.youtube.com/watch?v=JaV56DYy1NU 2) Pueblos en resistencia contra el megaproyecto eólico. Retrieved from http://www.youtube.com/watch?v=exCmqUbERZQ 3) Enfrentamiento en San Dionisio del Mar por un proyecto eólico. Retrieved from http://www.youtube.com/watch?v=8h3cyxtvPJg
	Social media: 1. Asamblea de Pueblos del Istmo (Assembly of the Isthmus People) Retrieved from https://www.facebook.com/pages/Asamblea-de-Pueblos-del-Istmo/183849978361582 2. La Voz de Charis (The Charis Voice) Retrieved from https://www.facebook.com/guixhiroautonomo Blog: Retrieved from http://tierrayterritorio.wordpress.com/2014/02/13/

affect the daily activities of the local communities, the project would enhance the region's development. However, violent acts involving the main three actors (i.e. the Mexican government, MNCs, and local communities) have persisted throughout attempts to build La Venta III. The following section presents the origin and evolution of the conflict.

5.5.1 The conflict

The CDA analysis highlighted a critical incident in the attempt to build La Venta III. Amnesty International (2011) reported that on October 28, 2011, community activists and members of the indigenous communities were injured when protesting

Table 5.2 **Sample involved in the fieldwork**

Ten interviews with members of elite groups	Twenty-four interviews with indigenous people	Four focus groups (FG)	Observations
Eight governmental officials in Mexico	Fourteen residents of San Mateo, Oaxaca	FG1: Five members of the Assembly of Indigenous People at Juchitán, Oaxaca	October 15–19, 2013 at San Mateo del Mar and Juchitán, Oaxaca
One governmental official in Denmark		FG2: Four members of the Assembly of Indigenous People at Juchitán, Oaxaca	April 8 10, 2014 at San Mateo del Mar and Alvaro Obregón, Oaxaca
One executive at IDB	Ten members of the Assembly of Indigenous People at Juchitán, Oaxaca	FG3: Seven residents of San Mateo, Oaxaca	
		FG4: Four members of the Assembly of Alvaro Obregón	

against the construction of the wind farm. Therefore, I researched and mapped the origins of the conflict to explore the different understandings and the power of the actors involved; Figure 5.2 presents a timeline for the sequence of events.

5.5.1.1 National regulations: changes in the use of the land

Mexican Agrarian Law (Ley Agraria, 2012) states that, in the case of modification and cancellation of the collective farm system, at least three-quarters of the ejidatarios (members of the communal assembly) must be present for the valid installation of the assembly that will decide the use of the land. The lands on which the project was to be built were ejidos (communal agriculture lands). The plan for the wind park implied a change in the use of the land from agricultural to industrial.

According to the report entitled "ESMR-Mareña Renovables Wind Project", the Mareña project would occupy a total area of 22.848 hectares in San Dionisio and 6.72 hectares in Santa Maria del Mar in order to install 132 turbines (IDB, 2011, p. 4). Of the 132 turbines, 102 were to be installed in the San Dionisio area of the Cabo de Santa Teresa key and 30 turbines were to be built at Santa Maria del Mar, which is located in San Mateo del Mar.

The IDB report entitled "Mareña Renovables: Environmental and Social Action Plan" states: "The client [Mareñas Renovables] organized 33 consultations (total attendance of 800 people) between August 2011 and August 2012" (IDB, 2012, p. 27).

The same report also states that "consultation activities have mainly focused on land acquisition; communities were fully informed about the consultation program, or project-related impacts that may affect them." However, the IDB reported:

Figure 5.2 **Timeline: conflict**

2011	2012	2013
• 28 August: Amnesty International reported injuries to indigenous people that protested against the project. • November: IDB recognizes lack of systematic consistency in the consultation process.	• Local newspapers reported increase of unemployment and lower agricultural and milk production in the region.	• 17 October: Destruction of resistance camps in Juchitán, Oaxaca. • 15 May: Vestas signed a prior agreement to postpone the project until 30 November, 2013. • 2013: Mareña Renovables entered in forbearance until 30 July, 2013

> To date [November 9, 2011] the consultation process did suffer from a lack of a systematic process to register issues, concerns and feedback of affected people. However, it is important to underline that usufruct agreements with Santa Maria and San Dionisio were publicly discussed in communal assemblies; minutes of such assemblies were attached to agreements signed before a Public Notary. (IDB, 2011, p. 35)

This report also indicates that "in the case of San Dionisio del Mar, three communal assemblies to the same end were called before obtaining the necessary audience requested by law for the assembly to be legal (an attendance of at least 50%)" (p. 35). However, according to Mexican Agrarian Law, Article 23, the attendance must exceed three quarters of the ejidatarios, not the 50% highlighted in the IDB's report. A governmental official commented on this:

> The consultations were characterized by a lack of coherence and adequate dialogue given the formal institutions established by the government to protect the local communities. For example, the consultations failed to consider the current Agrarian Law (Mexican governmental official).

In addition, none of the IDB's reports suggest that cultural and language aspects (Zapoteca and Huave) were considered in the consultations. A senior IDB executive commented:

> Consultations were carried out in compliance with Mexican law and the Bank's directives. However, we sub-contracted this process to a local [Mexican] consulting firm. To be honest, I do not know the details of the

procedure … but you know how these people operate … We acknowledge that there are some problems, but we are fixing them (Executive at the IDB's European branch).

International conventions. According to the interviews conducted, it appears that it is necessary to develop and implement a specific regulatory framework for the implementation of ILO Convention 169 in Mexico. One Mexican governmental official discussed this issue as follows:

Mexico has not yet enacted legislation or regulations covering the consultation provisions related to indigenous communities that are included in the Convention (Director of Affairs on Indigenous Communities).

Mexican officials stated that the state congress in Oaxaca had initiated a discussion on the reform of the Political Constitution of Oaxaca with regard to the rights of the region's indigenous and Afro-Mexican populations. However, the proposition remained under review and there were no signs of the potential introduction of mechanisms for its implementation.

The outcome from the CDA and the field work developed showed no evidence on how the MNCs involved in the wind park project met the UNGPs and the ILO Convention 169.

5.5.1.2 Social and environmental issues

Newspaper reports indicate that, by 2012, unemployment rates had increased in the La Ventosa region as a result of the leasing of the land, which had been utilized for agricultural purposes five years earlier (e.g. Moreno and Pérez-Alfonso, 2012):

In the community of Santo Domingo Ingenio, 120 people were employed in La Ventosa for the construction and installation of the windmills in 2004. However, in 2012, only 11 people worked for the wind park, half of whom were from other regions. Thus, many people lost their jobs and crime rates began to increase (Beas-Torres, La Jornada, November 3, 2012).

A resident in Oaxaca commented:

The Isthmus of Tehuantepec had previously produced the best cheese in the region but the limited amount of cattle feed had significantly decreased milk production by 2012. By 2012, unemployment rates had increased in the La Ventosa region as a result of the leasing of the land, which was utilized for agricultural purposes five years earlier (A Zapoteca resident of Juchitán, Oaxaca).

The above statement illustrates the argument against wind parks in Oaxaca. As presented above, 16 wind parks are located in the La Ventosa region (La Venta I, and La Venta II). However, by the time the La Venta III was to be built, the Zapoteca residents had entered into an alliance with the Huaves to oppose MNCs and governmental wind-energy projects. As a resident of San Mateo del Mar explained:

> The Zapotecas wanted to share their experiences with regard to the 16 wind parks already operating in the region. They [the Zapotecas] want to prevent us [the Huaves] from making the same mistakes that they made (Huave resident of San Mateo del Mar, Oaxaca).

The CDA offered no evidence of the consideration of the UNGPs in this project, as presented above. Principle 13 may be relevant in relation to ejidos (communal lands), as it suggests that developers must negotiate a land-lease payment that is fair and convenient for both parties. Another difficulty is preventing project-development processes from leading to speculation on land leases for wind farms:

> In Mexico, there is still no mechanism for regulation and standardization related to the development and operation of wind farms (LAERFTE, Article 8, 2013).

Various sources indicate that numerous wind turbines are needed if the level of energy production is to approach that produced by traditional thermal-power plants (LAERFTE, 2013). Turbines use only 1% to 3% of the land they occupy, whereas the remainder can continue to be used for agriculture or livestock (AIDA, 2009). However, the construction of mega-projects such as wind parks adversely affects territorial occupation, requires construction of infrastructure to access the wind parks, and requires new methods of energy transmission. These issues are highlighted in the following statement:

> Ejidatarios, or "members of the communal assembly," claim that animals, fish, and shrimp are frightened by the noise produced by wind turbines. They also claim that the output of farming and agriculture has decreased (Members of the Communal Assembly, focus group).

In contrast, Andrew Chapman, General Director of Mareña Renovables, stated:

> Turbines do not harm the lake. Turbines will be installed on land. They do not generate vibration or noise that affect fish, and they do not spill substances that are harmful to marine life. Although fishing activities are temporarily restricted in certain sections of the site, Mareña Renovables is committed to providing free transportation for fishermen to travel to free and secure sections (Mareña Renovables, 2013b).

A recurrent argument evident in the CDA and in the primary data focuses on the environmental impact of wind parks in Mexico. For example, a video produced by an independent film-maker includes the following script:

> Wind power has an effect on birds, which can collide with wind turbines and be displaced by the construction and operation of a wind farm. This problem is important in Oaxaca, which serves as a corridor for the passage of birds in southern Mexico. In addition, soil and water pollution can occur from the spilling and changing of thousands of litres of lubricating oil in the turbines (Video: Somos Viento, "We are Wind").

5.6 Responses

On May 15, 2013, Vestas announced that it had signed a forbearance agreement with Mareña Renovables that would push back the completion date of the wind park (SeeNews, 2013). Mareña Renovables also entered into a forbearance agreement with project lenders that ran until July 30, 2013 but could be extended. The contract with Vestas was scheduled to run until November 30, 2013:

> In May 2013, Vestas stated that access to the Oaxaca construction site was limited because the roads were blocked by opposition groups. The company added that this would delay considerably the development of the wind farm (Petrova, 2013).

The resistance group, which included Huaves and Zapotecas, built a resistance camp along the road to the Gulf of Tehuantepec, immediately outside the Zapoteca city of Juchitán, Oaxaca. The resistance camp blocked all the wind-energy firms' vehicles from accessing San Mateo del Mar.

> At 19:30 on October 17, 2013, 58 people including men, women [dressed in Tehuanas, a typical Zapotec dress] and children were in the resistance camp armed with machetes and wooden sticks. The camp was burned down the night before (Observation).

The adults discussed strategic options because the resistance camp was burned the previous night. One of the group's representatives stated that they were opposing the wind energy park project because they were not consulted or included in the development of the project. A member of the Assembly of the Indigenous Peoples of the Isthmus in Defence of Land and Territory stated:

> We do not believe that such a project will offer any of the benefits that the politicians and foreign firms claim our communities would receive. They [the MNCs] want to lease our land for MXN 132 (approximately US$10) per hectare annually, and they offer to share 1.94% of the revenue. I believe that this is an abuse. We know that the suggested land-lease payment is far less than what they pay in Europe. Our understanding of "sharing" is 50% of the profits! (Assembly Member).

Thereafter, news reports indicated that the Mareñas project would be built in another location in Oaxaca:

> The community [Huaves and Zapotecas] claims to have received assurances that the consortium, Mareña Renovables, now plans to move the project (McGovern, 2014).

A Mexican governmental official commented on this development as follows:

> Yes, it is true. However, it is important to remember that it was not solely the fault of the Mexican government, the MNCs, or the local communities. Everyone is responsible, as everyone lied. Nevertheless, the problem

has been resolved and the wind farm will be built (Senior member of the Mexican Government).

5.7 Discussion

The main research question presented for this chapter stated: What is the relation between consultation-consent and CSR? Based on the results presented, five issues were identified as the source of the conflict between the elite groups and indigenous people in Oaxaca, Mexico. This provided insights to map the relation between consultation-consent and CSR: 1) Ignorance and misinformation regarding wind energy mega-projects. The main issue is in relation to the 'fair lease pay' for the land. Ignorance of the details of the project appears to be the cause for mistrust, and for the attitudes of rejection or challenge from Huaves and Zapotecas towards elite groups. 2) Misdirected advice or the absence of advice on the consultation process from local and federal governmental officials, and external stakeholders. 3) Elite groups' failure to disseminate information on the actual impacts of wind farms on the social groups that are directly affected, for example on myths of the negative consequence to the environment of turbines. 4) Lack of clear, timely regulation. In Mexico, there remains no mechanism for regulation and standardization related to the development and operation of wind farms. 5) Legal problems related to land possession. A common problem in the Mexican countryside, particularly in the La Ventosa region, is the proper titles for the tenure of land. As a result of ignorance, a lack of sound advice or customs related to the inherited form of the property land, numerous communities, suburbs and families do not truly have juridical and legal ownership of large tracts of land.

The results suggest that the Zapotecas and Huaves, on the one hand, and governmental and economic elite groups on the other, have adopted different understandings of regional development, in this specific case, regarding wind parks. It may be argued that the MNCs are attempting to implement their business models in Oaxaca, which appears to overlook the basic concepts of CSR. For example, consultation and consent interaction with stakeholders on a voluntary basis and the CSR principles presented (e.g. European Commission, 2011) appear to be the origin of the conflict between elite groups and indigenous people. I interpret this as a traditional top-down strategy in which higher-level structures shape the behaviour of lower-level actors (Scott, 2008). However, the model is being reshaped by the indigenous communities (lower-level actors), a development that was not expected by the government or the MNCs (higher-level actors).

The Zapotecas and Huaves appear to have put their old land disputes aside to join forces to re-establish their usos y costumbres (practices and customs) with the objective of being involved in consultations that meet the requirements of Mexican law and ILO Convention 169. This move appears to be particularly important in an institutional context where a lack of the rule of law within the formal institutions (legal systems) appears to exist in Mexico. The Zapotecas and Huaves have blocked MNCs' access and demonstrated in public to fill the institutional voids found in Mexico.

At the same time, the MNCs involved in the conflict have other resources with which they could "fight" the indigenous people. For example, MNCs can protect their investments through contracts with Mexican officials. In addition, MNCs have access to tools, procedures, and even coaching from external stakeholders such as the United Nations, the IDB, or the ILO to assist in the implementation of such principles as those of ILO Convention 169, particularly with regard to con-sultations with and consent from local communities. One may wonder why MNCs do not utilize these tools. This challenges the assumption that foreign MNCs have transferred their management policies and practices, such as CSRs in Mexico, which have created a mimetic effect in Mexican firms. Why do investors not apply their own policies from home in their foreign direct investment (FDI)? It appears that these complexities tend to be more evident in mega-projects. For example, for Oaxaca, Mexico, it appears that power may be determined by clientelism, or patron-age arrangements, which are relationships based on subordination in exchange for material rewards. This may be the case across a wide range of hierarchical relations in this region (Fox, 1994, p. 153). In this context, indigenous people in Oaxaca have traditionally held little power or have been marginalized social actors, and their interests have been misaligned with the existing rules, structures and practices.

This lack of compliance challenges the CSR concept presented: "Respect for applicable legislation and for collective agreements between social partners" (European Commission, 2011, p. 6). In this respect, the findings presented here suggest that the policy related to the wind park project in Oaxaca lacks vertical coherence. The findings show the presence of a gap in the regulative policies necessary to implement international human-rights law and laws related to various other obligations, such as consultations and consent, and in the processes needed to regulate wind parks in Mexico. In addition, Mexico has no regulations governing land leases for wind parks. This has created a power-bargaining situa-tion among the MNCs and the ejidatarios (communal representatives). Most of the bargaining power is held by the MNCs, which propose the rents and the divi-sion of profits to the communal representatives, who have little power in the nego-tiation process. In addition, higher-level actors appear to lack horizontal policy coherence. The results suggest that, although economic elite groups normally have CSR and legal departments, they lack the knowledge needed to plan and imple-ment a mega-project that involves indigenous communities' consultation and consent. The lack of understanding of indigenous peoples' usos y costumbres to first develop a consultation process to then reach consent has led to conflict. Such conflict has national and international impacts, as the Mareñas Renovables con-sortium encompasses national and international stakeholders. Vestas appears to have overlooked its role as the business partner in the project. According to the UNGPs, the role of Vestas in the value chain should have included relationships with business partners, entities in its value chain, and any other non-state or state entities directly linked to its business operations, products or services (United Nations, 2011). This raises concerns regarding the lack of compliance of Vestas in the value chain for the Oaxaca wind park project. In addition to the neglect of principles of development, this requires the creation of wealth and the conservation of resources in addition to their fair distribution both between and within communities (Roseland, 2012); it also requires them to be responsible for the consequences of their actions. Members of the economic elite (MNCs) may be attempting to implement their business models in Oaxaca without considering the basic principles of CSR. In this regard, the governmental and economic elites appear to be actively manipulating the institutional context to alter the institutional demands. They also appear to be attempting to influence defined norms through active lobbying (Pache and Santos, 2010, p. 463). These activities have apparently given rise to positive results for Mexicans and MNCs; in January 2014, the Mexican congress approved an energy reform that allows the private sector to invest in energy. However, there have been no signs of a reform that would integrate the rights of the indigenous communities into the legislation in Mexico in relation to indigenous peoples' consultation and consent processes.

5.8 Conclusions and reflections on development-oriented CSR

This chapter highlights the role of indigenous communities as critical micro-level social actors (Morgan *et al.*, 2004) in mega-projects. Although several scholars have argued for the importance of considering the institutional context and CSR when conducting international business, scholars and practitioners have thus far lacked a fundamental understanding of these constructs, particularly regarding consultation and consent principles. This is exemplified by the fact that the government and economic elite groups have been unable to resolve the wind park conflict in Oaxaca, which appears to have fuelled the misleading stereotypes that indigenous communities and elite groups have of each another.

The case presented could help to develop an agenda on a development-oriented CSR. Elite groups function by public consent. Economic elite groups are expected to serve constructively the needs of society (CED, 1971). Based on the case presented, it could be argued that economic elite groups could function as a platform not only for job creation but also to reinstall basic FPIC principles. However, the responses of the government and MNCs presented appear to improperly engage institutional challenges in Mexico, where laws and procedures to build the wind park project need to be implemented. Surprisingly, the Zapotecas and Huaves are fighting to reinstall the basic principles of CSR in their institutional context, principles that elite groups appear to have ignored.

In this context, the role of the indigenous people, who have traditionally held little power or have been marginalized social actors, may be shifting. These groups may have the potential to serve as change agents (Seo and Creed, 2002). However, what are the mechanisms used by indigenous groups to shape institutions that rely on logic different from their own? Future research could integrate the concept of strategic agency (Giddens, 1984, p. 9) to study the power of institutional actors. This approach may help to unpack the processes through which actors not only render practical consciousness discursive but also interpret their political interests (Hensmans, 2003). The dynamic evident in this study between development and CSR appears to show connections among the institutional (formal and informal) linkages, as suggested by organizational theorists. However, I suggest that institutional contexts have an impact on the strategic responses of the indigenous populations and elite groups. In this regard, I urge researchers focused on emerging economies to consider how actors respond, develop strategies, and shape CSR in other transitioning economies.

In conclusion, the wind park project in Oaxaca reveals the struggles of the indigenous communities that are challenged by questionable patronage arrangements introduced by the political and economic elite groups. The Oaxaca saga provides fertile ground for further development of various elements in studies to design strategies that reflect the interactions between development and CSR that appear to confront one another in different national contexts.

Bibliography

AIDA (Interamerican Association for environmental Defense) (2009). The Challenges of Deploying Wind Energy in Mexico. The case of the Isthmus of Tehuantepec. Retrieved from http://www.aida-americas.org/sites/default/files/Challenge%20Wind%20Energy%20Mexico%20Final.pdf.

Amnesty International (2011). Document—Mexico: Further Information: Protesters at Risk of Unfair Prosecution. Retrieved from http://www.amnesty.org/en/library/asset/AMR41/069/2011/en/6f41ef6b-84ca-4eb7-8655-2b822a0e19a1/amr410692011en.html, last accessed 5 June 2013.

Asociación Mexicana de Energía Eólica (2008). An Overview of the Wind Energy in Mexico. Retrieved from: http://www.amdee.org/.

Banerjee, S.B. (2000). Whose land is it anyway? National interest, indigenous stakeholders, and colonial discourses. The case of the Jabiluka uranium mine. *Organization & Environment,* 13(1), 3-38.

Beas-Torres, C. (2012) Tres mitos del mega proyecto eólico del Istmo de Tehuantepec [Three myths of the wind park project at the Isthmus of Tehuantepec]. (Mexico: La Jornada). Retrieved from http://www.jornada.unam.mx/2012/11/03/opinion/023a1est.

Bowen, H.R. (1953). *Social Responsibilities of the Businessman.* New York: Harper & Row.

Bowen, J.D. (2011). Multicultural market democracy: elites and indigenous movements in contemporary Ecuador. *Journal of Latin American Studies,* 43(3), 451-483.

Carroll, A.B. (1991). The pyramid of corporate social responsibility: toward the moral management of organizational stakeholders. *Business Horizons,* 34(4), 39-48.

Carroll, A.B. (1999). Corporate social responsibility evolution of a definitional construct. *Business & Society*, 38(3), 268-295.

CDI (Comision Nacional para el Desarrollo de los Pueblos Indígenas) (2009). Huaves - Mero Ikooc [National Commission for the Development of Indigenous Peoples]. Retrieved from http://www.cdi.gob.mx/index.php?option=com_content&task=view&id=595&Itemid=62.

CED (Committee for Economic Development) (1971). Social responsibilities of business corporations. Retrieved from https://www.ced.org/reports/single/social-responsibilities-of-business-corporations.

Colchester, M., & Ferrari, M.F. (2007). Making FPIC Work: Challenges and Prospects for Indigenous Peoples, Forest Peoples Programme (FPP). Retrieved from http://www.forestpeoples.org/topics/civil-political-rights/publication/2010/making-fpic-free-prior-and-informed-consent-work-chal.

Cotula, L., & Vermeulen, S. (2011). Contexts and procedures for farmland acquisitions in Africa: what outcomes for local people? *Development*, 54(1), 40-48.

CTBR Staff Writer (2012). Vestas secures 90 MW wind turbine order from Enel green power. Retrieved from http://wind.cleantechnology-business-review.com/news/vestas-secures-90mw-wind-turbine-order-from-enel-green-power-281212.

Dickert, N., & Sugarman, J. (2005). Ethical goals of community consultation in research. *American Journal of Public Health*, 95(7), 1123-1124.

Driscoll, C. (2006). The not so clear-cut nature of organizational legitimating mechanisms in the Canadian forest sector. *Business & society*, 45(3), 322-353.

Dye, T.R., & Pickering, J.W. (1974). Governmental and corporate elites: convergence and differentiation. *The Journal of Politics*, 36(4), 900-925.

European Commission (2011). Communication from the Commission to the European Parliament, the Council, the European Economic and Social Committee and the Committee of the Regions. A renewed EU strategy 2011-2014 for Corporate Social Responsibility (Brussels: European Commission, 25.10.2011). COM(2011) 681 final. Retrieved from http://eur-lex.europa.eu/LexUriServ/LexUriServ.do?uri=COM:2011:0681:FIN:EN:PDF.

Fairclough, N. (2005). Peripheral vision discourse analysis in organization studies: The case for critical realism. *Organization Studies*, 26(6), 915-939.

Fox, J. (1994). The difficult transition from clientelism to citizenship: lessons from Mexico. *World Politics*, 46(2), 151-184.

Gellert, P.K., & Lynch, B.D. (2003). Mega-projects as displacements. *International Social Science Journal*, 55, 15-25

Giddens, A. (1984). *The Constitution of Society: Outline of the Theory of Structuration*. Cambridge: Blackwell Publishing Ltd.

Hensmans, M. (2003). Social movement organizations: a metaphor for strategic actors in institutional fields. *Organization Studies*, 24(3), 355-381.

IDB (Inter-American Development Bank) (2011). Mareña Renovables ESMR-Wind. Project Number ME-L1107. Retrieved from http://idbdocs.iadb.org/wsdocs/getdocument.aspx?docnum=36537741.

IDB (Inter-American Development Bank) (2012). Mareña Renovables: Environmental and Social Action Plan. Project Number ME-L1107. (25 January, 2012). Retrieved from http://www.iadb.org/en/projects/project-description-title,1303.html?id=ME-L1107, last accessed 5 June 2013.

ILO (International Labour Organization) (2009). Indigenous and Tribal Peoples' Right in Practice – A Guide to ILO Convention No. 169. Retrieved from http://www.ilo.org/indigenous/Resources/Guidelinesandmanuals/WCMS_106474/lang--en/index.htm.

Khanna, T., & Palepu, K. (1999). The right way to restructure conglomerates in emerging markets. *Harvard Business Review*, 77, 125-135.

LAERFTE (2013). Ley para el Aprovechamiento de Energías Renovables y el Financiamiento de la Transición Energética [Law for the Use of Renewable Energy and Energy Transition Financing]. Retrieved from http://www.cre.gob.mx/documento/1523.pdf, last accessed 5 June 2013.

Ley Agraria [Agrarian Law] (2012). Cámara de Diputados del H. Congreso de la Unión. Estados Unidos Mexicanos [Chamber of Deputies of the H. Congress, United Mexican States], DOF (09-04-2012). Retrieved from http://www.diputados.gob.mx/LeyesBiblio/pdf/13.pdf.

Matten, D., & Moon, J. (2008). Implicit and explicit CSR: A conceptual framework for a comparative understanding of corporate social responsibility. *Academy of Management Review*, 33(2), 404-424.

Mareña Renovables (2013a). Mareña Renovables. Retrieved from http://marena-renovables.com.mx/.

Mareña Renovables (2013b). El Proyecto del Parque Eólico Istmeño San Dionisio Fortalecerá a las Comunidades del Istmo Juchitán Zaragoza, Oaxaca, México. Retrieved from http://marena-renovables.com.mx/wp-content/uploads/2012/12/Bolet%C3%ADn-Mare%C3%B1a-Renovables-11-02-13.pdf, last accessed 5 June 2013.

McGovern, M. (2012). Developers face escalating militant opposition in Oaxaca. *Windpower*. Retrieved from http://www.windpowermonthly.com/article/1124476/developers-face-escalating-militant-opposition-oaxaca.

McGovern, M. (2014). Analysis: Macquarie's Mareña project on the brink. *Windpower*. Retrieved from http://www.windpowermonthly.com/article/1227498/analysis-macquaries-marena-project-brink.

Moreno, H., & Pérez-Alfonso, J.A. (2012). Anuncian manifestaciones en Oaxaca contra parques eólicos [Announce protests in Oaxaca against wind farms]. (Mexico: La Jornada). Retrieved from http://www.jornada.unam.mx/2012/10/30/estados/032n1est.

Morgan, G., Kristensen, P.H., & Whitley, R. (Eds.). (2004). *The Multinational Firm: Organizing Across Institutional and National Divides*. Oxford: Oxford University Press.

Oxford Dictionaries (2014). Definition of consult in English. (Oxford University Press). Retrieved from http://www.oxforddictionaries.com/definition/english/consult

Pache, A., & Santos, F. (2010). When worlds collide: the internal dynamics of organizational responses to conflicting institutional demands. *Academy of Management Review*, 35(3), 455-476.

Peinado-Vara, E. (2006). Corporate social responsibility in Latin America. *Journal of Corporate Citizenship*, 21, 61-69.

Petrova, V. (2013). Vestas agrees delay of 396-MW wind farm in Mexico. (London: SeeNews Renewables). Retrieved from http://renewables.seenews.com/news/vestas-agrees-delay-of-396-mw-wind-farm-in-mexico-353412.

Preneal (2011). Preneal cierra la venta de dos proyectos eólicos en Oaxaca (México). [Preneal closed the sale of two wind projects in Oaxaca (Mexico)]. Retrieved from http://www.preneal.es/en/news/3-noticias/71-preneal-cierra-la-venta-de-dos-proyectos-eolicos-en-oaxaca-mexico-por-89-millones-de-dolares.

PROMÉXICO (2013). Energías alternativas en México [Alternative energy in Mexico]. Retrieved from http://www.promexico.gob.mx/desarrollo-sustentable/energias-alternativas-en-mexico.html.

Porter, J. (1957) The economic elite and the social structure in Canada. *Canadian Journal of Economics and Political Science*, 23(3), 376-394.

Porter, M.E., & Kramer, M.R. (2006). The link between competitive advantage and corporate social responsibility. *Harvard Business Review*, 84(12), 78-92.

Quijano, A. (2000). Coloniality of power and Eurocentrism in Latin America. *International Sociology*, 15(2), 215-232.

Rojas, R. (2012). Proyecto de parque eólico desata pugnas entre pobladores del Istmo [Wind farm project unleashes conflicts between people of the Isthmus] (Mexico: La Jornada, 39). Retrieved from http://www.jornada.unam.mx/2012/01/17/sociedad/039n1soc.

Roseland, M. (2012). *Toward Sustainable Communities: Solutions for Citizens and Their Governments*. Gabriola Island, BC, Canada: New Society Publishers.

Sassen, S. (2004). Local actors in global politics. *Current sociology*, 52(4), 649-670.

Scott, W.R. (2008). Approaching adulthood: The maturing of institutional theory. *Theory and Society*, 37(5), 427-442.

SeeNews, R. (2013). Vestas agrees delay of 396-MW wind farm in Mexico (London: SeeNews Renewables). Retrieved from http://renewables.seenews.com/news/vestas-faces-further-delay-for-396-mw-mexican-wind-deal-393420.

Seo, M., & Creed, W.D. (2002). Institutional contradictions, praxis, and institutional change: a dialectical perspective. *Academy of Management Review*, 27(2), 222-247.

United Nations (2011). Guiding Principles on Business and Human Rights. Implementing the United Nations Protect, Respect and Remedy Framework (New York and Geneva: United Nations). Retrieved from http://business-humanrights.org/en/un-guiding-principles.

Vestas (2012). Vestas wins order for largest wind energy project in Latin America. 396-MW order for Mexico underlines Vestas intention to lead wind industry in Latin America. News release No. 3/2012. Madrid: Vestas.

Wind Power (2013). Parque eólico La Venta I (México) The Wind Power, 2013. 07/2013. Retrieved from http://www.thewindpower.net/windfarm_es_4092_la-venta-i.php.

6

Migrants' engagement in CSR
The case of a Ghanaian migrants' transnational social enterprise

Daniela Bolzani[1] and Selenia Marabello[2]
University of Bologna, Italy

Academic debate has questioned whether CSR norms and practices are globally converging and highlighted the need to develop a south-centred CSR agenda. Drawing on the concept of co-development, we analyse the extent to which immigrant-led transnational businesses can implement southern-driven CSR actions to address development needs in developing countries. We study the case of Ghanacoop, a transnational agro-food cooperative owned by Ghanaian immigrants in Italy, which implemented philanthropic and corporate responsibility innovation actions. Our analyses are based on 18 months' ethnography carried out in Italy and Ghana from 2007 to 2009. We discuss several key aspects of CSR from a management and anthropological view, applying an interdisciplinary discipline. We show how immigrant-led transnational businesses, being rooted both in western and southern institutional contexts, can lead CSR practices to globally converge, but also how diaspora engagement in CSR does not necessarily guarantee the

---

1 Author of the Introduction and paragraphs 6.2.1, 6.2.2, 6.2.3, 6.2.4 and 6.3.1.
2 Author of paragraphs 6.1, 6.1.1, 6.1.2 and 6.3.

conception and implementation of southern-driven CSR discourses and actions.

In the last decades, management researchers have begun to question whether management practices, among them corporate social responsibility (CSR), are converging or diverging around the world (Matten and Moon, 2008). Although it is clear that national institutional frameworks and contextual factors are essential for differentiating CSR norms and practices (Egri and Ralston, 2008; Dobers and Halme, 2009), few micro-level CSR analyses can be found in the literature (Lund-Thomsen, 2004) especially outside OECD countries (Belal and Momin, 2009). Mainstream literature therefore reports on concepts, debates and research strategies from the north, without considering the voices of the "peripheral" south (Connell, 2007). In this manner, the opportunity to contribute and challenge theoretical development is partially missed.

Therefore, several authors have acknowledged that a southern perspective is required in the debate concerning CSR policies and practices (Ward and Fox, 2002). With a south-centred agenda it is possible to understand local CSR drivers and constraints, the human and institutional capacity needed to manage these drivers and the CSR tools to address local stakeholders' concerns (Fox, 2004) and thus to contribute to sustainable development (Idemudia, 2011). A key issue that emerges from this approach concerns the engagement of southern stakeholders in the dialogue with companies (Blowfield and Frynas, 2005). This is required in order to identify and address local needs and priorities and to assure that CSR initiatives are perceived as relevant and legitimate, thus ensuring a correct allocation of resources from companies and avoiding the crowding-out of local authorities' policy actions (Blowfield and Frynas, 2005; Barkemeyer, 2007).

This chapter examines how and to what extent a southern perspective on CSR can be brought forward by immigrant-led transnational businesses. Immigrants can foster development in their countries of origin by engaging in forms of co-development. It is also discussed whether immigrant-led transnational businesses, acting as "brokers" crossing northern and southern boundaries, can embody and address relevant development problems in developing countries through CSR.

With the aim of answering this question, we analyse the case of a business and co-development project named "Ghanacoop", which created a cooperative company owned by Ghanaian immigrants in Italy, and active in transnational activities in the agro-food sector between Ghana and Italy. The company incorporated CSR in its business model as well as promoting it through philanthropic actions. Our analyses are based on an 18-month anthropological fieldwork project carried out between 2007 and 2009 in Italy and Ghana by one of the authors, which was aimed at assessing the role of immigrants' transnational engagement in co-development. In an interdisciplinary perspective, we re-analysed the data applying a management—and an anthropological—view on the CSR activities of the company. Through the chapter, we use the term CSR as an umbrella term, which recognizes the company's responsibility for its own and business partners' actions and the need to manage its relationship with the wider society (Blowfield and Frynas, 2007).

The first part of the chapter discusses the theme of migration and development, specifically describing the Ghanacoop project, and provides some information about Ghanaian migration to Italy. The second part of the chapter presents an introduction to the issue of CSR convergence/divergence, some background information concerning the Ghanaian context for CSR, our research design and an analysis of Ghanacoop's CSR practices. The final part provides a critical discussion of the case and some final reflections on development-oriented CSR.

6.1 Migration and development

The link between migration and development has gained remarkable relevance in the discourses of international organizations (e.g. the United Nations and its agencies[3]), which celebrate the role of immigrants as new cultural and social brokers (Olivier de Sardan, 2005; Lewis and Mosse, 2006), who act as development agents for the countries of origin. An important set of transnational activities refers to "co-development", that is the policies and practices of development involving actors and institutions below the level of the state (Grillo, Riccio, 2004). Co-development is a concrete expression of migrants' political engagement and produces a plurality of representations concerning development, identity and political action. Co-development is based on the idea that migrants can be development actors for their countries of origin, mobilizing social and cultural knowledge from different social contexts, also involving other institutions in both the sending and the receiving countries (e.g. NGOs, municipal authorities, village associations and local communities) (Marabello, 2013), as well as achieving positive outcomes for the migrants themselves (Weil, 2002; Agunias, 2006).

6.1.1 Ghanaian migration to Italy

Ghanaian migration to Italy started in the 1980s, following the military coups d'état and the economic downturn in the country. Although immigrants first arrived as asylum seekers (Manuh, 2006), since the late 1990s migratory movements have been due to economic reasons or family reunifications (Riccio, 2008). Over

---

3 For some examples, see the website of the Joint Migration and Development Initiative (http://www.migration4development.org/) or the Global Forum for Migration and Development (http://www.gfmd.org/).

the last two decades, Ghanaian diaspora has been seen as an opportunity for development in Ghana (Mohan, 2006). This occurred thanks to the election of a new government (in 2001) championed by diaspora citizens, the recognition of dual citizenship (since 1997), the recognition of Ghanaian associations in the countries of emigration and the engagement of local traditional political authorities (the *chiefs*) that aimed at attracting investments and resources for developing their homeland.

In Italy most Ghanaian immigrants settled in the northern part of the country. Approximately twelve thousand Ghanaians, demographically balanced in terms of gender, reside in the Emilia-Romagna region (Regione Emilia-Romagna, 2013) and almost 53% live in the province of Modena (Regione Emilia-Romagna, 2013), which is the city where Ghanacoop was founded.

6.1.2 The "migration for development in Africa" (MIDA) project

In 2002 the International Organization for Migration (IOM), together with the Italian Ministry of Foreign Affairs, launched a program involving Ghanaian and Senegalese immigrants in Italy called "MIDA Ghana/Senegal". The aim of the program was to identify and support the implementation of immigrants' initiatives for local development in their countries of origin, especially those regarding income-generating activities and rural development. It consisted in creating bottom-up partnerships, providing technical assistance and matching funds from Italian national and regional authorities and involving immigrants' associations and other private and public actors (Stocchiero, 2008). The program selected twelve projects to be supported, five of which were promoted by Ghanaian groups.

6.1.2.1 The Ghanacoop project

Ghanacoop was founded as a cooperative enterprise in May 2005 by the Ghana National Association in Modena. Ghanacoop was envisaged as an import-export company in the agro-food sector. The agro-food market was seen as a viable opportunity for exploitation by the Ghanaians, even though they did not have any direct experience in the sector. The business model was initially to include two lines of activities: first, the importing of exotic fruits from Ghanaian fair-trade labelled producers; second, the promotion of sustainable tourism in/from Ghana. In time, the business plan changed, focusing only on the agro-food component. The company therefore engaged in three activities: the importing of agro-food Ghanaian products, the exporting of Italian products and the management of a small pepper plantation in Ghana.

In 2006, the company started to import fair-trade labelled pineapples, sold under the brand "Miss Ghananas" in large retail stores in three cities in Emilia-Romagna, and ethnic food, sold in the African shops in the north of Italy. The company was highly active in the promotion of the image of Ghana and of their commercial activity, involving voluntary members of the Ghanaian Association. In the same year, the company established an operative subsidiary in Ghana, named Ghanital Multiporpouse Ltd. In 2007, the company started to export Italian products (e.g. wine, Parma ham) to Ghana, selling them through new distribution chains to the new élites and the foreigners residing in the country. By the end of 2007, the company established a pepper plantation in the village of Gomoa Simbrofo, catering for the national market. In July 2009, Ghanacoop closed down after a fraud by one of the main customers and a series of internal conflicts among the leaders.

On establishment, the company was managed by the same leaders of the Ghanaian Association. However, this activity was never warmly welcomed by the volunteer members of the association and their dual engagement as business managers and association leaders generated some degree of misunderstanding about the goals of the company and those of the association. In July 2006, an Italian social cooperative with a long experience in foreign countries and development joined the management of the company with a control agreement. Some Italian partners subsequently joined the company and some entered the board of directors. Besides the aid received from IOM, Ghanacoop was heavily supported by the city government, which provided contacts with other private and public actors and public visibility.

The company's socially responsible activities were an integral part of the business. As already mentioned, two of the main business activities of Ghanacoop (i.e. fair-trade fruit importing and the pepper plantation management) were based on a form of "corporate responsibility innovation" (Halme and Laurila, 2009). In 2006, the company launched a new branding system to certify that the products were based on the immigrants' initiative for development (MIDCO—Migrants Initiatives for Development of the Country of Origin). In addition, the company carried out "philanthropic" CSR actions (Halme and Laurila, 2009), such as building an emergency room for the hospital in Apam and financing a photovoltaic plant in Gomoa Simbrofo (2007). The development of socially responsible activities was accompanied by intense network relationships with other private and public organizations in Italy and in Ghana. In particular, Ghanacoop was supported by other Italian cooperatives (for the distribution of fair-trade pineapples in Italy; for the building of an emergency room at the Apam Catholic Hospital), by the University of Modena (ideation of the MIDCO branding), and finally, by an Italian cooperative bank (for providing the solar panel in Gomoa Simbrofo).

Important international bodies, such as the IOM and the United Nations presented it as a best practice[4] and international broadcasters, CNN and the BBC, devoted time on their media networks to present the case.

---

4 For some examples: Key Migration Issues Workshop Series: Contributions of Diasporas (New York, 2006), organized by the United Nations Institute for Training and Research (UNITAR); United Nations Population Fund (UNFPA); International Organization for Migration (IOM); Venice Forum (Venice, 2008).

6.2 Empirical evidence: CSR in the Ghanacoop case

6.2.1 Convergence–divergence of CSR

A recent academic debate has questioned whether CSR norms and practices are globally converging or diverging. In fact, although CSR is expected to converge due to global institutional pressures, CSR trends are expected to diverge due to enduring differences in national business systems (Jamali and Neville, 2011; Matten and Moon, 2008). The complexity of this issue also led to the development of a "cross-vergence" perspective (Ralston, *et al.*, 1993), whereby the interaction of national differences and global influences result in complex hybridized CSR solutions (Jamali and Neville, 2011).

In this debate, it is useful to distinguish between explicit (voluntary programs and strategies carried out for societal interests) and implicit (values, norms, rules resulting in mandatory and customary collective obligations for companies) CSR practices (Matten and Moon, 2008). Studies have shown that CSR convergence is mainly "cosmetic", that is, regarding the adoption of explicit CSR in developing countries, even if it depends on the strength of traditional local institutions and governments (Matten and Moon, 2008). Implicit CSR interpretations remain closely attuned to local institutional norms and pressures (Jamali and Neville, 2011, p. 617), such as cultural, religious, tribal, or family values.

New insights can be brought into this debate by investigating the case of Ghanacoop. In fact, as an immigrant-led transnational company rooted both in northern and southern social contexts, it responds to different institutional expectations and embodies the various interpretations of CSR norms and practices, holding implications for a development-oriented CSR.

6.2.2 The local context: CSR in Ghana

In Ghana, the recognition of the private sector as an engine of growth, development and solving societal problems has emerged only in the last decade (Amponsah-Tawiah and Dartey-Baah, 2011; Kragelund, 2004;). Because of the socialist orientation characterizing the years after independence from the United Kingdom (1957), the state–business relationships in Ghana were marked by a strong anti-capitalist rhetoric, state-led industrialization (e.g. state-owned enterprises), poorly designed privatization programs and extensive corruption (Kragelund, 2004).

CSR did not receive any specific regulation or official promotion until 2006, after which the Ghana Business Code (GHBC)[5] (Atuguba and Dowuona-Hammond,

---

5 See   http://investinkumasi.com/wp-content/uploads/2013/09/ghana_business_code.pdf.

2006) and the Extractive Industries Transparency Initiative (GHEITI)[6] were started (Amponsah-Tawiah and Dartey-Baah, 2011). However, CSR is to date not included in any comprehensive regulatory framework regarding corporate governance and appears to be poorly understood or just regarded as a "philanthropic add-on" (African Peer Review Mechanism, 2005). CSR in the country is indirectly encouraged through tax deductions for companies sponsoring charities, sports development and promotion, educational scholarships, and rural and urban community development projects (Atuguba and Dowuona-Hammond, 2006). Companies are, however, required to devolve a "development tribute" to local authorities, as a form of royalty payment peculiar to the country.

6.2.3 Research design

Our analyses are based on an anthropological fieldwork carried out in 2007–2009 by one of the authors, aimed at examining the role of diasporas for co-development and the specific case of Ghanacoop as an example of migrants' civic, political and economic transnational engagement. The anthropologist played an "observer as participant" role (Junker, 1960)[7] in the ethnographic project (Mosse, 2004). The ethnography, as continued vis-à-vis relation between researcher and informants, enabled us to learn about the culture of the migrants under study and understand the meaning of their actions in the context of Ghanacoop (Hammersley and Atkinson, 1995). The researcher participated in daily work-related Ghanacoop routines for 18 months in Italy and Ghana, informal meetings (e.g. holy masses, shops, etc.), the monthly meetings of the Ghanaian association as well as national and international conferences. The data were collected by means of participant observation, informal conversations, semi-structured interviews and secondary sources (e.g. project reports, newspapers, press releases, Ghanacoop website, Chamber of Commerce documents, etc.). In-depth, longitudinal semi-structured interviews were carried out with 12 members of the cooperative, four Ghanaian migrants' associations and national networks and 41 stakeholders (12 employees, three customers, three suppliers, 20 family members, three policy-makers). The interviews were conducted in Italian, English and Twi (Akan) language and were tape-recorded and transcribed. Participant observation took place mainly in Modena (Italy) and Accra (Ghana), but data were also gathered in Apam, Gomoa Simbrofo, Agona Swedru (Ghana), Rome, Vicenza, Mantua and Castelfranco Emilia (Italy). The selection of participants was carried out as an emergent and slow process aimed at amplifying the understanding of the culture and the context studied and at gaining trust, favoured by Ghanacoop's leaders (key informants).

6 See http://www.gheiti.gov.gh/.
7 She gained access to the field since she was recruited by CE.SPI (Centro Politica Internazionale) and IOM as a consultant for evaluating the implementation of the MIDA project.

Table 6.1 **Dimensions of CSR analysed**

1	Types and conception of CSR
2	Vision, motivating principles and values governing the business and CSR
3	Stakeholder management Integration of CSR processes
4	Outcomes of CSR Improvement of CSR processes

For an in-depth discussion of the theoretical perspectives underlying each of these dimensions, see Jamali *et al.* (2009).

As already mentioned, the original anthropological fieldwork was aimed at assessing the role of immigrants' transnational engagement regarding co-development. Taking an interdisciplinary perspective, we envisaged a great opportunity in merging a management and an anthropological view of the CSR activities of the company. Our analyses need therefore to be read as a double challenge: first, to apply a cross-disciplinary lens to the already-gathered data (the specific theme of CSR was not discussed with respondents); second, to select the relevant information and insights from hundreds of hours of field observations, interviewing, participation and interpretation. In ethnography, the researcher provides a personal interpretation of the participants' world, by participating actively in the field and the continual iteration of data collection, data interpretation, and thematic development (Down, 2006). We interpreted the data by means of an informal coding methodology (similar to McCann *et al.*, 2013). We read and re-read each document separately, selected sentences in the text that were relevant to our research question and formulated provisional analytical categories with regard to the dimensions outlined by Jamali *et al.* (2009) (see Table 6.1).

We identified patterns of convergence and divergence in the statements regarding each of the identified dimensions provided by the respondents. During this stage, we did not make use of data-analysis software for three reasons. First, three languages (Italian/English/Twi) would have been difficult to manage in the same textual record; secondly, we did not want to impose arbitrary structures on the emerging meaning of data (McCann *et al.*, 2013); third, we felt that the importance of themes was determined by their connection to a broader context of respondents' accounts rather than their frequencies (Down, 2006). We then compared our analyses of data and selected ethnographic materials, by aligning our own disciplinary-driven points of view and answering to the research question in an informal and exploratory manner.

In the next section, we describe the case of Ghanacoop by adopting the analytical framework proposed by Jamali *et al.* (2009), which integrates several theoretical perspectives in order to obtain a nuanced vision of CSR dimensions. Given the demanding task of ethnographic writing (Geertz, 1973), we decided to make extensive use of the parts of the interviews that are most relevant for discussing our research question.

6.2.4 CSR dimensions in the Ghanacoop case

6.2.4.1 Types and conceptions of CSR

According to the managers of Ghanacoop, CSR was entirely embedded in the cooperative's business model. The company was, in fact, identified as "a transnational enterprise committed to development"[8]. This is also confirmed by some of the partners, who viewed Ghanacoop as "the operative arm of the Ghanaian Association",[9] as well as a development actor active on a transnational level, that is both in Italy and Ghana. In particular, in Italy the cooperative was seen as a business making it possible to carry out important initiatives or launching other entrepreneurial activities to create job opportunities for immigrants. For Ghanaian immigrants in Italy, being leaders or members of Ghanacoop meant having numerous opportunities, meeting important people, being invited to public events, and therefore having opportunities for social mobility in the Italian and Ghanaian contexts. In Ghana, the CSR activities of the company received a more nuanced and confused representation. The employees of Ghanital reported several interpretations of the project:

> Ghanacoop received money from the Italian Government to help immigrants.[10]

> In Ghana, Ghanacoop is known only for its social projects, while Ghanital is known only in the business environment. Maybe Ghanacoop will stop making social projects and will only deal with business, since not all its partners are interested to social projects.[11]

The pepper plantation workers did not have a clear idea of the Ghanacoop project, apparently only understanding that it was a company owned and managed by Ghanaian migrants. The local village chief also did not show a clear understanding of Ghanacoop, providing only brief comments on his perception of the company and of the projects, such as "Ghanacoop? Better living"[12], echoing a "developmental" slogan used during the 2008 presidential elections by J.E.A. Mills. These different conceptions of CSR from the "internal" and the "external" stakeholders of the company show evidence of the issue of stakeholders' expectations (Idemudia, 2011; Blowfield and Frynas, 2007), an issue that we will tackle below.

The types of CSR implemented by Ghanacoop, in the narratives by managers and partners, appear to be part of the ethical and discretionary responsibility (Carroll, 1991). As highlighted above, socially responsible activities were strongly intertwined in the cooperative's business model, having a sense of morality, justice,

8 Interview with A.T., partner and manager of Ghanacoop, June 2007, Modena (Italy).
9 Interview with Mr G., individual partner of Ghanacoop, December 2008, Modena (Italy).
10 Interview with P., employee of Ghanital, June 2009, Accra (Ghana).
11 Interview with S., employee of Ghanital, June 2009, Accra (Ghana).
12 Interview with Nana A., deputy chief of the village of Gomoa Simbrofo, June 2009, Gomoa Simbrofo (Ghana).

rightfulness and fairness (Carroll, 1991). Using the typology described by Halme and Laurila (2009), Ghanacoop implemented CR innovation. The business idea was based on a win-win model. In addition to this, the company implemented discretionary responsibility, that is, it provided optional philanthropic contributions. Philanthropy implies an emphasis on charitable actions and the use of corporate resources for "doing good" (e.g. donations, sponsorships, charity, etc.), with no direct relation to the core business. Paradoxically, however, the accounts of managers and employees demonstrate that, even if implementing "higher-level" CSR actions (in Carroll's pyramid), Ghanacoop partially failed to implement economic and legal responsibility. In fact, the salaries of managers and employees were very low and the employees in Ghana did not have any written contract with Ghanital or Ghanacoop.

6.2.4.2 Vision, principles and values governing the business and CSR

The founders of Ghanacoop played a very strong role in the definition of the vision and of the motivations for the CSR involvement of the company. For them the locus of responsibility (Hemingway and Maclagan, 2004) is found at the individual level, since they exercise stewardship and influence the pursuit of CSR actions. With regard to this, being immigrants was seen as the key to drive effective CSR actions in the country of origin. The motivation for CSR actions undertaken by Ghanacoop were basically altruistic (Hemingway and Maclagan, 2004), aiming at providing genuine aid for the population in the country of origin. The business was seen as a means to provide benefits to Ghanaians, even if those benefits are not always those expected or believed by the local community, as we will see below.

As reported by some of the managers:

> We, as diaspora, do good for people, we're proud to be able to do something to contribute to development. (...) Ghanaians often have suspicions about what we're doing, but we are Ghanaians too, we believe in development and we can use our knowledge and our know-how to make them live better, we're always open to talk to everyone but none of us should accept political offices, even when they are offered to us, we are businessmen and we believe that the price of our sacrifices in Italy should be partially returned to those who couldn't leave, those who can't make a living. We produce development for people in Ghana.[13]

> Here they often ask us to go talk to the politicians, and we do it for Ghana and for the Ghanaians who live in Italy. In Ghana, especially, where we built some things, people are very grateful, you see it when we arrive there, well, sure ... they think we are an NGO ...[14]

The importance of individual discretionary motivation for CSR can be explained, in the Ghanaian cultural framing, by the importance of the characteristics of "big

---

13 Interview with A.T., manager of Ghanacoop, June 2007, Modena (Italy).
14 Interview with O. N., manager of Ghanacoop, April 2008, Modena (Italy).

men" and of the collective leaders (Lentz, 1998). To this regard, being entrepreneurs and producing economic and financial wealth, being offered political positions, and having extended networks of relationships, describe the ideal characteristics needed to be legitimized to act as development actors in the Ghanaian context.

6.2.4.3 Stakeholder management and integration of CSR processes

Analysing how Ghanacoop managed stakeholders provides a very interesting account about the different perceptions of internal and external stakeholders. Following the representations of managers and partners of the cooperative, on one hand, because Ghanacoop was run by immigrants, it knew what was the best for the Ghanaian communities. However, it also needed information and a contact with local stakeholders in order to appropriately decide which actions to implement in Ghana.

> We know what's good for them and what they need, so before laying out a feasibility plan we ask, we get information, but then we decide what is best for that community. Often some organizations in Italy ask us: "We'd like to do something", and so we tell them what can be done, how to invest their money so that it won't be wasted or stolen ...[15]

This vision was also confirmed by the employees of Ghanital, the "daughter" company established in Ghana. This company did not appear as being independent from Ghanacoop, but rather, being in a relationship characterized by hierarchy, complementary and reciprocal solidarity (Sahlins, 1986).

> Ghanital and Ghanacoop are almost the same thing. More or less like you and your mother. We think about Ghanacoop as the mother, we, children, do what Ghanacoop decides (...). Ghanital is not strong enough to work alone, we depend on Ghanacoop.[16]

> I believe that Ghanacoop makes the best choices, and it cannot happen that we do not agree with Ghanacoop's ideas or projects. They know what is the best for us and what we have to do.[17]

Interestingly, for Ghanacoop having a subsidiary in Ghana did not serve as a connection with the local community. The relationship between the two companies and with its leaders was characterized by a "kinship" terminology (e.g. Ghanacoop as a mother; its managers as "uncles" for employees), which can also be explained by the young age of the Ghanaian employees. Furthermore, the employees of Ghanital were personally dependent on Ghanacoop and its leaders. They had a feeling of trust towards their employer: although they did not have a written job contract, they had been financially helped by one of the leaders of the cooperative to solve

---

15 Interview with A.T., manager of Ghanacoop, June 2007, Modena (Italy).
16 Interview with P., employee of Ghanital, June 2009, Accra (Ghana).
17 Interview with J., employee of Ghanital, June 2009, Accra (Ghana).

personal problems (e.g. housing or health issues). Therefore, there was no feedback from the local Ghanaian subsidiary on the CSR vision adopted by Ghanacoop leaders, nor a formal integration in the strategies or in the management of operating practices (Waddock *et al.*, 2002) in the two companies. The decisions were taken in Italy and implemented with no critical approach by the local subsidiary.

Analysing the perceptions of Ghanacoop's CSR actions by the local community, there are different accounts of the actions undertaken by the cooperative. On one hand, Ghanacoop emerged as a real development broker, able to display and exploit direct relationships with the beneficiaries in Ghana. For example, a large Italian retailer decided to finance a project in the health sector in Ghana and Ghanacoop guided the decision about which type of project to finance, through contacts with the local church. On the other hand, there was tension between what was seen as good in the eyes of the company and its leaders and what was really needed by the local community. This emerges in particular with regard to the philanthropic projects like that dealing with the building of a solar energy plant in the village of Gomoa Simbrofo. As reported by the village chief:

> ... they decided to build a solar plant to give light to the village (...) They showed me what they thought to do and they asked me whether we would like that kind of energy (...). They decided everything on their own. Now they have to change the batteries of the plant, they should change them, they promised it, but they still haven't done it.[18]

In this case, building the solar plant was not negotiated between the company and the chief, neither was there an evaluation about the impact on the local community. In fact, two years after the installation of the plant, the government installed electricity cables in the area. The company decided autonomously about the social interventions to be achieved. The real needs of the community were not elicited by the company, which consequently made a useless, unsustainable investment in the long term.

6.2.4.4 Outcomes of CSR and improvement of CSR processes

Although Ghanacoop was a project supported by several international and national institutions, the company did not have a fully institutionalized and operational corporate social policy. It did not systematically measure the outcomes of its CSR activities, for example through social indicators or a social balance sheet. These results compare well with findings in other developing countries (e.g. Jamali *et al.*, 2009; Kourula and Halme, 2009).

In the words of managers and partners of the company, the CSR involvement of Ghanacoop showed three types of outcomes. First, the company contributed to the development of Ghana through business activities, launching processes of job generation and social change. The commercial activities implemented by the company

18 Interview with Nana K., village chief of Gomoa Simbrofo, May 2008, Modena (Italy).

favoured local suppliers of fair-trade fruits and generated some job opportunities, even if very limited in number, duration and benefits. Second, the company alleviated the needs and problems of the local deprived population, through charity and transfer of goods. Third, the CSR activities provided a positive feedback to migrants themselves, as people in charge of a "right" task, and to the company, especially in 2009, after the fraud from a large client:

> The recent economic crisis and the mistakes almost made us close down, we came very close to losing our jobs. It was terrible. (...) Fortunately during these years we have done a lot of good, and we built strong relationships, so now everybody is trying to find a way to help and to advise us.[19]

6.3 Conclusions

By analysing the case of Ghanacoop, we have highlighted the key CSR dimensions characterizing an immigrant-led transnational company. This case is particularly valuable for advancing our knowledge on the issue of CSR in developing countries, especially in the under-researched African context (Kolk and Van Tulder, 2010).

The extensive ethnography from which we employed data is methodologically sound for investigating the impact of development policy or programs (Olivier de Sardan, 2005) and for studying CSR and its micro-level dynamics. As any other method employed in social sciences, we have to account for reflexivity and for the dialogical nature of fieldwork, even if long periods of time spent on the field can change the preconceptions of ethnographers concerning people and settings (Hammersley and Atkinson, 1995). Since ethnography produces deep insight and various possible interpretations rather than definite versions of events (Geertz, 1973), we do not claim that our interpretation is superior to others. However, the author involved in fieldwork had several opportunities for comparing and presenting her insights to project participants and other researchers.

A number of interesting considerations can be made when analysing the case within the theoretical debate about the convergence/divergence of CSR norms and practices.

First, as a transnational actor, Ghanacoop was involved in different networks of local stakeholders, located in both northern and southern areas of the world. However, CSR and development discourses were mainly taking place in the north. Therefore, the company used CSR to manage primary northern stakeholders (Barkemeyer, 2007), such as customers, media, Italian local authorities or international organizations. Indeed, internal stakeholders of the company mirrored, translated (Lewis and Mosse, 2006) and strategically performed a CSR and development

19 Interview with A.T., manager of Ghanacoop, July 2009, Modena (Italy).

language typical of the expectations of national and international organizations from western countries.

Second, the company executives played fundamental roles in guiding the vision and motivations for CSR, as observed in other studies concerning SMEs (e.g. Heugens *et al.*, 2008; Jamali, *et al.*, 2009). In particular, they were able to contemporarily represent Ghanacoop as a company and as a development agent, by adopting both a business and a development idiom. As an entrepreneurial actor, Ghanacoop embodied the collective image of success and upward social mobility projected on entrepreneurial figures for both Italians and Ghanaians. As a development actor, it mobilized the "moral community" of diasporic actors for development their homeland (Kleist, 2008).

Third, the case shows the gap between CSR "action" and "discourse". In fact, although the discourses concerning CSR mirrored the language of development and the willingness to break power asymmetries in Ghana, in practice the actions implemented by the cooperative did not change or weaken those asymmetries. This is due to various factors. First, the concepts of CSR and of development were blurred. The same company implemented CSR activities which appeared to be CR innovation as well as simple philanthropy/charitable actions in Ghana. Second, and paradoxically, since immigrants were managing Ghanacoop, it was not making use of a decentralized autonomous structure in Ghana, but CSR initiatives were basically identified in Italy with few feedback loops from Ghanaian stakeholders.

To sum up, the case of Ghanacoop seems to suggest that immigrant-led transnational businesses have the potential to bring a convergence of CSR practices, as they are rooted both in western and southern institutional contexts. Since mainstream CSR discourses take place in the north, such companies try to be accountable to northern stakeholders and implement CSR actions in line with their expectations. At the same time, as they are aware of the fragile interpretations given to CSR in the country of origin and of the weak local institutional context, these companies transfer their interpretation of CSR as a positive contribution to the development of the country.

6.3.1 Reflections on development-oriented CSR

This chapter describes how an immigrant-led transnational business, Ghanacoop, was envisaged as a potential "development broker". Literature on transnational companies is gaining momentum in management research (Drori *et al.*, 2009), but to our knowledge no study has been carried out on how immigrants can implement CSR actions in their countries of origin.

Building on the concept of co-development, diaspora engagement in CSR activities with the countries of origin would allow for the mobilization of social and cultural knowledge directed to the development of the country of origin. By analysing the case of Ghanacoop, it was observed that diaspora engagement in CSR with developing countries, per se, does not necessarily ensure the conception of "southern-driven" CSR discourses and actions, the involvement of relevant southern stakeholders and the best allocation of resources. However, some positive aspects can be found by interpreting northern-driven CSR norms and practices. In fact, being accountable to strong northern stakeholders could generate an engagement in substantive socially responsible behaviours when operating in weak institutional environments such as those of developing countries (Campbell, 2007; Jamali and Neville, 2011).

It is difficult to measure the outcomes of CSR activities on local development. Ghanacoop implemented various types of CSR and had the opportunity of impacting on various types of stakeholders and poverty (Newell, Frynas, 2007). Nevertheless, the profound needs for economic development, social justice and the eradication of poverty in the country cannot be solved by the private sector alone (Jamali *et al.*, 2009). To this regard, the involvement of diaspora in transnational social business initiatives could be useful for mobilizing and sensitizing entire communities and their socio-political ties.

Bibliography

African Peer Review Mechanism (2005). Country review report of the Republic of Ghana, (Midrand: African Union). Retrieved from http://www.afdb.org/fileadmin/uploads/afdb/Documents/Project-and-Operations/00798283-EN-APRM-GHANA-REVIEW-REPORT-JUNE-2005.PDF.

Agunias, D.R. (2006). *From a Zero-Sum to a Win Win Scenario? Literature Review on Circular Migration*, (Washington, USA: Migration Policy Institute). Retrieved from http://www.migrationpolicy.org.

Amponsah-Tawiah, K., & Dartey-Baah, K. (2011). Corporate social responsibility in Ghana. *International Journal of Business and Social Science*, 2(17), 107-112.

Atuguba, R., & Dowuona-Hammond, C. (2006). Corporate Social Responsibility in Ghana. Friedrich Ebert Foundation (FES) Report, Ghana.

Barkemeyer, R. (2007). Legitimacy as a Key Driver and Determinant of CSR in Developing Countries. Paper presented at 2007 Marie Curie Summer School on Earth System Governance.

Belal, A.R., & Momin, M. (2009). Corporate social reporting (CSR) in emerging economies: A review and future direction. *Research in Accounting in Emerging Economies*, 9, 119-143.

Blowfield, M., & Frynas, J.G. (2005). Setting new agendas: critical perspectives on corporate social responsibility in the developing world. *International Affairs*, 81(3), 499-513.

Campbell, J. (2007). Why would corporations behave in socially responsible ways: an institutional theory of corporate social responsibility. *Academy of Management Review*, 32(3), 946-967.

Carroll, A.B. (1991). The pyramid of corporate social responsibility: toward the moral management of organizational stakeholders. *Business Horizons*, 34, 39-48.

Connell, R. (2007). *Southern Theory: The Global Dynamics of Knowledge in Social Science*. Cambridge, UK: Polity.

Dobers, P., & Halme, M. (2009). Corporate social responsibility and developing countries. *Corporate Social Responsibility and Environmental Management*, 16(5), 237-249.

Down, S. (2006). *Narratives of Enterprise: Crafting Entrepreneurial Self-identity in a Small Firm*. Cheltenham, UK: Edward Elgar.

Drori, I., Honig, B., & Wright, M. (2009). Transnational entrepreneurship: an emergent field of study. *Entrepreneurship Theory and Practice*, 33(5), 1001-1022.

Egri, C.P., & Ralston, D.A. (2008). Corporate responsibility: a review of international management research from 1998 to 2007. *Journal of International Management*, 14(4), 319-339.

Fox, T. (2004). Corporate social responsibility and development: in quest of an agenda. *Development*, 47, 26-36.

Geertz, C. (1973). *The Interpretation of Cultures*. New York, NY: Basic Books.

Grillo, R., & Riccio, B. (2004). Translocal development: Italy-Senegal. *Population, Space and Place*, 10, 99-111.

Halme, M., & Laurila, J. (2009). Philanthropy, integration or innovation? Exploring the financial and societal outcomes of different types of corporate responsibility. *Journal of Business Ethics*, 84, 325-339.

Hammersley, M., & Atkinson, P. (1995). *Ethnography: Principles in Practice*. London, UK: Routledge.

Hemingway, C., & Maclagan, P. (2004). Managers' personal values as drivers of corporate social responsibility. *Journal of Business Ethics*, 50, 33-44.

Heugens, P., Kaptein, M., & van Oosterhout, J. (2008). Contracts to communities: a processual model of organizational virtue. *Journal of Management Studies*, 45(1), 100-121.

Idemudia, U. (2011). Corporate social responsibility and developing countries: moving the critical CSR research agenda in Africa forward. *Progress in Development Studies*, 11(1), 1-18.

Jamali, D., & Neville, B. (2011). Convergence versus divergence of CSR in developing countries: an embedded multi-layered institutional lens. *Journal of Business Ethics*, 102, 599-621.

Jamali, D., Zanhour, M., & Keshishian, T. (2009). Peculiar strengths and relational attributes of SMEs in the context of CSR. *Journal of Business Ethics*, 87, 355-377.

Junker, B.H. (1960). *Field Work: An Introduction to the Social Sciences*. Chicago, IL: University of Chicago Press.

Kleist, N. (2008). In the name of diaspora: between struggles for recognition and political aspirations. *Journal of Ethnic and Migration Studies*, 34(7), 1127-1143.

Kolk, A., & Van Tulder, R. (2010). International business, corporate social responsibility and sustainable development. *International Business Review*, 19(2), 119-125.

Kourula, A., & Halme, M. (2009). Types of corporate responsibility and engagement with NGOs: an exploration of business and societal outcomes. *Corporate Governance*, 8(4), 557-570.

Kragelund, P. (2004). The embedded recipient and the disembedded donor: private-sector development aid in Ghana. *Forum for Development Studies*, 31(2), 307-335.

Lentz, C. (1998). The chief, the mine captain and the politician: legitimating power in northern Ghana. *Africa*, 68(1), 46-67.

Lewis, D., & Mosse, D. (2006). *Development Brokers and Translators: the Ethnography of Aid and Agencies*. Bloomfield, NJ: Kumarian Press.

Lund-Thomsen, P. (2004). Towards a critical framework on corporate social and environmental responsibility in the south: The case of Pakistan. *Development*, 47, 106-113.

Manuh, T. (2006). *An 11th Region of Ghana? Ghanaians Abroad*. Accra, Ghana: Ghana Academy of Arts and Sciences.

Marabello, S. (2013). Translating and acting diaspora: looking through the lens of a co-development project between Italy and Ghana. *African Studies*, 72, 207-227.

Matten, D., & Moon, J. (2008). Implicit and explicit CSR: a conceptual framework for a comparative understanding of corporate social responsibility. *The Academy of Management Review*, 33(2), 404-424.

McCann, L., Granter, E., Hyde, P., & Hassard, J. (2013). Still blue-collar after all these years? An ethnography of the professionalization of emergency ambulance workers. *Journal of Management Studies*, 50, 750-776.

Mohan, G. (2006). Embedded cosmopolitanism and the politics of obligation: the Ghanaian diaspora and development. *Environment and Planning A*, 38, 867-883.

Mosse, D. (2004). Good policy is unimplementable? Reflections on the ethnography of aid policy and practice. *Development and Change*, 35(4), 639-671.

Olivier de Sardan, J.P. (2005). *Anthropology and Development: Understanding Contemporary Social Change*. London: Zed Books.

Ralston, D.A., Gustafson, D.J., Cheung, F.M., & Terpstra, R.H. (1993). Differences in managerial values: a study of US, Hong Kong and PRC managers. *Journal of International Business Studies*, 24(2), 249-275.

Regione Emilia-Romagna (2013). L'immigrazione Straniera in Emilia-Romagna (Bologna, Osservatorio regionale sul fenomeno migratorio). Retrieved from http://sociale.regione.emilia-romagna.it/immigrati-e-stranieri/dati/losservatorio-regionale/dati-immigrazione.

Riccio, B. (2008). West African transnationalisms compared: Ghanaians and Senegalese in Italy. *Journal of Ethnic and Migration Studies*, 34(2), 217-234.

Sahlins, M. (1986). *Island of History*. Chicago, IL: Chicago University Press.

Stocchiero, A. (2008). Learning by Doing: Migrant Transnationalism for Local Development in MIDA Italy-Ghana/Senegal Programme. Working Paper n. 48 (Roma, Italy: CeSPI).

Waddock, S., Bodwell, C., & Graves, S. (2002). Responsibility: the new business imperative. *Academy of Management Executive*, 16(2), 132-147.

Ward, H., & Fox, T. (2002). Moving the Corporate Citizenship Agenda to the South (London: International Institute for Environment and Development). Retrieved from file:///C:/Users/Admin/Desktop/Ward%20and%20Fox.pdf.

Weil, P. (2002). Towards a coherent policy of co-development. *International Migration*, 40(3), 13-53.

7

CSR, mining and development in Namibia

David Littlewood
Henley Business School, UK

Jo-Anna Russon
Queens University Management School, UK

This chapter explores relationships between mining, corporate social responsibility (CSR) and development in the case of Namibia. Drawing upon extant literatures, it first conceptualizes relationships between mining, CSR and development. With reference to case examples and in-country fieldwork, this conceptualization is then applied as a framework to critically consider mining's historic and contemporary development impacts in Namibia and the role of CSR within these. This chapter concludes with reflection on the potential for more "development-oriented" CSR, particularly in mining, offering insights and implications for practitioners, policy-makers, and academics.

Few industries are as controversial, attract as much critical attention, and are as important to the economies of so many developing nations, as mining. For mining advocates, natural resources are a blessing with the potential to fuel national economic growth and prosperity (ICMM, 2014). For its critics, mining is associated with conflict, negative environmental impacts, and underdevelopment (Bebbington *et al.*, 2008). The relationship between mining and development is complex and contentious at various spatial scales. At a global level, debate about the need for and implications of ever more mineral extraction is ongoing (Mason *et al.*, 2011), while at a national level the "resource curse" (Auty, 2002) effects of mining, particularly in the developing world, remain a contested subject (McFerson, 2009), as are mining's local community level "resource curse" impacts (Littlewood, 2014). Corporate social responsibility (CSR) is advocated as an important mechanism for addressing some of these historic and ongoing tensions between mining and development. However, the relationship between CSR and development is also much debated. Proponents argue that there is a "business case" for CSR with "shared value" (Porter and Kramer, 2011) creating opportunities for businesses that innovate to solve development and poverty alleviation issues. Opponents counter that CSR still rarely goes beyond business as usual (Banerjee, 2008) with a host of development issues overlooked in prevailing CSR agendas and practices.

This chapter contributes to debates about the relationships between mining, CSR and development in a number of ways. It first responds to calls in the literature for more CSR research in developing world contexts (Kolk and Van Tulder, 2010) as part of moving the CSR research agenda forward and giving it a more "southern" orientation (Idemudia, 2008, 2011). Moreover, it has been argued that scholars should look at more specific industries (e.g. mining), and at original developing world contexts going beyond relatively well-studied countries such as South Africa and Nigeria (Jeppesen and Lund-Thomsen, 2010). At a country level, Namibia remains under-represented within mainstream management and CSR literature, yet as a case it has the potential to offer insights for other developing countries. Building upon extant literatures, a conceptualization of the relationships between mining, CSR and development is also outlined, and then applied to Namibia, with potential salience for other future studies. The chapter's final contributions relate to its reflections on and suggestions for a more "development-oriented" CSR in the mining industry in Namibia, and further afield.

The chapter is informed by three research questions: (1) How can relationships between mining, CSR and development be conceptualized? (2) What are the historic and contemporary development impacts of mining in Namibia, and what is the role of CSR within these? (3) To what extent is CSR in the mining industry in Namibia "development-oriented", and how might this be enhanced?

In structure, this chapter first reviews the state of the field with a particular focus on CSR, mining and development in Southern Africa and Namibia. Drawing upon extant literatures, a conceptualization of the relationships between mining, CSR and development is then presented. This framework is then applied to consider historic and contemporary mining activity in Namibia, its development impacts, and the role of CSR within these, drawing upon four case study examples. Finally, implications of the Namibian case for wider policy-makers, practitioners and academics are identified, as well as reflection on the potential for a more development-oriented CSR.

7.1 Mining, CSR and development in Africa

Africa's economy is now growing faster than any other continent, with the African Development Bank recently identifying more than a third of African countries with growth rates exceeding 6% (ADBG, 2013). While such impressive growth is not uniform across the continent, the overall outlook is positive, leading some observers to identify Africa as the next frontier for business (*The Economist*, 2013). While this recent boom is linked to expansion across a number of sectors, a key driver of this growth has been further investment in mining and natural resource extraction. In Southern Africa, average GDP growth for the states of the Southern African Development Community in 2011 was 5.14% (SADC, 2012), with particularly high levels in emerging resource economies like Mozambique (7.4% in 2012), but also in more established ones like Zambia (7.3% in 2012) (World Bank, 2014). However, resource extraction has a long and controversial history in Africa and while some countries like Botswana (Pegg, 2010) have been relatively successful in harnessing the development potential of their natural resources, for others such as the Democratic Republic of the Congo, Equatorial Guinea, Gabon and Nigeria (McFerson, 2009), natural resources have been a curse. Ensuring that the benefits of mining are equitably distributed while avoiding its negative social and environmental externalities are therefore key concerns for African policy-makers.

There is a well-established literature exploring relationships between mining and development globally (Bebbington *et al.*, 2008). At a country level, this work has often focused on "resource curse" theories, which posit that natural resource abundance creates various economic, social and political distortions which ultimately undermine its contribution to national development (Auty, 2002; Williams, 2011). At sub-national levels, work has also explored the relationships between mining and regional and community development (Garvin *et al.*, 2009; Kapelus, 2002; Kemp, 2010). Through initiatives like the Mining, Minerals and Sustainable Development Project, and bodies like the International Council on Mining and Metals (ICMM), the mining industry has been at the forefront of the global CSR movement. This can be at least partially attributed to the controversial nature of many mining investments, but also to the fact that mining increasingly takes place in the developing world, often in countries with weak institutions and legislation (Kolk and Lenfant, 2012). Alongside the now significant body of work on mining and development, there are a growing number of studies which add CSR to this equation (Hilson, 2012). Important themes in this research include: CSR and its community development impacts (Campbell, 2012; Hilson and Yakovleva, 2007; Kemp, 2012 and Owen); CSR, development and macro-level issues like taxation and resource governance (Prno and Slocombe, 2012); and CSR, development and environmental justice concerns (Wan, 2014). While many studies on mining, CSR and development view their relationship quite sceptically, some authors suggest at least some companies have improved their developmental performance, and highlight the potential for positive outcomes where mining companies engage with

CSR more strategically, and enter into innovative multistakeholder partnerships (Kolk and Lenfant, 2012; Warhurst, 2001).

A growing body of work explores mining, CSR and development in Africa more specifically. In relation to Southern Africa, this work has often focussed on South Africa (Campbell, 2012; Hamann, 2003; Kapelus, 2002), although studies have also examined other countries in the region (Lungu, 2008; Perks, 2012). Social, environmental and development issues around mining in Namibia have also received some attention. For example, Kempton and Du Preez (1997) discuss state-firm relations in Namibia before and after independence with reference to the diamond industry, while Claasen and Roloff (2011) consider intersections between responsibility and legitimacy with reference to De Beers. Finally, there is a body of practitioner-oriented work examining issues like mining's environmental impacts (Barnard, 1998), employee health (Shindondola-Mote, 2009), and export processing zones (Jauch, 2002). The mining industry is also a frequent subject in national media. Nevertheless, an overarching conceptually informed examination of CSR, mining and development in Namibia has yet to be undertaken.

7.2 Conceptualizing mining, CSR and development

CSR has been described as an "essentially contested concept" (Okoye, 2009), with its definition complicated by a variety of factors, including but not limited to: the wide variety of issues that can be considered under its rubric (Blowfield and Murray, 2011); variations in its meaning, salience and practice in different organisational and geographical contexts (Crane *et al.*, 2014); and the emergence of alternative, complementary, and competing terminologies such as sustainability and corporate citizenship (Matten and Crane, 2005). Reflecting on this complexity, in this chapter we draw upon the definition of CSR offered by Blowfield and Frynas (2005), who describe it as:

> An umbrella term for a variety of theories and practices, all of which recognize the following (a) that companies have a responsibility for their impact on society and the natural environment, sometimes beyond legal compliance and the liability of individuals; (b) that companies have a responsibility for the behaviour of others with whom they do business (e.g. within supply chains); and that (c) business needs to manage its relationship with wider society, whether for reasons of commercial viability or to add value to society (p. 503).

In this chapter, we are particularly concerned with the activities of mining companies in Namibia, and with examining the extent to which CSR (e.g. this notion that companies have responsibilities to manage their impacts on society and the natural environment, that these responsibilities include legal compliance but also potentially go beyond it, and encompass relationships with a wide variety of stakeholders) has informed historic and contemporary mining practices, and is embedded within the operations and decision-making of mining companies in Namibia, and the implications of this for development.

The relationship between CSR and development has been examined and conceptualized by various authors. For example, Frynas (2008) unpacks the relationship between CSR and international development, arguing that while increasing claims are being made about the positive development contribution of CSR, there remains a lack of empirical evidence to support them. Frynas (2008) further contends that this contribution is also limited by an overemphasis on the "business case", while various corporate governance issues, and concerns around the wider role of business in society and development, are too often ignored. In another important contribution, Idemudia (2008) conceptualizes the relationship between CSR and development suggesting that company CSR obligations for development include: (1) negative injunction duties, whereby companies have an obligation to avoid and correct any social injury they cause; and (2) affirmative duties, requiring the pursuit of moral and social good. Other important contributions to the field include: work by Kolk and Van Tulder (2006) examining the CSR development commitments of "forerunner" multinationals, and Jamali and Mirshak (2007) who consider CSR in developing country contexts.

However, to understand the relationship between CSR and development it is necessary to also consider the wider relationship between business and development. Reflecting this fact, in an important early contribution, Jenkins (2005) identifies three principal channels through which he suggests business can contribute to poverty alleviation, an "enterprise channel" (e.g. job creation), a "distribution channel" (e.g. base of the pyramid (BoP) ventures), and "a government revenue channel" (e.g. paying tax). He then discusses the implications for development of the addition of CSR to each of these channels, concluding that despite claims to the contrary the overall link between CSR and positive development outcomes remains limited. In a more recent work addressing this issue, Blowfield and Dolan (2014) present a framework for understanding and analysing business's role as a development actor, distinguishing between "business as a development tool" and "business as a development agent" (Blowfield, 2012). Blowfield and Dolan (2014) define a business development "agent" as a business that consciously deploys capital with the intention of delivering outcomes that contribute to international development goals. They suggest that this is dependent on giving primacy to the benefits of the poor and being held accountable for developmental outcomes (Blowfield and Dolan, 2014). However, the extent to which companies can truly be considered accountable development agents remains limited due to the instrumental nature of development oriented CSR which tends not to give primacy to development outcomes for intended beneficiaries (Blowfield, 2012; Blowfield and Dolan, 2014). Consequently, the relationship between CSR and development is both problematic and complex.

As discussed in the previous section, the relationship between mining and development has been the subject of significant academic attention while recent frameworks have also been introduced in practitioner communities aiming to unpack this relationship. For example, in 2006 the ICMM launched its Resource Endowment Toolkit, with the most recent 2011 version *Mining: Partnerships for Development Toolkit* identifying six priority partnership themes where mining companies can look to enhance their positive development contributions (through engagement with CSR) and minimize negative impacts. This toolkit, and work by the WBCSD, in turn informed the 2013 ICMM report on *Approaches to Understanding Development Outcomes from Mining* which identifies four principle ways in which mineral development may contribute to human and social development: (1) core business activity; (2) dual purpose; (3) direct social investment; and (4) macro-economic contributions (ICMM, 2013).

Drawing upon these varied extant studies and frameworks, we identify two principal ways of conceiving relationships between mining, CSR and development. The first of these relates to whether or not through their practices companies are avoiding and/or correcting any social harm they cause "negative injunction duties" (Idemudia, 2008), in effect through their activities and decision making, do they avoid contributing to underdevelopment, or after Blowfield (2012) being a "cause of poverty". Second, are companies addressing their more "affirmative duties" and responsibilities (Idemudia, 2008) in the development sphere, this encompasses a role as both "tools" of development (e.g. they are providing needed employment, paying taxation and royalties), but also as proactive "agents" of development (e.g. through community development activities, inclusive pro-poor supply chains

Figure 7.1 **Conceptualizing mining, CSR and development**

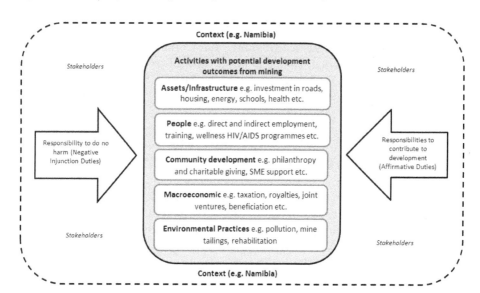

etc.). In the following discussions, we will consider the extent to which companies are avoiding causing harm and are contributing to development in five key areas of mining activity, which are in turn drawn from recent practitioner frameworks (e.g. Mining: Partnerships for Development Toolkit 2011 and the ICMM Resource Endowment Toolkit 2013). The five aspects of mining company activity considered are: (1) assets or infrastructure investments; (2) people, for example, employment, training; (3) community development activities; (4) macroeconomic aspects, for example, resource governance, taxation; and (5) environmental practices. Figure 7.1 provides an overview and more detail on this conceptualization.

7.3 Methodology

This chapter is based on research carried out from 2007 to 2014 and the continued monitoring of industry developments. Four case study mining companies were examined, with the approach informed by writing on case study research (Yin, 2009). These cases were selected to include some of the largest mining companies operating in Namibia at the time of the research, operating in different parts of the country, extracting different minerals, and all had significantly engaged with CSR through community development activities and by operating sustainable development departments. Background on the four case studies is provided in Table 7.1. Qualitative research methods were primarily employed, with semi-structured interviews the principal method of data collection. Interviews were conducted with representatives of key stakeholder groups including: company staff; government representatives; local service providers; community and civil society representatives; and employee representatives. In total 90 interviews were undertaken across the cases, with a largely even distribution. Interviews were recorded when possible.

Focus groups were a secondary method of data collection, with nine undertaken. Additionally, observation research was carried out, and a research diary kept over a 12 month fieldwork period. Data analysis involved first transcription, and then annotation and thematic coding utilizing NVIVO data analysis software, through a largely inductive sense making process.

7.4 Mining CSR and development in Namibia

The mining industry is central to Namibia's economy, latest figures estimate mining provides permanent employment for around 7,898 people, with a further 478 temporary employees and 5,176 contractors (Chamber of Mines Namibia, 2012). In 2012, the industry paid N$1.12 billion (US$105.2 million) in corporation tax and N$957.7 million (US$89.96 million) in royalties, and contributed 11.5% to Namibia's GDP (Chamber of Mines Namibia, 2012). Mining has occurred in Namibia for over

Table 7.1 **Background on Namibia case study mines**

Case study	Background
Namdeb	• Diamond mining, located in Sperrgebiet and town of Oranjemund • Founded 1994 joint venture De Beers and Government of Namibia, previously Consolidated Diamond Mines (CDM) • Namdeb Foundation established in 2010, amalgamation of previous arrangements (Namdeb Social Fund, Oshipe Development Fund, etc.) • Former company town of Oranjemund proclaimed 2011 • Affiliate De Beers Marine Namibia, Namgem diamond manufacturing • Value addition through the Namibia Diamond Trading Company
Skorpion zinc mine	• Zinc mine located in Rosh Pinah company town, Karas region. • Construction began 1999, operations commenced 2001. Originally owned by Anglo-American and from 2010 Vedanta Resources Plc • Anglo-American Namibia Foundation (AANF) established in 2009 • Global Vedanta Foundation
Rössing uranium	• Located in Arandis, Erongo region • Arandis former company town handed over to government 1994 • Established 1976, uranium mining operation • Rio Tinto Group the majority shareholder • Industry leader in community development through the Rössing Foundation
Rosh Pinah zinc	• Located in Karas Region, lead and zinc mine • Mine constructed 1969 with Rosh Pinah established as a company town • Varied historic ownership including Incor, Kumba Resources, Exxaro Resources and Glencore Xstrata plc

a century. However, while the industry's historic, contemporary and future economic significance is undoubted, its role in Namibia's development has been and remains controversial.

7.4.1 Assets and infrastructure: CSR and Namibia's ghost mining towns

Company towns, defined by Lucas (1971) as communities owned and administered by an industrial employer, have historically been a feature of mining in Namibia (Littlewood, 2014). Examples include the diamond towns of Oranjemund and Kolmanskop (now abandoned, see Figure 7.2), Arandis, Rosh Pinah and Uis among others. In recent times, mining companies in Namibia have moved away from operating models requiring the creation of company towns. Nevertheless, some company towns still exist or have been handed over to the state and, as in Namibia and elsewhere, what happens to such towns when mining ceases or during downturn periods remains a significant development issue.

Figure 7.2 **Kolmanskop ghost mining town in Namibia**

At present, and considered in relation to notions of negative injunction responsibility, mining companies in Namibia have a positive record of meeting the development needs of their direct employees. Companies generally provide good wages, free or subsidized housing, and high quality health and education provision. However, where things become more problematic and contested is in relation to the potential affirmative development responsibilities of companies, particularly in relation to wider stakeholders.

The Rosh Pinah case provides an illustration of this. Mine development has spurred the growth of a large informal community known as Tutungeni, attracting economic migrants who often work for mine contractor companies. Access to high quality private local health and education services and infrastructure investments for such stakeholders may be constrained, while their influx has created significant strain on existing public services, as illustrated by the following interview quotations:

> The government clinic is available but it is not to the standard it should be. When you are sick in the night, you have to wait for a long time before being treated. The private hospital that is available is expensive and not everybody can afford it especially the contractors and the people living in Tutungeni (Focus Group with Tutungeni Residents).

> They are not doing it out of the kindness of their hearts, they need these things to get workers down here. The private clinic, the private school, they are all meant for the workers. They view them as their responsibility. A lot of the community investment and what is done for their employees is presented in a way like it is done for the wider good, it is not, it is done for them (Interview Local Community Representative).

This case illustrates the potential for negative "unanticipated consequences" and development implications resulting from mining. Considered through a lens of affirmative responsibility, mining companies in Namibia might also be criticized for missing opportunities to collaborate with the state and other actors in the creation of assets to have a more significant development impact. Such assets might also be more sustainable and viable in the longer term if developed in partnership, although the "reciprocal responsibilities" of the state to instigate such ventures and to meet local needs must also be recognized.

Company towns in Namibia have historically been controversial. In the pre-independence period (before 1990), to varying extents, mining companies failed to address their negative injunction responsibilities through practices like the migrant labour system, and use of hostel accommodation. Furthermore, in Namibia during periods of low commodity prices, or as resource profiles decline, company towns have frequently been handed over to the government. For example, Arandis was handed over in 1994 while more recently in 2011, Oranjemund was handed over by Namdeb. Littlewood (2014) identifies four key areas of challenge that actors in such communities face in their efforts to foster sustainability and viability including: (1) Challenges of dependency (e.g. the reliance of local businesses, people, infrastructure on mine subsidies); (2) Challenges of location, the remote physical location of these communities; (3) Challenges of community, for example many people reside in these communities purely for work; (4) Challenges of purpose, what is the rationale for these communities after mining. These types of community have widely struggled post-handover and as mining has reduced, as illustrated by the following quotation:

> It was done before with Arandis and it was a failure. We couldn't maintain the municipality and so forth. They couldn't maintain the infrastructure, the water and the electricity they couldn't pay for it, they couldn't generate enough money to be viable and sustainable (Interview Government Representative).

The sustainability and viability of these types of community was a significant concern across the cases. To varying extents companies had engaged with these issues within their CSR programs. For example, in 2005 the Rössing Foundation opened an office in the Arandis community recognizing various risks associated with the community's decline including reputational damage, threats to its "licence to operate", and instability in its operating environment. Thereafter, the Foundation and company began working with local government and key stakeholders in partnership through the Arandis Sustainable Development Project to safeguard the town's future.

Viewed in isolation, such CSR activities suggest a significant commitment to ensure the sustainability and development of these communities. Yet such activities must be understood in light of the role the companies have played in creating these communities, and their long term development challenges, as well as company desire to hand over responsibility for them to other actors. Essentially, while it might be argued that through voluntary CSR interventions, the case study companies are attempting to address their negative injunction responsibilities in relation to such communities, these efforts are significantly undermined by their past practices and historic relationships with these communities which have been characterized by unsustainability.

7.4.2 People—employment, empowerment and wellness

Historically, and at present, the mining industry has been a key source of direct and indirect employment in Namibia. The relatively high wages in the industry have allowed those employed to support often large numbers of spatially dispersed dependants with significant positive implications for development. Broadly, it can therefore be argued that companies are addressing their negative injunction responsibilities in this area, although if discussed historically this might be contested, due to the questionable health and safety practices employed by some mines before independence and illustrated by the following interview quotation, with ongoing material legacies (e.g. post-employment ill-health):

> There was none. It was just get a guy from Ovamboland, put him under-ground for a month or two. We show the guy on the drilling machine "yes come you work here". So there was no formal training, or awareness training, or induction. The injuries were up to here (Interview Mine Manager).

Progress in engaging with affirmative development responsibilities in respect of employment has perhaps been more limited among the case studies and industry as a whole. Nevertheless, some progress has been made in; 2003, for example, three southern mines initiated the Namibian Preferential Procurement Council, which aimed to develop supplier relationships between mines and local businesses, with an emphasis on those run by previously disadvantaged Namibians. The success of this industry led initiative as a vehicle for inclusion of the poor was mixed, but it was launched in the context of limited empowerment legislation, prior to the 2011/12 release of Namibia's New Equitable Economic Empowerment Framework (NEEEF).

NEEEF is Namibia's affirmative action policy, akin to Broad Based Black Economic Empowerment (BBBEE) legislation in South Africa. Hamann *et al.* (2008) argue that such is the prominence of BBBEE in dominant discourse around corporate responsibility in South Africa, that to a large extent it corresponds to the locally negotiated definition of CSR. While NEEEF is much newer, the wider notion of empowerment and "Namibianization" is a key component of the locally negotiated definition of CSR in a Namibian context. A final aspect of activity to note, are engagements by mining companies in Namibia with HIV/AIDS (Namibia's HIV/AIDS prevalence in 2012 was estimated at 13.3%; UNAIDS, 2014). The case study companies and wider mining industry in Namibia have for the last decade engaged significantly and affirmatively with this challenge, with positive implications for development.

7.4.3 Community development—funds, foundations and partnerships

Community development activities by the case study companies can largely be conceived as addressing affirmative development responsibilities. Such practices have evolved over time driven by advances in best practice. Some companies have established in-house projects, others channel donations through partners while others provide business support with the aim of integrating local enterprises into supply chains. However, perhaps the most common approach has been to develop semi-autonomous foundations (e.g. the Rössing Foundation, Namdeb Foundation, Anglo-American Namibia Foundation).

Strengths and weaknesses in community development activities by mining companies have been widely studied in the literature (Bebbington *et al.*, 2008; Hamann, 2003; Kapelus, 2002). Across the cases variation was similarly encountered. Some recurrent limitations identified included: the questionable sustainability of some interventions, particularly where they were in-house programs or heavily subsidized; duplication and inefficient use of resources; limits in understanding and assessing impact, and following up on interventions, which was often linked to lack of resources and staffing for community development; project identification and a lack of strategy (e.g. for many years, Namdeb funnelled its charitable support through various social funds with assistance provided reactively and to a huge number of causes but with little overarching strategy).

Across the industry in Namibia, there is growing consensus around the benefits of a semi-autonomous foundation approach to community development, where foundations employ mixed funding regimes (e.g. social enterprise type models), have dedicated staff with development expertise, and work in partnership with other actors. This convergence can partially be attributed to the historic successes of the Rössing Foundation which has been an industry leader in community development in Namibia, adding value to stakeholders and also Rössing Uranium, as illustrated by the following interview quotation:

> The assistance that the Foundation is providing has the potential to provide very useful information for best practice in ETSIP[1] and info about how companies can assist with the government in implementing educational improvement. (Interview Rössing Foundation staff member)

This quotation relates to the Rössing Foundation's work on education, with the foundation engaging in partnership with Namibia's government informed by the framework of the national Education and Training Sector Improvement Programme. Interactions between the foundation and government are underpinned by a reciprocal understanding of responsibility (e.g. the foundation is seeking to complement rather than duplicate the activities of the state, strategically supporting school improvement). This reciprocal understanding of responsibility

---

1 Education and Training Sector Improvement Programme.

is evident in things like the signed memorandum of understanding outlining the respective roles and areas of activity of all parties.

7.4.4 Macroeconomic—taxation, royalties and governance

Recognition of the corporation as a political actor has emerged as an important theme in recent CSR research, with studies addressing subjects like: corporate political lobbying, corporate accountability, tax avoidance, the wider limits of self-regulation. From a development perspective these are critical issues; for example, a recent Christian Aid (2014, p. 24) report argued that "The absence of effective taxation systems in sub-Saharan Africa is directly responsible for the unacceptably high levels of poverty suffered by so many on the continent". The payment of taxation and royalties, which can be used by the state for developmental purposes, is perhaps the most significant contribution to development that mining companies in Namibia can make; it might also be conceived as a fundamental negative injunction responsibility. Yet, in practice, there is considerable ambiguity and debate about what that tax contribution should be, whether mining companies are and have historically made a fair contribution and, if not, who is responsible.

In the pre-independence period, mining industry actors faced considerable criticism for suggested collusion with the apartheid administration and paying what critics argued was a "ridiculously low" rate of taxation (Kempton and Du Preez, 1997). Such concerns have particular salience in relation to mining given the non-renewable nature of the resources extracted. At present, payment of taxation and royalties by mine industry actors remains a key subject of debate and confrontation in Namibia. In 2006, new mining royalties were introduced by the government, but, faced with industry opposition and lobbying, they were amended and reduced. More recently in 2012, Namibia's government proposed a 5% export levy on raw materials (including minerals) but again industry lobbying and threats of disinvestment have seen the levies fall to 0–2%. These instances illustrate the role of mining companies in Namibia as political actors, and their power, and the power of international investors to negotiate their development responsibilities.

A host of further issues can be considered within the macroeconomic domain including: beneficiation and value addition (e.g. are raw materials just exported from Namibia or are they also processed and used in production?) joint-venture shareholdings (e.g. between Namibia's government and De Beers in the case of Namdeb); and resource governance (e.g. should and if so how can mining companies encourage better use of resource rents?). These largely fall within the sphere of affirmative development responsibilities and to date in Namibia engagement with them has mostly been on a voluntary basis and on industry terms.

7.4.5 Environment—abandonment, liability and rehabilitation

The Chamber of Mines Namibia (2010) estimates there are over 200 abandoned mines in the country, with liability for their rehabilitation transferred to the state.

From a development perspective, this is a drain on already stretched government resources while also creating potential local level negative health outcomes. The case of Tsumeb Corporation Ltd (TCL) amply illustrates this problem. When the mine closed in 2001, it is reported that only 30% of the true closure cost requirement had been set aside by TCL. At present the environmental impacts of over 100 years of copper mining in and around Tsumeb are still being unearthed.

Historic environmental problems relating to mining partially reflect a weak pre-independence governance of the industry but also slow progress after independence in enacting new stronger legislation, as well as limits in government monitoring capacity. For example, it was only in 2007 that a comprehensive Environmental Management Act was introduced and 2012 that the Act fully came into effect. The situation at present remains precarious with suggestions that environmental protection is still subordinate to the interests of mining as illustrated by the following quotation:

> The mines and energy act overrides all other acts in the country. If they discover they can mine petroleum in the middle of the Sperrgebiet then it will be, because that gives you more economic development than tourism does and scenery does (Interview Environmental Advocate).

Planned large-scale investment in uranium mining in the Erongo region, currently on hold due to a fall in global uranium prices, also has potentially significant environment and development related impacts (for more detail, see SAIEA, 2011). Addressing and mitigating environmental externalities and their development impacts is a key negative injunctive responsibility of mining companies. However, weaknesses in legislation, the government's pro-mining orientation, and power imbalances between mining companies and local civil society may curtail corporate accountability.

7.5 Towards a more development-oriented approach

This chapter illustrates how context informs the nexus of mining, development and CSR. In Namibia, their intersection is mediated particularly by issues of legacy, empowerment and temporality. More broadly, legacy is a key component of corporate responsibility for mining companies, given that the resources they extract are finite and non-renewable, and mine closure is inevitable. Ensuring that before, during and after mining, stakeholders and the environment are not harmed, is a basic negative injunctive responsibility for mining companies and also state actors (e.g. in the design and enforcement of appropriate legislation). Historically, in Namibia there have been failings in this respect by both parties, with negative development outcomes. Mining companies in Namibia as political actors have also at times worked to undermine this policy formation process; yet, in other instances, they have sought to encourage the formation of an enabling environment for engaging with affirmative development responsibilities (e.g. on preferential procurement). In Namibia, as in other developing countries, there is a danger of mining companies juxtaposing engagement with aspects of their affirmative development responsibilities (e.g. community development assistance), while failing to address their negative injunctive responsibilities in other areas (e.g. not paying their full tax contribution, building and then handing over unsustainable company towns). Such approaches open companies up to criticism of "greenwashing".

To be more effective agents of development, a development-orientation needs to be embedded in the values, structures, practices and decision-making of mining companies. Our tentative suggestions for how this might be achieved in Namibia and more widely include: (1) stronger legislation and enforcement preventing companies avoiding their negative injunctive responsibilities, coupled with legislation that enables or even makes mandatory certain aspects of affirmative development responsibility, widespread adoption across developing countries is needed to reverse "race to the bottom" approaches to attracting mining investment (e.g. tax incentives, reducing labour standards etc.); (2) inclusive mining ventures where low income groups or communities have a shareholding in the company, and significant influence in governance and decision-making, perhaps as an alternative to public/private partnerships, transparency and real accountability to stakeholders and beneficiaries is critical; (3) social assets (e.g. schools and clinics) developed strategically in partnership or embracing innovative social enterprise models balancing company and wider stakeholder needs; (4) taxation for the explicit purpose of addressing mining's historic negative environmental impacts in Namibia and funding enforcement.

Bibliography

ADBG (2013). *Annual Development Effectiveness Review.* African Development Bank Group.

Auty, R. (2002). *Sustaining Development in Mineral Economies: the Resource Curse Thesis.* London: Routledge.

Banerjee, S.B. (2008). Corporate social responsibility: the good, the bad and the ugly. *Critical Sociology,* 34(1), 51-79.

Barnard, P. (1998). *Biological Diversity in Namibia.* (Namibian National Biodiversity Task Force).

Bebbington, A., Hinojosa, L., Bebbington, D.H., Burneo, M.L., & Waarnars, X. (2008). Contention and ambiguity: mining and the possibilities of development. *Development and Change,* 39(6), 887-914.

Blowfield, M.E. (2012). Business and development: making sense of business as a development agent. *Corporate Governance: The International Journal of Business in Society,* 12(4), 414-426.

Blowfield, M., & Dolan, C.S. (2014). Business as a development agent: evidence of possibility and improbability. *Third World Quarterly*, 35(1), 22-42.

Blowfield, M., & Frynas, J.G. (2005). Setting new agendas: critical perspectives on corporate social responsibility in the developing world. *International Affairs*, 81(3), 499-513.

Blowfield, M.E., & Murray, A. (2011). *Corporate Responsibility* (2nd edition). Oxford: Oxford University Press.

Campbell, B. (2012). Corporate social responsibility and development in Africa: redefining the roles and responsibilities of public and private actors in the mining sector. *Resources Policy*, 37(2), 138-143.

Chamber of Mines Namibia (2010). Namibian Mine Closure Framework. Retrieved from http://www.chamberofmines.org.na/fileadmin/downloads/Final_Reports/Mine_Closure_Framework.pdf.

Chamber of Mines Namibia (2012). Chamber of Mines Namibia Annual Review. Retrieved from http://www.chamberofmines.org.na/main/publications/annual-reports.html.

Christian Aid (2014). Africa Rising? Inequalities and the Essential Role of Fair Taxation. Report commissioned by Tax Justice Network Africa and Christian Aid.

Claasen, C., & Roloff, J. (2012). The link between legitimacy and responsibility. The case of DeBeers in Namibia. *Journal of Business Ethics*, 107(3), 379-398.

Crane, A., Matten, D., & Spence, L.J. (2014). *Corporate Social Responsibility, Readings and Case in a Global Context* (2nd edition). Routledge: London.

Frynas, J.G. (2008). Corporate social responsibility and international development: critical assessment. *An International Review*, 16(4), 274-281.

Garvin, T., McGee, T.K., Smoyer-Tomic, K.E., & Aubynn, E.A. (2009). Community-company relations in gold mining in Ghana. *Journal of Environmental Management*, 90, 571-586.

Hamann, R. (2003). Mining companies' role in sustainable development: the "why" and "how" of corporate social responsibility from a business perspective. *Development Southern Africa*, 20(2), 237-54.

Hamann, R., Khagram, S., & Rohan, S. (2008). South Africa's charter approach to post-apartheid economic transformation: collaborative governance or hardball bargaining. *Journal of Southern African Studies*, 34(1), 21-37.

Hilson, G. (2012). Corporate responsibility in the extractive industries: experiences from developing countries. *Resources Policy*, 37, 131-137.

Hilson, G., & Yakovleva, N. (2007). Strained relations: a critical analysis of the mining conflict in Prestea, Ghana. *Political Geography*, 26(1), 98-119.

ICMM (2013). Approaches to Understanding Development Outcomes from Mining. International Council on Mining and Metals.

ICMM (2014). International Council on Mining and Metals. Retrieved from http://www.icmm.com/.

Idemudia, U. (2008). Conceptualizing the CSR and development debate. *Journal of Corporate Citizenship*, 29, 91-110.

Idemudia, U. (2011). Corporate social responsibility and developing countries: moving the critical CSR research agenda in Africa forward. *Progress in Development Studies*, 11(1), 1-18.

Jamali, D., & Mirshak, R. (2007). Corporate social responsibility (CSR): theory and practice in a developing country context. *Journal of Business Ethics*, 72(3), 243-262.

Jauch, H. (2002). Export processing zones and the quests for sustainable development: a Southern African perspective. *Environment and Urbanization*, 14(1), 101-113.

Jenkins, R. (2005). Globalization, corporate social responsibility and poverty. *International Affairs*, 81(3), 525-540.

Jeppesen, S., & Lund-Thomsen, P. (2010). Special issue on new perspectives on business, development and society. *Journal of Business Ethics*, 93(2), 139-142.

Kapelus, P. (2002). Mining, corporate social responsibility and the "community": the case of Rio Tinto, Richards Bay Minerals and the Mbonambi. *Journal of Business Ethics*, 39, 275-296.

Kemp, D. (2010). Mining and community development: problems and possibilities of local-level practice. *Community Development Journal*, 45(2), 198-218.

Kempton, D.R., & Du Preez, R.L. (1997). Namibian De Beers state firm relations: co-operations and conflict. *Journal of Southern Africa Studies*, 23(4), 585-613.

Kolk, A., & Lenfant, F. (2012). Business–NGO collaboration in a conflict setting: partnership activities in the Democratic Republic of Congo. *Business and Society*, 51(3), 478-511.

Kolk, A., & Van Tulder, R. (2006). Poverty alleviation as business strategy? Evaluating commitments of forerunner multinational corporations. *World Development*, 34(5), 789-801.

Kolk, A., & Van Tulder, R. (2010). International business, corporate social responsibility and sustainable development. *International Business*, 19(2), 119-125.

Littlewood, D. (2014). Cursed Communities? Corporate social responsibility (CSR), company towns and the mining industry in Namibia. *Journal of Business Ethics*, 120(1), 39-63.

Lucas, R.A. (1971). *Minetown, Milltown, Railtown: Life in Canadian Communities of Single Industry*. Toronto: University of Toronto.

Lungu, J. (2008). Socio-economic change and natural resource exploitation: a case study of the Zambian copper mining industry. *Development Southern Africa*, 25(5), 543-560.

Mason, L., Prior, T., Mudd, G., & Giurco, D. (2011). Availability, addiction and alternatives: three criteria for assessing the impact of peak minerals on society. *Journal of Cleaner Production*, 19(9-10), 958-966.

Matten, D., & Crane, A. (2005). Corporate citizenship: towards an extended theoretical conceptualization. *Academy of Management Review*, 30, 166-179.

McFerson, H. (2009). Governance and hyper-corruption in resource-rich African countries. *Third World Quarterly*, 30(8), 1529-1548.

Okoye, A. (2009). Theorising corporate social responsibility as an essentially contested concept: is a definition necessary? *Journal of Business Ethics*, 89(4), 613-627.

Owen, J.R., & Kemp, D. (2012). Assets, capitals and resources: frameworks for corporate community development in mining. *Business and Society*, 51(3), 382-408.

Pegg, S. (2010). Is there a Dutch disease in Botswana? *Resources Policy*, 35(1), 14-19.

Perks, R. (2012). How can public–private partnerships contribute to security and human rights policy and practice in the extractive industries? A case study of The Democratic Republic of Congo (DRC). *Resources Policy*, 37(2), 251-260.

Porter, M.E., & Kramer, M.R. (2011). Shared value: how to reinvent capitalism—and unleash a wave of innovation and growth. *Harvard Business Review*, 89(1-2), 62-77.

Prno, J., & Slocombe, D.S. (2012). Exploring the origins of "social license to operate" in the mining sector. Perspectives from governance and sustainability theories. *Resources Policy*, 37(3), 346-357.

SADC (2012). CCBG Macroeconomic Information, Southern African Development Community. Retrieved from http://www.sadc.int/about-sadc/overview/sadc-facts-figures/.

SAIEA (2011). Southern African Institute for Environmental Assessment – Strategic Environmental Assessment for the Central Namib Uranium Rush. Retrieved from http://www.saiea.com/uranium/.

Shindondola-Mote, H. (2009). Uranium Mining in Namibia: The Mystery Behind "Low Level Radiation". Windhoek: Labour Resource and Research Institute (LaRRI).

UNAIDS (2014). Namibia | UNAIDS. Retrieved from http://www.unaids.org/en/regions countries/countries/namibia/.

The Economist (2013, April 6). Investing in Africa. The Hottest Frontier.

Wan, P.M.J. (2014). Environmental Justices and Injustices of Large-scale Gold Mining in Ghana: A study of Three Communities Near Obuasi. *The Extractive Industries and Society*, 1(1), 38-47.

Warhurst, A. (2001). Corporate citizenship and corporate social investment: drivers of tri-sector partnerships. *Journal of Corporate Citizenship*, 1(1), 57-73.

Williams, A. (2011). Shining a light on the resource curse: an empirical analysis of the relationship between natural resources, transparency, and economic growth. *World Development*, 39(4), 490-505.

World Bank (2014). The World Bank open data. Retrieved from http://data.worldbank.org/.

Yin, R.K. (2009). *Case Study Research: Design and Methods* (4th edition). Thousand Oaks, CA: Sage.

8

CSR and the development deficit

Part of the solution or part of the problem?

Nonita T. Yap

School of Environmental Design and Rural Development, Canada

The globalization of production and consumption systems has increased the geographic reach of corporations. As investors, employers and lobbyists, corporations impact local economies and local environments in the most remote of communities. This is seen as problematic by many. Others see development opportunities through corporate social responsibility. This chapter looks at the CSR practices of three corporations—Vale in Brazil, Newmont in Ghana, and Philex in the Philippines—and examines what each has done to address the basic needs of the community, to minimize its environmental impact, and to promote accountable and democratic governance. The CSR practices of Newmont and Philex demonstrate that responsible corporations can be part of the solution to the development deficit. Vale's CSR practice in Brazil showcases the fundamental limitation of voluntary instruments. In the absence of countervailing policy and social forces allowing private enterprise to define what development can and cannot mean is problematic.

The notion that business has social responsibilities beyond creating jobs is not new. The Code of King Hammurabi introduced around 1700 BC imposed penalties including death, on builders for faulty construction, and on farmers for irrigation facility malfunctions (Nagarajan, 2011). In the 18th century, Robert Owen, a capitalist who made his fortune in the cotton trade, campaigned for improving the working conditions of factory workers and providing education for their children (The History Guide, nd).

What is new are debates on the scope of the social contract and how it is to be evaluated. Most of the literature is on OECD countries (Egri and Ralston, 2008). This is not for lack of interest among developing countries. In the late 1960s, leaders of newly independent nations in Asia and Africa called on the UN to establish a code of conduct for transnational corporations (TNCs). The efforts faltered with the shift in the tenor of the debate on TNCs towards collaboration and partnership, and were abandoned in the early 1990s with the dismantling of the UN Centre for TNC (Jenkins, 2005). The UN's Global Compact was a salutary example of the voluntary approach to international corporate governance. Many more self-regulatory instruments have since been introduced covering human rights, labour standards, environment, and anti-corruption. Most instruments are voluntary (e.g. Extractive Industries Transparency Initiative—EITI) and a few are mandatory for clients (e.g. Equator Principles) or subscribers (e.g. ISO 26000).

This shift to "soft law" is embraced by many, including donor agencies, as an opportunity for directing the organizational, technological, and financial resources of corporations to address the development deficit (Jamali, 2007; Smith, 2003). Others are more measured. For CSR to make a significant contribution to development, "the CSR agenda needs to address the structural and policy determinants of underdevelopment and the relationship of TNCs to those determinants" (Utting, 2005, p. 385).

The question for this chapter is whether CSR can be aligned with development, and how it can be mobilized more effectively to serve sustainable development goals. This chapter looks at three mining companies with established CSR policies, operating in resource-rich countries with high levels of power asymmetry and income disparities, and examines three questions. What has the company done to help address the basic needs of the community? How has it minimized its environmental impacts? How has it contributed to accountable and democratic governance? The mining sector is chosen because it is a major economic sector in many developing countries and one beset with a long litany of sustainability challenges. The three cases are Vale S.A. in Itabira, Brazil, Newmont Ghana Gold Ltd (NGGL) in Brong-Ahafo, Ghana, and Philex Mining Corporation in Padcal, Philippines. These companies were selected as they are widely recognized as models of responsible corporations. Their CSR activities and outcomes can thus be argued as representing what is possible. The countries represent contexts with similarities and differences. Brazil and the Philippines share a Latin colonial history lasting several centuries; Ghana was under the British crown for 55 years. The population of all three are predominantly of the Christian faith. As seen in Table 8.1, Brazil, a

Table 8.1 **Country profiles**

Country	Population (10⁶) 2014	GDP/ cap (USD)	GINI coefficient	Poverty rate (%)	2013 HDI (out of 187)	Literacy rate (%)	Corruption perception index (2013)
Brazil	203.308	11,298	0.527 (2012)	21.4 (2009)	0.744 (79)	91.3	72 (177)
Ghana	27.043	1,850	0.428 (2006)	28.5 (2007)	0.573 (138)	71.5	63 (177)
Philippines	100.410	2,765	0.430 (2012)	26.5 (2009)	0.660 (117)	95.4	94 (177)

Sources: various

http://data.worldbank.org/indicator/SI.POV.GINI

http://en.wikipedia.org/wiki/List_of_countries_by_population

http://en.wikipedia.org/wiki/List_of_countries_by_literacy_rate

http://hdr.undp.org/en/content/human–development–index–hdi–table

http://www.transparency.org/country

middle-income country, with the highest GDP per capita of the three also has the highest GINI coefficient and a poverty rate not much lower than the other two.

The information on the companies was gathered largely from reviews of peer-reviewed journals, students' theses, company annual reports, and websites. This was complemented by field research notes in the case of Vale. The analysis of the company CSR activities is guided by a framework developed from research and development work on cleaner production, environmental impact assessment and sustainable development, and informed by the insights of those who have argued for development-oriented CSR (e.g. Blowfield, 2005; Jenkins, 2005; Utting, 2005; Banerjee, 2008).

The chapter is organized in four sections. The first is a brief summary of relevant CSR literature. The second is a discussion of the elements and rationale for the framework used to structure the analysis of the three case studies. The discussion of the case studies starts with a summary of the sustainability challenges in the mining sector. This is done to situate the CSR practices of the three companies in the broader context of the sector. The chapter closes with comments on the patterns and issues emerging from the case studies and reflections as to whether the CSR practice of Vale in Itabira, Newmont in Brong-Ahafo, and Philex in Padcal are successful examples of development-oriented CSR, and in what respects they fall short.

8.1 CSR: what, why, how and impacts

> There is little point in blaming pigs for not being able to fly … Judging … corporate performance requires an examination of whether a business is doing what it can do given its range of external options and internal competencies.

> (Zadek, 2001, p. 9)

> To operate with sustainability is to act with conscience and responsibility throughout the lifecycle of our activities.

> Vale Sustainable Development Policy[1]

> The West [read CSR] may be trying to distribute cake, when what is truly needed is bread.

> (Kemp 2001, p. 33)

There is no agreement on what constitutes corporate social responsibility, nor what drives it (Banerjee, 2008; Rowe, 2005; Yap *et al.*, 2007; Zadek, 2001), Nor is there agreement on its benefits (Rajak, 2006; Smith, 2003).

There are differences and similarities in CSR practices in different countries. A survey of human resource managers in the US, Canada, Mexico, Australia, China, India and Brazil identified "donations to local charities" and "donations to natural disasters" as the top two CSR activities in all seven countries. The third priority for the US, Canada, Australia, China and India was "company-sponsored community volunteer projects". For Brazil and Mexico, it was "fair labour practices" (SHRM, 2007), not dissimilar to that identified for Asia by CSR experts, CEOs and owners of supply chains (Welford, 2005). In Africa, companies focus on health, education and community development (Ite, 2007; Rajak, 2006) as do large corporations in the Philippines (Maximiano, 2005; Talisayon, 2009). The patterns appear to reflect the host country's stage of industrialization. A company's CSR practice may also vary from one country to another, for example Newmont in Ghana and Peru (Triscitti, 2013), suggesting that local policies and politics do matter.

---

1 Retrieved from: http://www.vale.com/PT/aboutvale/sustainability/links/LinksDownloa dsDocuments/Politica_de_Desenvolvimento_Sustentavel.pdf, last accessed 5 June 210.

8.2 A framework for evaluating the development impacts of CSR

The World Business Council on Sustainable Development (WBCSD) defines CSR as "the commitment of business to contribute to sustainable economic development, working with employees, their families, the local community and society at large to improve their quality of life" (WBCSD, 2001, p. 6). What are the implications for CSR practice of a development orientation and sustainability perspective?

A development orientation would require that a company assist the host community to meet its basic needs. In many low income countries, these mean food, shelter, education, health, cultural identity, choice, and increasingly, peace and security. A sustainability perspective imposes additional requirements. The pursuit of sustainability may be pictured as one of achieving a balance between population and patterns of consumption on one side and the mix of environmental goods and services on the other, with technology as a non-rigid pivot and the other human system variables (community) as the bar (Figure 8.1). The more resilient the bar (community) is, the greater its ability to maintain the balance. A sustainability assessment therefore means evaluating the impacts of company operations on: (a) the local ecological capital; (b) the local aggregate human demand; and (c) community resilience. Effective pursuit of sustainable economic community development will require exercise of prudent resource and environmental stewardship, enhancement of community resilience, that is, community capacity for transformation and adaptation, and the existence of an accountable and democratic

Figure 8.1 **Sustainability teeter totter (adapted from Yap, 1990)**

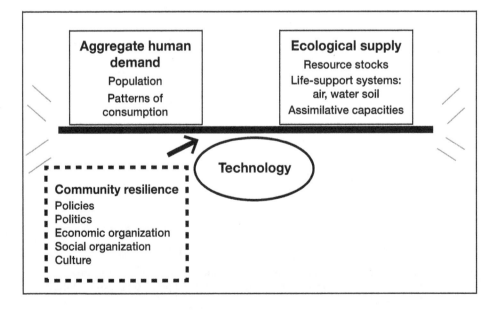

Figure 8.2 **Preconditions for sustainable development**

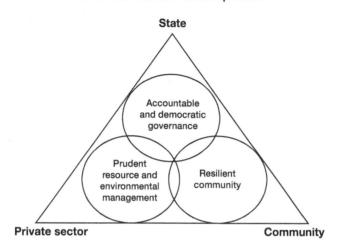

system of governance that enables the exercise of such stewardship and the development of such capacities (Figure 8.2).

These three preconditions are also consistent with the principles underlying ISO 26000, the WBCSD's Breaking New Ground, the Extractive Industries Transparency Initiative (EITI), and the IFC's sustainability framework. A CSR assessment checklist with selected indicators is suggested in Table 8.2.

8.3 The Case Studies

8.3.1 Sustainability challenges of the mining sector

The mining industry has seen a major resurgence in the 21st century, driven by the dramatic growth in demand for consumer products, facilitated by the relaxation of mining and environmental legislation, and in many developing countries, greater security provided to mining operations by military or paramilitary forces (Holden and Jacobson, 2007). The list of community concerns around mining remains long, with acid drainage, toxic contamination and water scarcity, the most frequently cited. Pollution burdens and landscape destruction preclude employment in traditional and non-market livelihoods (Martinez-Alier, 2001). Workplace health and safety, the hiring of non-local residents and wage gaps between those who work for the mine and those who do not, are a source of tension (Azapagic, 2004). Frequently, the industry brings dramatic changes in a very short time in areas without the necessary infrastructure (Knobblock, 2013). Conflict can arise from competition for

Table 8.2 **CSR evaluation checklist**

A. Prudent resource and environmental stewardship	B. Community transformative and adaptive capacity	C. Accountable and democratic governance
• Minimization of waste along the whole supply chain • Remediation of damage—past, present and future • Implementation of impact monitoring and emergency response programs • Protection of critical natural capital	• Maximization of local employment and local value chain • Development of skills necessary for economic diversification • Replacement of depleted natural capital with other forms of capital	• Compliance with local laws but adhering to international standards • Provision of relevant and accurate information to stakeholders, e.g. production outputs, revenues, taxes • Respect for civil and political liberties, cultural autonomy, social, economic freedoms, and personal security

vital community resources like farmland, drinking water and the mineral resource itself. The potential for conflict can be reduced if the economic benefits are shared with the community, resource depletion compensated by economic diversification, and environmental and landscape impacts minimized (Da Silva Enriquez, 2007).

8.3.2 Vale Itabira (Brazil)

Vale S.A., state owned and operated until 1996, is the world's largest iron producer and second largest minerals and mining company. Founded during World War II as Companha Vale do Rio Doce (CVRD), Vale now operates in five continents with interests in iron, copper, nickel, coal and phosphate rock. It contributes 86% of Brazil's iron production. The Itabira mine (state of Minas Gerais) has operated for 60 years and anticipated to operate for another 75. Vale is the only Latin American member of the Carbon Disclosure Project. Its Sustainability Report has received an award for two years for Transparency in Communication from the Global Compact. In 2010, it won the Global Reporting Initiative (GRI) Reader's Choice Civil Society Award (Tubino *et al.*, 2011).

8.3.3 Mining policy and regulatory context in Brazil

In 1986, one year after the end of 21 years of military rule, the Brazilian government passed CONAMA Resolution 01/86 which required environmental assessment and environmental licensing (Licença de Operação Corretiva—LOC) for activities that cause or could potentially cause environmental harm. This was followed by CONAMA Resolution 09/87 requiring public participation in Environmental Assessment (EA). Both are implemented by the state government.

8.3.3.1 Vale's resource and environmental management

The city of Itabira lies approximately 100 km northeast of the state capital, Belo Horizonte. Sixty years of mining operations, mostly in a regulatory vacuum, have left scars—loss of biodiversity, agricultural land, and culturally significant land-forms. The proximity of mine sites to urban neighbourhood has impacts on the quality of life from dust, noise and traffic. In 1982, the community launched a civil suit against Vale referencing air pollution and landscape destruction. While not successful in exacting compensation, it brought together different groups around environmental issues. In 1994, Vale was required to apply for LOC. It obtained the LOC 6 years later with extensive community engagement. Fifty-two conditions were attached, 80% of which dealt with repairing past damage and addressing current concerns (Tubino *et al.*, 2011). The LOC was renewed in 2004 behind closed doors. The operations are now ISO 14001 certified.

Unfortunately, many LOC conditions proved to be ambiguous and the differ-ent stakeholders, including Vale, are holding firm to their own interpretation. Vale seems content to simply meet, not exceed the LOC conditions. The issue of drink-ing water scarcity is a case in point. The lowering of the water table (a cumulative impact of mining) is among the biggest threats to community well-being and eco-nomic diversification in Itabira. There is broad recognition that infrastructure for a new water supply is needed but there is no agreement as to who is responsible, nor the political will to work together.

8.3.3.2 Contribution to community resilience

Relative to non-mining neighbouring communities, Itabira has a higher level of municipal revenues, lower level of income inequality, higher literacy rate albeit a low average level of education (Da Silva Enriquez, 2007). Vale is not only Itabira's leading employer, but also the leading source of municipal revenue. Taxes and royalties from Vale are estimated to contribute to 80% of municipal revenue (Wasylycia-Leis *et al.*, 2014).

As the state-owned CVRD, Vale was heavily involved in service provision—housing, clinics, schools and recreation. Once privatized, the company transi-tioned from a provider to an enabler of social welfare. As Vale delivered on the LOC environmental conditions, community activism waned (Tubino *et al.*, 2011). This, combined with Vale's continuing economic dominance seems to have resulted in collective inertia, particularly in relation to economic diversification. Wasylycia-Leis *et al.*'s (2014, p. 490) quote one resident "… the Itabirano does not have a cul-ture of entrepreneurship … we are raised to become a Vale employee".

8.3.3.3 Contribution to accountable and democratic governance

Vale, a member of EITI, has successfully appealed fines in Itabira over noncom-pliance and had them reduced or eliminated (Wasylycia-Leis, *et al.*, 2014). Most recently, it successfully appealed taxes assessed by the Brazilian government

(Mining.com, 2014). In January 2012, Vale was elected the world's worst company in terms of human rights and environment, beating Japan's TEPCO. It was awarded the *Oscar of Shame*, organized by Greenpeace and Berne Declaration.

8.3.4 Newmont Ghana Gold Ltd—NGGL (Ghana)

Newmont Mining Corporation is headquartered in Colorado, US and has core operations in the US, Australia, Peru, Indonesia and Ghana. Founded in 1921 and publicly traded since 1925, Newmont Mining became the world's largest gold producer in 2002 (Newmont, nd). Newmont's operations in Ghana are ISO 14001 certified. In 2012, it was recognized for transparency for the third year by the Carbon Disclosure Project. The first gold mine company selected to be part of the Dow Jones Sustainability World Index, Newmont has been named to the Index seven consecutive years.

8.3.4.1 Mining policy and regulatory context in Ghana

Part of the Structural Adjustment Program introduced in Ghana in 1986 was the liberalization of the century-old mining sector. Section 48(1) of the Minerals and Mining Act 2006 protects mining leaseholders for up to 15 years from "any enactment, order or action that have the effect or purport to have the effect of imposing obligations" including custom duties, royalties, taxes, transfer of capital and dividends remittance. The Act also grants the leaseholder the right "to stack or dump a mineral or waste product as approved in the holder's Environmental Impact Statement". But Section 50 requires the lease holder to submit a program of "localisation" (i.e. a training program to replace expatriate personnel with Ghanaian personnel), and Section 74(2) requires that in instances of compulsory acquisition of property, "payment ... be prompt, and compensation ... fair and adequate".

Mining job growth has averaged over 4% annually since 2002. In 2009, the mining sector contributed 43% of Ghana's exports, almost 20% of national tax revenue, and 6.3% of its GDP (Kapstein and Kim, 2011). In 2011, Ghana became the 10th largest gold producer in the world with five foreign companies accounting for 90% of the production. Newmont Mines is among the top three (Hauschildt, 2008).

8.3.4.2 Newmont's resource and environmental management

The Brong-Ahafo region is in south Ghana, bordered to the north by the Black Volta River and to the east by Lake Volta. Newmont occupies nearly 2,000 hectares. Open pits are the most visible land disturbance but stockpiles and waste dumps, water and tailings reservoirs, and facilities, roads and other infrastructure are also visible. During its application to mine in the region, Newmont deposited $4 million in an account with a $34 million letter of credit for final reclamation. Abandoned mine sites are partially reclaimed. In 2009, Newmont decided to reassess and withdraw its application to mine in the Ajenjua Bepo Forest Reserve (Newmont, nd).[2] However, in 2009 Newmont was fined $4.9 million when process waters containing cyanide overflowed from containment ponds resulting in fish kills in the Subri River. Newmont initially claimed that the cyanide was introduced by residents for fishing[3] (Boateng, 2012) but has since established a cyanide management system linked to its ISO 14001 certification.

8.3.4.3 Contribution to community resilience

Newmont's lease covers ten communities with 208,000 inhabitants, mostly subsistent farmers with 50% adult literacy rate. The ore deposit was located beneath an area settled by about 1,700 households. The company compensated the residents financially, provided them with new homes, schools and titles to land.[4] Resettled farmers were encouraged to restart farming, provided with inputs and access to alternative land. Those who did reportedly enjoy higher yields (Kapstein and Kim, 2011).[5] Another program, funded at US$3.5 million assisted residents who lost their livelihoods because of the mine to seek alternative livelihoods (Kapstein and Kim, 2011). In 2008, the Newmont Ahafo Development Foundation (NADeF) was established between NGGL and the Ahafo Social Responsibility Forum. Funded through annual contributions from NGGL ($1 for every ounce of gold sold and 1% of profits from Ahafo mine), NADeF supports community development programs. Since 2013, 63 infrastructural projects have been completed and scholarships awarded to over 4,000 students at the senior high school and tertiary levels. A 2011 impact study of NGGL concluded that NGGL: (a) generates nearly 10% of Ghana's total exports, 4.5% of its total FDI, and 1.3% of GDP; (b) produces around 48,000 direct and indirect jobs; and (c) in 2009 alone provided 99 local companies with nearly US$6 million in contracts; 39% of its workers are local, 11% are women. Wage and benefits are above the regional average (Kapstein and Kim, 2011). Its local procurement fund increased from $1.7 million in 2006 to $14 million in 2010 benefiting 373 local businesses. NGGL also worked with Ghana Chamber of Mines on an import substitution strategy for products currently imported that can realistically be produced in Ghana such as mill liners and grinding media.[6]

In April 2014, NGGL was named the Most Outstanding Community Interaction Company in West Africa (www.newmont.com).

---

2 Ajenjua Bepo Forest Reserve is not classified as a "protected forest reserve" and mining is allowed.
3 The use of cyanide for fishing is also practised in the Philippines.
4 How this land ownership was legally possible is not explained in any of the documents used.
5 Yaro (2010) noted that the arrangement was only for two years after which they either had to leave or pay rent.
6 Source: http://www.commdev.org/files/2759_file_Newmont_Developing_a_Local_Procurement_Policy__IFC_Sustainability_Exchange_V_29_6_11.pdf.

8.3.4.4 Contribution to accountable and democratic governance

As part of its commitment to EITI, NGGL allows local stakeholders and investors to monitor how revenues are distributed and spent. All reports—internal and independent—are posted on the company website. However, Newmont's commitment to accountable and democratic governance was challenged by Yaro (2010). She quotes a youth leader:

> The company has bought all our chiefs and officers by giving them fat envelopes, buying them cars, houses and employment. ... if you send your problem to them [the chiefs], they will ... accuse you of talking against the chiefs and gods of the land thereby requesting you to slaughter a sheep to pacify the gods (p. 28).

NGGL explained these contributions (between US$4,000 to US$6,000 annually) as compensation for time spent on the company activities. Since 2008, these agreements have been posted on the company website (Newmont, nd).

8.4 Philex Mining Corporation (Philippines)

Philex Mining Corporation (PX) was incorporated in the Philippines in 1955 and listed with the Philippine Stock Exchange in 1956. It is now the Philippine's largest gold and copper producer (NASSA, 2012). The Padcal copper and gold mine in the highland province of Benguet is PX's main site, operated since 1958. In 2011, further exploration activities in Padcal and its vicinities were pursued. Reserves in three ore bodies were certified and the mine's life was extended beyond 2020.

8.4.1 Mining policy and regulatory context in the Philippines

The Philippine Mining Act of 1995 provides for 100% foreign-ownership and 100% repatriation of mining capital and profits for up to 50 years (Holden & Jacobson, 2007). Mining in the Philippines is dominated by large companies, mostly foreign owned, and limited to extraction. Once extracted, the raw ores are processed mainly in China (Gorre *et al.*, 2012). Not surprisingly and in sharp contrast to that in Ghana, the contribution to employment from the Philippine's 27 large scale mines[7] has ranged from 0.5% to 0.6% (2008 to 2011), with a backward linkage index of only 0.46, and forward linkage of 0.82. From 2003 to 2012, its contribution to the GDP has ranged from 0.6% to 1% (Estremera, 2011).[8]

---

7 There are an estimated 400,000 small-scale miners in the Philippines.
8 A proposed revenue-sharing scheme will see the government taking 55% of the industry's net revenues or 10% of gross revenue (currently 2%), whichever is higher. (http://www.prrm.org/publications/gmo2/mpotential.htm).

An important player in Philippine economic social and political development is its dynamic social movement, the largest in Asia and most diverse in terms of interests and advocacies.[9] These include very active sustainable mining advocacy groups.

Mining proponents must obtain an environmental compliance certificate (PD 1586), consult with local governments and communities to obtain social acceptability (DENR 96-37), and in areas covered by ancestral domains, secure the free and prior informed consent (FPIC) of the indigenous community (DENR AO 96-40). If an FPIC is granted, the company must pay the indigenous community a royalty of at least 1% of the gross output, 90% for community development, and 10% for R&D of mining technology and geosciences. Both social acceptability and FPIC need to be renewed regularly. The Local Government Code of 1991 requires participation of municipal councils in monitoring mining activities. In 2010, an administrative order (AO 2010-21) was introduced under Section 136 of the Philippine Mining Act. It requires leaseholders to submit a five-year Social Development Management Program for the "sustained improvement of the living standards of the host and neighbouring communities by creating responsible, self-reliant and resource-based communities ... in a manner consistent with ... people empowerment".

In spite of its comprehensive set of environmental regulation and inclusive approach to environmental governance, the Philippines has several hundred "legacy" mines and suffers one mining accident after another (MAC, 2013). Stark *et al.* (2006, p. 1) explain: "The implementation and enforcement of Philippine mining laws ... are inconsistent and weak" (see also Table 8.1).

8.4.2 Philex's resource and environmental management

The first Filipino mining company certified under ISO 14001, Philex spends 5.5% of its total mining and milling cost on environmental protection, exceeding the government requirement of 3–5% (Brown, nd). A logged over area before 1958, the Padcal site now has more than 2,000 hectares reforested with about 7 million trees. The company invests roughly US$74,000 annually on reforestation (Philex Mining Corporation, nd). Philex undertakes immediate and progressive rehabilitation of disturbed areas. One decommissioned tailings pond is fully revegetated with various land uses such as grazing, bamboo propagation, and a mini-golf course. A fog cannon suppresses dust. Engineered silt traps help control downstream sedimentation. Regular quality monitoring is done for surface and drinking water sources, and effluent monitoring is conducted regularly at strategic sampling points in and outside of the camp. However, these did not prevent a breach of the company's only operating tailings pond (TP3) in August 2012. The spill, triggered by heavy rains and two typhoons but likely exacerbated by the fact that TP3 was past its structural prime, is considered the worst mining disaster in Philippine history (NASSA,

---

9 Source: http://en.wikipilipinas.org/index.php/Philippine_Non-Government_Organizations.

2012). The breach was not effectively plugged for a month resulting in the release of 20 million metric tons of tailings, wiping out artisanal fishing and gold panning downstream. The tailings eventually reached and lodged in the dead storage of the San Roque multipurpose dam, reducing its capacity (NASSA, 2012).

Philex maintained that the spill was force majeure but paid the US$23 million fine for a Mining Act violation. This covered the cost of rehabilitation on the upstream including the tailings dam, construction of an open spillway, clean-up of the Agno River and Balog creek. Two years after the disaster, Philex reports having constructed riprap walls, footpaths on rugged terrain and hanging bridges, concrete pathways, and elevated walkways down the Balog creek, to attract tourists. The company also constructed a pond seeded with 30,000 tilapia fingerlings (Emirates24/7News, 2014). As of March 2014, Philex was still negotiating the reduction of an additional US$5 million fine for Clean Water Act violation.

8.4.3 Contribution to community resilience

Philex's Padcal mine operation straddles two barangays.[10] The two barangays receive US$44,000 a month from Philex Mines and officials from the two councils participate in identifying, planning and implementing community development projects. Philex deals with three neighbouring communities outside the campsite proper. One consists of those who settled before the mine operation, largely from the Ibaloi clan. Another include descendants of the Kalanguya and Kalakana-ey families who came before and shortly after world war II, and the third are migrants who came to engage in small scale gold mining. Philex pays royalties to the indigenous communities (Chaloping-March, 2006).

During the 1980s Philex invested heavily in local philanthropic activities, particularly in agriculture. Its CSR program now covers health, education, livelihoods and public infrastructure (HELP). In 2014, HELP was allocated US$1.93 million. The health program reportedly serves an average of 350 out-patients daily with free consultation, medicines and treatment. Free private elementary education is provided, initially only to mine workers but later extended to neighbouring communities. PX subsidizes the private Philex-Saint Louis High School. The elementary school has graduated more than 12,000 since the 1960s and the high school, around 7,000 students since the 1970s. Full scholarships are awarded at both college and vocational levels. Philex's wage rates (2,145 full time and 482 contractors) are 21 to 61% higher than the regional average (Brown, nd).

Philex has received government awards for providing workers, equipment and fund-raising in response to natural disasters in the country. In April 2014, Philex Mining Corp. was named one of the Philippine's top companies by the Hong Kong-based Finance Asia Magazine for its social and environmental projects. It was ninth in the Best CSR category (InterAksyon.com, 2014).

---

10 Barangay is the lowest level of public administration in the Philippines.

8.4.4 Contribution to accountable and democratic governance

Philex Mining regularly posts information on its website on production data, payments, and others. It reports having paid US$208 million in taxes (1956–2006) and US$23 million in excise taxes (1991–2007), the latter divided 60/40 between the national and local government (Brown, nd). Its monthly payments to the two barangays are reported to community members at community assemblies (ANSA-EAP, 2014).

8.5 Are these examples of development-oriented CSR?

Table 8.3 summarizes the main features of the CSR practice of the three companies.

8.5.1 How have the companies helped address the community's basic needs and promoted community resilience?

Newmont Ghana and Philex Mines, through their investments in health and agriculture are bringing "bread" to their host communities. Both companies are exercising prudent environmental stewardship and paid the fines when they have slipped. Their education and scholarship programs are opening alternative livelihood opportunities for the next generation. In its patronage and stimulation of local businesses and employment creation, Newmont certainly goes far beyond "its range of external options and internal competencies" (Zadek, 2001) as arguably Philex does with its reforestation program. Vale, on the other hand, has opted not to go beyond legal compliance.

8.5.2 In what respects do they fall short?

Both Newmont Ghana and Philex invest heavily in infrastructure projects, agriculture, health and education, in effect replacing the state. This will likely create dependency or a sense of entitlement (Rajak, 2006) and erode the legitimacy of local systems of governance (Hauschildt, 2008) before the communities. It is, however, difficult to fault the companies. It can be argued that both are simply aligning their CSR programs with national and local development goals. In all three cases, the national government receives the lion's share of the company taxes, but unfortunately in all three the national and the local government seem content to leave social welfare provisioning to the company. In both Ahafo and Padcal, as in many developing countries, there is strong preference among government officials—national and local—for infrastructure building as the development priority. Roads, schools and clinics are no doubt important for rural development. Buildings and

Table 8.3 **Summary of main features of CSR practice**

Company	Environment and resources stewardship	Community basic needs and resilience	Accountable and democratic governance	Development orientation (L, M, H)
Vale	• ISO 14001 certified • Complies with LOC conditions • Drinking water scarcity an outstanding sustainability problem	• Primary source of employment in Itabira. • Contributes 80% of municipal revenues • Drinking water scarcity not addressed • Outreach to local college • No community development program	• Member of EITI • Sustainability reports awarded for transparency • Several appeals of corporate taxes	Low
Newmont Ghana	• ISO 14001 certified • Letter of credit for final rehabilitation • Partial rehabilitation of abandoned sites • Cyanide management system linked to ISO certification	• Compensated displaced residents, housing and access to land • Encourage alternative livelihoods with funding • High number of jobs created on and off mine • Wages above regional average • Very generous local procurement (>$6 million) • Heavy investment in education and infrastructure	• Member of EITI • High contribution to government revenues and employment • Posts all payments paid to national and local governments • Addresses local concerns • Paid fines for violations	High
Philex	• ISO 14001 certified • Heavy investment in reforestation • Rehabilitates abandoned sites • Regular water quality and effluents monitoring at strategic sites	• Compensated displaced residents, housing and access to land • Wages above national average • Heavy investment in health, education and infrastructure benefiting employees, host and neighbouring communities • Creates alternative land uses and livelihoods with rehabilitated sites	• Member of EITI • Royalties to indigenous communities exceeds requirement • Posts all payments paid to national and local governments • Paid fines for violations	High

roads are also visible and therefore useful during political campaigns, and construction projects are a lucrative and reliable source of influence. Companies by themselves cannot eliminate governance failure, but companies committed to development ought not contribute to, nor seek to benefit from it. From the information gathered for this chapter, there is no evidence that either Newmont or Philex has deliberately contributed to governance failure. On the other hand, Vale's repeated and successful appeals of its corporate taxes make it vulnerable to speculation that it is (Wasylycia-Leis *et al.*, 2014).

This raises the need for nuance in the call for "aligning CSR with local and national development goals" or for a "southern perspective in CSR". Development is a contested term. There are many, frequently differing development visions in the south and many different voices at the local.

8.5.3 Can corporations become genuine agents for long-term development?

The CSR practice and outcomes of Newmont Ghana and Philex Mining demonstrate that responsible private corporations can contribute importantly to local economic and social development objectives. It does require a state with a development vision and welfare orientation (as appears to be the case in Ghana) or strong social groups that manage to countervail organized business interests and corporate leadership with a sense of moral responsibility (as appears to be the case with Philex), consistent with Utting's (2005) observation. Vale's performance in Itabira, on the other hand, showcases the fundamental limitation of CSR—its voluntary nature. The community's demand for drinking water security is not asking "the pig to fly". Vale has extracted tremendous rents and exacted enormous costs in Itabira. One might have expected a company with tremendous resources and globally recognized as a corporate leader, to have a conscience and go beyond responsibility. But Vale does not have to and appears to have chosen not to.

Corporations will not address the development deficit significantly unless there are forces that can effectively countervail and temper corporate profitability interests. Corporate leaders need to be encouraged, or driven, to give back to the communities where they derive their fortunes and on whom they exact enormous and frequently irreversible costs, not out of social responsibility but out of a moral debt. The developmental state needs to be strengthened. Equally important, independent civil society groups need to be supported.

Bibliography

ANSA-EAP (2014). Key stakeholder groups in Benguet buy into constructive engagement in mining. Retrieved from http://www.ansa-eap.net/learning-in-action/constructive-engagement/key-stakeholder-groups-in-benguet-buy-into-constructive-engagement-in-mining/.

Azapagic, A. (2004). Developing a framework for sustainable development indicators for the mining and minerals industry. *Journal of Cleaner Production*, 12, 639-662.

Banerjee, S.B. (2008). Corporate social responsibility: the good, the bad and the ugly. *Critical Sociology*, 34(1), 51-79.

Blowfield, M. (2005). Corporate social responsibility: reinventing the meaning of development? *International Affairs*, 81(3), 515-524.

Boateng, K.A. (2012). Newmont spills cyanide again? *Modern Ghana*. Retrieved from http://www.modernghana.com/news/370015/1/newmont-spills-cyanide-again.html.

Brown, W.W. (n.d.). Implementing corporate social responsibility. Policies & Practices. The Philex Mining Corporation experience. Unpublished paper.

Chaloping-March, M. (2006). Collaboration towards social sustainability: the case of a mining corporation, its surrounding communities, and local government in Benguet, Philippines. *Int. J. Environment and Sustainable Development*, 5(2), 109-125.

Da Silva Enriquez, A.M.R. (2007). Maldição ou Dadiva? Os dilemmas do desenvolviment sustentavel a partir de uma base mineira. (Curse or Blessing? The sustainable development dilemmas from a mining base). PhD Thesis, Universidade de Brasilia.

Egri, C.P., & Ralston, D.A. (2008). Corporate responsibility: a review of international management research from 1998 to 2007. *Journal of International Management*, 14, 319-339.

Emirates24/7News (2014). Filipinos mining Itogon for tourist gold. Retrieved from http://www.emirates247.com/news/philippines/filipinos-mining-itogon-for-tourist-gold-2013-01-14-1.491034.

Estremera, S.A. (2011). Mining sector can't deliver jobs: study. *Sun Star*. Retrieved from http://www.sunstar.com.ph/davao/local-news/2011/12/02/mining-sector-cant-deliver-jobs-study-193743.

Gorre, I., Magulgad, E., & Ramos, C.A. (2012). Philippines: Seizing Opportunities. Revenue Watch Institute, Working Paper Series 2012.

Hauschildt, A.L.S. (2008). Corporate Social Responsibility in a Local African Context. A Critical Perspective. M.A. Thesis, University of Arrhus.

Holden, W.N., & Jacobson, D. (2007). Mining amid armed conflict: nonferrous metals mining in the Philippines. Retrieved from http://onlinelibrary.wiley.com/doi/10.1111/j.1541-0064.2007.00193.x/pdf.

InterAksyon.com (2014). Philex Mining named one of PH's best in CSR advocacy. Retrieved from http://www.interaksyon.com/business/84461/philex-mining-named-one-of-phs-best-in-csr-advocacy.

Ite, U.E. (2007). Partnering with the state for sustainable development: Shell's experience in the Niger Delta, Nigeria. *Sustainable Development*, 15, 216-228.

Jamali, D. (2007). The case for strategic corporate social responsibility in developing countries. *Business and Society Review*, 112(1), 1-27.

Jenkins, R. (2005). Globalization, corporate social responsibility and poverty. *International Affairs*, 81(3), 525-540.

Kapstein, E., & Kim, R. (2011). *The Socio-Economic Impact of Newmont Ghana Gold Limited* (pp. 7-52). Accra: The Authors and Newmont Ghana Gold Limited.

Kemp, M. (2001). Corporate Social Responsibility in Indonesia. A Quixotic Dream or Confident Expectation? United Nations Research Institute for Social Development Technology Business and Society Programme, Paper No. 6. Retrieved from http://digitalcommons. ilr.cornell.edu/codes/11.

Knobblock, E. (2013). Organisation changes and employment shifts in the mining industry: Towards a new understanding of resource-based economies in peripheral areas. *Journal of Rural and Community Development*, 8(1), 125-144.

MAC (Mines and Communities) (2013). Philippines: one mine disaster after another. Retrieved from http://www.minesandcommunities.org/article.php?a=12143.

Martinez-Alier, J. (2001). Mining justice, environmental justice, and valuation. *Journal of Hazardous Materials*, 86, 153-180.

Maximiano, J.M.B. (2005). The state of corporate social responsibility in the Philippines. Paper presented at the 12th Annual Conference, Australian Association for Professional and Applied Ethics, Adelaide, 28–30 September.

Mining.com (2014). Brazil appeals court rules in Vale's favour over $10 billion tax bill. Retrieved from http://www.mining.com/brazil-court-rules-in-vales-favour-over-10bn-tax-bill/.

Nagarajan, K.V. (2011). The Code of Hammurabi: an economic interpretation. *International Journal of Business and Social Science*, 2(8), 108-118.

NASSA (National Secretariat for Social Action Justice and Peace (2012). The Philex Mine Tailings Spill of 2012: an Independent Fact-finding Mission Report. Retrieved from http://nassa.org.ph/?p=2064, last accessed 24 April 2014.

Newmont (nd). Newmont provides facts about payments to traditional councils and the Ajenjua Bepo production forest. Retrieved from http://www.newmont.com/features/our-communities-features/traditionalcouncils.

Rajak, D. (2006). The gift of CSR. Power and the pursuit of responsibility in the mining industry. In W. Visser, M. McIntosh, & C. Middleton (Eds). *Corporate Citizenship in Africa* (pp. 190-200). Sheffield, UK: Greenleaf Publishing.

Rowe, J.K. (2005). Corporate social responsibility as business strategy. In R. Lipschutz & J.K. Rowe (Eds). *Globalization, Governmentality and Global Politics: Regulation for the Rest of Us?* (pp. 200-225). London: Routledge.

SHRM (Society for Human Resource Management) (2007). 2007 Corporate Social Responsibility: United States, Australia, India, China, Canada, Mexico and Brazil. A Pilot Study. Virginia: SHRM.

Smith, N.C. (2003). Corporate social responsibility. Not whether but how? Centre for Marketing Working Paper No. 03-701. London: London Business School.

Stark, J., Li, J., & Terasawa, K. (2006). Environmental Safeguards and Community Benefits in Mining: Recent Lessons from the Philippines. USAID and Foundation for Environmental Security and Sustainability. Working paper no. 1. 18p.

Talisayon, S.D. (2009). Corporate Social Responsibility and Emergent Models in Management of Stakeholder Capital in Philippine Conglomerates. Paper presented at the Fifth International Research Workshop on Asian Business, Singapore, 13 April.

The History Guide (nd). Lectures on European Intellectual History. Robert Owen: 1771–1858; Retrieved from http://www.historyguide.org/intellect/owen.html.

Triscitti, F. (2013). Mining, development and corporate-community conflicts in Peru. *Community Development Journal*, 48(3), 437-450.

Tubino, D.S., Yap, N.T., & Devlin, J.F. (2011). Vale and its corporate social performance in Itabira, Brazil: is the glass half full or half empty? *Impact Assessment and Project Appraisal*, 29(2), 1-7.

Utting, P. (2005). Corporate responsibility and the movement of business, *Development in Practice*, 15(3-4), 375-388.

Wasylycia-Leis, J., Fitzpatrick, P., & Fonseca, A. (2014). Mining communities from a resilience perspective: managing disturbance and vulnerability in Itabira, Brazil. *Environmental Management*, 53, 481-495.

WBCSD (World Business Council for Sustainable Development) (2001). The Business Case for Sustainable Development: Making a Difference Towards the Johannesburg Summit 2002 and Beyond. Retrieved from http://www.wbcsd.org.

Welford, R. (2005). Corporate social responsibility in Europe, North America and Asia. 2004 survey results. *Journal of Corporate Citizenship*, 17, 33-52.

Yap, N.T. (1990). Sustainable development. Exploring the contradictions. *Current*, (Winter), 4-5.

Yap, N.T., Devlin, J.F., Wu, C.C., & Ton, S. (2007). Corporate environmental innovation and public policy: case studies from Taiwan. In: S. Parto & B. Herbert-Copley (Eds.). *Industrial Innovation and Regulation. Developing Workable Solutions* (pp. 22-50). Tokyo: United Nations University.

Yaro, I.J. (2010). The Impact of Mining on Livelihoods of Local Communities: A Case Study of Newmont Ahafo South Mining Project of Brong Ahafo Region of Ghana. M.A. Thesis. International Institute of Social Studies. The Hague, Netherlands, 58p.

Zadek, S. (2001). *The Civil Corporation*. London: Earthscan Publications Ltd.

9

Social and environmental accountability in developing countries

Ataur Rahman Belal
Aston Business School, UK

The principal aim of this chapter is to undertake a critical review of the social and environmental accountability of global business activities in developing countries. While global business activities have contributed to the economic development of developing countries, they have many adverse social and environmental consequences which are often under-studied. I explore the role of accounting in making those consequences visible. This chapter, however, concludes that while social and environmental accounting has the potential to raise the visibility of social and environmental impacts of corporate activities, it often fails to do so particularly under the current voluntary disclosure regime where corporations can choose what to report and how to report. This is even more pronounced in the developing countries because of their vulnerabilities arising from various social and environmental problems. This chapter argues for a case of "surrogate accountability" as an alternative to the current corporate driven form of accountability.

The principal aim of this chapter is to undertake a critical review of the social and environmental accountability of global business activities in developing countries.

These global business activities not only contribute to the socio-economic development of developing countries but also bring with them many adverse social and environmental consequences (Belal, *et al.*, 2013). I examine the role of accounting in making those consequences visible with a view to promote transparency and accountability of business activities (Cooper and Owen, 2007; Medawar, 1976) in developing countries. I also highlight the corporate motivations for social and environmental accounting and accountability exercises. For this purpose I draw on the extant social and environmental accountability literature to achieve the aim and objective of this chapter.

The chapter is structured in six sections. In the next section I highlight the social and environmental consequences of global business activities in developing countries (Jamali, 2010; Jamali and Mirshak, 2006). Here I argue that while these activities have brought in some benefits in the form of socio-economic development (including employment and tax revenues), they have also created significant undesired social and environmental consequences (e.g. environmental pollution and negligence of various labour issues including health and safety) for the people and the environment of these developing countries (Derry, 2012). Section 9.2 articulates the need for corporate accountability for these social and environmental impacts (Belal *et al.*, 2013). This is done based on work that has been carried out so far in the social and environmental accountability literature from the context of developing countries. Given the failure of the voluntary reporting regime to promote transparency and accountability, particularly in the context of developing countries, section 9.3 offers the potential of "surrogate accountability" as a possible way forward. Section 9.4 briefly explores the potential of development-oriented corporate social responsibility (CSR). Section 9.5 summarizes the discussion in the chapter and offers some concluding thoughts.

9.1 Social and environmental consequences of global business activities in developing countries

While globalization and its principal agent multinational enterprises (MNEs) have created many opportunities in developing countries in terms of economic development, tax revenues for the national exchequer of the host government and employment generation, they have also resulted in adverse social and environmental impacts. Eden and Lenway (2001) have referred to these impacts as the "dark side" of globalization. Given the vulnerability of developing countries (Belal *et al.*, 2013), these impacts could be potentially very significant. The vulnerabilities of developing countries arise from widespread poverty, corruption, fragile natural environment and weak governance and regulatory system.

Global corporations are spreading around the world in search of efficiency and cost-effective operations (Sikka, 2008). The destinations often include developing countries with exploitable resources (Sikka, 2011). Global capital is good at exploiting these resources located within the developing countries as a profitable venture. These resources can take the forms of oil and gas, mining and cheap labour (Sikka, 2011). However, the vulnerabilities of the developing countries are such that in that process the citizens of these countries and their livelihood might be endangered via adverse social and environmental impacts (Belal *et al.*, 2013). I provide illustrative examples of these adverse consequences in the following paragraphs.

Many of these developing countries (for example, China, Bangladesh and Vietnam) have adopted an export led strategy to pursue their economic development objectives. After China, Bangladesh is known as the second largest exporter of garments and textile products. After its initial start in the late 1970s, this is now a US$20 billion industry with the potential to reach US$36–42 billion by 2020 (McKinsey, 2011). There are 5,000 factories in Bangladesh employing 3.6 million workers, 90% of whom are women. More than 80% of total export proceeds of the country come from this sector (McKinsey, 2011). Thus the economic contribution of the sector towards the national economy of Bangladesh is significant. However, even more significant is the adverse social and environmental impacts created from this export-led economic growth. We now turn our attention to these impacts.

The appalling working conditions in the garment factories within the supply chains of large Western clothing retailers located in the poor developing countries like Bangladesh is well known and well documented. The health and safety of the workers is an issue of particular concern. In Bangladesh alone, hundreds of workers have died from health and safety related incidents. The latest incident took place on 24 April, 2013 which shook the world (Epstein and Buhovac, 2014) when a building in Dhaka city, called Rana Plaza, collapsed[1] killing over 1,100 people and leaving hundreds more injured. Rana Plaza housed five garment factories which were supplying a number of European and North American retailers including Walmart, Primark, C&A, Benetton and Cato Fashions. This incident took place only five months after the Tazreen Factory Fire incident which took the lives of 112 garment workers. Tazreen was believed to be supplying goods for Walmart (*New York Times*, 10 December, 2012).

While the labour related issues in the Bangladeshi garments sector, such as child labour, forced labour, fair wages and health and safety, have attracted the attention of the international media and other stakeholders, environmental pollution created by the garments manufacturing activities have received much less attention (Matin, 1995). A local newspaper recently ran a story on the environmental pollution created by the Dhaka Export Processing Zone in Ashulia where most of the garment factories are located (Saha, 2014). In this report, it was suggested that environmental pollution from these factories had affected nearby village canals,

---

1 This was due to structural faults within the building which housed these factories, it was suggested.

created public health hazards for the local villagers and other visible losses in the form of rust on the tin rooftops of the poor village homes. In a *New York Times* feature article on another industrial zone in the suburb (Savar area) of Dhaka where a number of garment factories are located, Yardley (2013) noted that discharge of untreated wastes was causing a major "water pollution disaster" and was destroying the rice paddies. It is also reported that fish stocks were dying in the nearby water bodies.

Bangladeshi garment manufacturers supply the international retailers mainly competing on price. The cheap labour cost is the main attraction of Bangladesh where it is believed to have the lowest labour cost in the world with the monthly wage of a garments worker at roughly US$37 a month (*New York Times*, 24 April, 2013). However, the cheap garment prices enjoyed by Western consumers comes from the dire working conditions of desperately poor workers and critical environmental resources detailed above.

Another example of major environmental degradation is to be found in the Hazaribagh area of Dhaka where 206 tanneries are located. The export earnings from the leather sector are worth billions of dollars and are desperately needed by this poor country. However, untreated toxic wastes discharged from these tanneries have created a major public health hazard in the area once known as "thousands flowers" (Hazaribagh) (Motlagh, 2013). The titles of two international media reports on these tanneries say it all: "Hell for leather: Bangladesh's toxic tanneries ravage lives and environment" (Motlagh, 2013) and "Bangladesh's toxic tanneries turning a profit at an intolerable human price" (Renton, 2012). According to Maurice of the World Health Organization (Maurice, 2001), 90% of the workers of these tanneries die before the age of 50 due to gastrointestinal, dermatological and other diseases arising from the significant pollution caused by these tanneries. Children and adults work in these tanneries largely unprotected to supply cheap high-quality "Bengali black" leather which is in high demand from the European leather retailers and fashion designers (Renton, 2012). Millions of litres of largely untreated waste pass through the neighbourhood and agricultural land destroying the paddies, then into one of the main rivers of the country, the Buriganga. Due to the pollution, the Buriganga has become "clinically dead" and endangers the livelihoods of the poor citizens of the country who depended on the river for fishing, boating and bathing (Belal, 2008; Belal and Owen, 2007).

The ship-breaking industry emerging on the shores of India, Pakistan and Bangladesh turns billions of dollars for the national economies. However, it comes at intolerable human and environmental costs. Ten kilometres long, the massive Gadani ship-breaking yard in Pakistan is known as one of the world's largest ship-breaking yards. Miller (2013) reported that workers at Gadani toil for a mere £2 a day. The working conditions are reported to be inhumane and dangerous. Within the Bangladeshi ship breaking industry located in Chittagong, fatal accidents are commonplace. Widespread damage is reported to have been caused to the local environment through effluent discharge from the ships and hazardous materials (asbestos, PCB and lead) leeching into the shore and the sea (EIU, 2012; Hossain and Islam, 2006). In addition to earning billions of dollars for the national coffer, this industry meets the significant demands for metal in the growing construction industry of these nations.

In addition to the above labour-intensive industries, natural-resource-based industries (e.g. oil and gas, mining, etc.) are common in developing countries. Due to corruption, funding constraints and lack of expertise, the governments of developing countries are often unable to extract these resources to the best advantage of its citizens. This desperate situation allows the multinational corporations (MNEs) to come in and exploit these resources in a way where commercial considerations lead to the neglect of the environment, communities and human rights (Khavul and Bruton, 2013; Newenham-Kahindi, 2011; Sikka, 2011). Weak, often corrupt, regulatory and governance regimes in these countries mean that the nations interests are not always best served by the governments and MNEs involved in the exploration activities.

A prime example is the Magurcharra incident in Bangladesh which never received the international attention that it should have. The incident, a gas well blowout, caused billions of dollars of natural gas to be wasted and serious environmental damage was inflicted on the nearby neighbourhood and communities. It happened in June 1997, during the process of gas exploration by the US oil company Occidental. The massive blowout created havoc in Magurcharra and the nearby villages and communities. Much of the flora in the vicinity, including the Lawacharra Reserve Forest, was destroyed. In all, 96 acres of the Lawacharra forest was burnt and rare biodiversity of the adjoining areas was lost to the continuous forest fires that persisted for 17 days after the incident (Siddiqui, 2001). According to The National Committee to Protect Oil-Gas-Mineral Resources and Port of Bangladesh, 245 billion cubic feet of gas was burnt in the explosion resulting in a nine billion Taka[2] loss to the nation (The New Nation, 13 June, 2006). While full compensation is yet to be received, the gas exploration activities in Bangladesh by the MNEs continue. In 2005, two similar incidents took place in Tangratila, Bangladesh, during exploration activities by a Canadian multinational company, Niko (Islam and Islam, 2011). The incidents resulted in millions of cubic feet of gas being wasted, which was valued at US$50–60 million according to one estimate (Nasreen *et al.*, 2006, cited in Islam and Islam, 2011). Tens of thousands of villagers in the nearby areas had to flee their homes for fear of life. Ordinary people demonstrated on the streets demanding compensation for the loss of their homes and livelihoods. However, very little was paid in the form of compensation to the villagers and the state. Niko officials, at first, attempted to escape paying any compensation by collaboration with some dubious government officials. Gas exploration by another US company, Chevron, in the Bibiyana gas field met with local resistance by the people who lost their lands and received very little in return (Gardner *et al.*, 2012). Chevron's exploration activities in the environmentally sensitive areas of Bangladesh have received

---

2 US$1 = 80 Taka approximately.

Table 9.1 **Social and environmental consequences of global business activities: summary and a case of Bangladesh**

Business activity types	Examples of social and environmental consequences
Garments manufacturing and export	Poor working conditions, child labour, human rights violation; health and safety concerns (e.g. Rana Plaza factory building collapse noted above); environmental degradation
Leather processing and export	Environmental pollution arising from toxic discharges; extreme public health hazards (e.g. Hazaribagh tanneries)
Emerging ship-breaking industry	Poor working conditions; health and safety concerns (e.g. ship-breaking industries in Chittagong)
Natural resource extraction	Environmental accidents leading to loss of local flora and fauna (e.g. Magurcharra disaster); loss of local community lands and homes during gas exploration process

widespread criticism and resistance from affected people. However, their activities still continue, resulting in significant social and environmental costs that are hardly taken into account. Table 9.1 provides a selective summary of the social and environmental consequences of global business activities in Bangladesh. The table captures the social and environmental consequences of global business activities in developing countries by exhibiting Bangladesh as a case in point.

The social and environmental consequences of global business activities are not limited to Bangladesh. The story is similar elsewhere. In Nigeria, Shell's oil exploration activities in Niger Delta led to significant environmental damage, displacement of the local people and the human rights violations of the Ogoni people. Some of these companies are so powerful that even the host states are sometimes unable to hold them to account. Corporate accountability is even more difficult to achieve when some of these states are crippled by corruption and weak institutions (Sikka, 2011). Moreover, sometimes these developing nation states are smaller than the large corporations creating power differentials. For example, in 2011 the annual gross domestic product (GDP) of Nigeria was US$235.923 billion while the total revenue of Shell was US$484.480 billion. The company ranked 26th on the list of the world's top 175 economic entities while Nigeria ranked only 52nd (http://dstevenwhite.com/2012/08/11/the-top-175-global-economic-entities-2011). Such disparity in power and size between the corporations and the host government indicates that some of these poor developing nation states are often unable to protect their own citizen's interests in various investments contracts agreed with these powerful corporations (Lauwo and Otusanya, 2014).

In Tanzania, gold mining activities by the multinational companies have displaced local communities, led to violation of human rights and significant impacts on the local natural environment (Gifford et al. 2010; Lauwo and Otusanya, 2014). Various tax incentives and stabilization clauses inserted in the mineral development agreements (MDAs) have adverse social and environmental impacts. Lauwo and Otusanya (2014) have examined the Tanzanian MDA of Barrick Gold Mining (a Canadian multinational) and expressed concern about the lack of transparency in the process of signing the contract. Their study focused on Barrick's operations in the Buzwagi Gold Mine (BGM) of Tanzania. Mining operations required the eviction of local residents from their lands and thus violating their human rights. It has also led to resistance movements, conflicts with the mining company and widespread health hazards arising from environmental pollution caused by heavy metals and hazardous chemicals. The rights of local residents to a clean environment and safe water supply has been affected. The terms and conditions of the MDA (including the stabilization clauses) with Barrick constrained the ability of the Tanzanian state to uphold it's own citizens rights (Lauwo and Otusanya, 2014).

The social and environmental consequences of global corporate activities in developing countries, as highlighted above, raise issues of serious concern. These impacts arise from the process of globalized production and exploration activities. How do we hold the global capital to account for these adverse social and environmental impacts? This is where accounting and accountability have a greater role to play. If we accept that global capital is responsible for these impacts, then we could demand accountability thereof and discuss an appropriate form of accountability required to make global capital accountable to people. In the next section, I discuss the possibilities of these accountabilities (or the lack of it).

9.2 Corporate social and environmental accountability in developing countries

Traditionally, the discipline of accounting is preoccupied with the economic performance of organizations. The traditional accounting model does not allow for the social and environmental consequences highlighted in the previous section. By relaxing some of the constraints of the traditional accounting model, social and environmental accounting can have the emancipatory potential (Gallhofer *et al.*, 2006) of promoting the visibility of social and environmental consequences arising from global corporate activities (Belal, 2008; Gray *et al.*, 2014a; Unerman, 2003). The fundamental objective of social and environmental accounting is to enhance the transparency and accountability of organizations (Medawar, 1976). Thus, social and environmental accounting is linked to the discharge of accountabilities related to the social and environmental performance of organizations. This should empower the stakeholders affected by the adverse social and environmental performance of organizational activities and thereby could be considered as a mechanism for holding organizations to account. However, given the power differentials between organizations and the stakeholders to what extent the emancipatory potential of accounting can be realized is a moot question.

Publication of CSR reports[3] by various organizations is a contemporary phenomenon and has become a mainstream activity amongst the larger corporations. According to the latest KPMG survey of CSR reporting (KPMG, 2013), 71% of 4,100 companies included in the survey have published such reports. This phenomenon is not only noticeable in developed countries but also in emerging and developing countries as well. KPMG surveys have found significant growth in the reporting of Indian, Chinese and Taiwanese companies.

Most of these reports are published voluntarily. Why do they do so? A significant body of research exists which explores the underlying motivations for CSR reporting. A dominant explanation in the social and environmental accounting research is that corporations use CSR reports as a tool for legitimizing their activities (Cho, 2009; Cho and Patten, 2007; Deegan, 2002; Deegan *et al.*, 2002; Kamal and Deegan, 2013). Most of the researchers concluded that CSR reporting is an exercise aimed at the management of powerful stakeholders while it was meant to be aimed at discharging accountability to all stakeholders irrespective of their power (Belal, 2002; Belal and Owen, 2007; Cooper and Owen, 2007).

Voluntary reporting regimes meant that corporations could cherry pick and choose what to report resulting in incompleteness of reporting. Incomplete reporting defeats the fundamental objectives of CSR reporting, namely, transparency and accountability. Belal and Cooper (2011) observed that significant omission occurred in the CSR reporting of Bangladeshi companies on the issues of child labour, equal opportunities and poverty alleviation. They argued that these omissions might be deliberate attempts by business or an indication of their unwillingness to engage with issues of national and international significance.

These issues are not only significant in the national context of Bangladesh but also in many other developing countries. In the context of Tanzanian gold mining industries, Lauwo and Otusanya (2014) note that the issues of human rights abuse and serious environmental pollution have not been disclosed in the CSR reports of the mining company under study. Most of these issues affect the poor and vulnerable stakeholders such as local villagers and community peoples in the neighbourhood where operations of global companies take place. These stakeholders bear the brunt of the "dark side" of the globalized corporate activities and include the destitute workers of textile factories and shipyards, community peoples

3 Also known as social reports, environmental reports and social and environmental reports. There are many other labels for it. Currently, most reports are labelled as sustainability reports or integrated reports. CSR refers to the corporate commitment to conduct their operations in a social, ethical and environmental friendly manner. According to a Green Paper published by the European Commission (EC, 2001), it refers to "a concept whereby companies integrate social and environmental concerns in their business operations and in their interaction with their stakeholders on a voluntary basis". Corporations may undertake CSR activities but might not necessarily report those activities in the public domain. However, in recent times corporations have started to provide an account of their CSR activities via their websites and stand-alone CSR/sustainability reports. KPMG surveys periodically track such developments in reporting.

in the neighbourhood of Hazaribagh and Niger Delta and the villagers affected by the Tanzanian mining activities. They do not speak English nor do they have the powers to seek redress and hold these mighty corporations to account (Belal *et al.*, 2016).

Corporate reporting of social and environmental performance have so far failed to deliver the desired level of transparency necessary to ensure accountability to the powerless vulnerable stakeholders noted above. Given the disparity in power, these stakeholders themselves are unable to hold the corporations to account. Power and size of the large corporations, weak regulatory regimes and corruption in state governance result in an unwillingness or inability of the developing country governments to reign in the activities of the global corporations (Lauwo and Otusanya, 2014; Sikka, 2011).

9.3 Surrogate accountability and its potential for developing countries

The discussion reveals that corporate reluctance, unable governments and powerless stakeholders of developing countries do not provide much hope for social and environmental accountability of corporate activities under the current voluntary corporate reporting regime. However, alternative possibilities of providing "counter-accounts" from non-corporate sources such as civil societies including non-governmental organizations (NGOs), pressure groups and trade unions, could be a better hope for the future. In this context, the concept of "surrogate accountability" (Rubenstein, 2007) might be worthy of examination. According to Rubenstein (2007), it:

> … involves an actor—a surrogate—who substitutes for accountability holders during one or more phases of the accountability process: setting *standards*, finding and interpreting *information*, and, most importantly, *sanctioning* the power wielder if it fails to live up to the relevant standards (p. 617).

Here it must be noted that "surrogate accountability" cannot be a replacement for direct standard accountability whereby accountability holders can hold power wielders to account and impose appropriate sanctions for failure to discharge appropriate accountabilities. Rubenstein (2007) contends that it is generally inferior to standard accountability. In her paper, it is instead proposed as the "second-best" form of accountability as opposed to no accountability at all. In the context of developing countries, victims of corporate activities (e.g. workers and affected marginalized communities) can often find themselves unable to sanction the power wielders due to a lack of power arising from prevalent inequalities, rampant corruption, weak governance and widespread poverty. These power differentials can often make direct standard accountability mechanisms ineffective leading to a lack of accountability. We note that while these power differentials are unlikely to be resolved in the near future, empowering the civil societies with a view to sanction the power wielders via surrogate accountability might be a reasonable way forward.

Civil societies which often represent the rights of the vulnerable stakeholders may act as a surrogate for the victims of globalized corporate activities and demand accountability from the corporations on behalf of the weaker constituents in developing countries. Civil societies can also prepare independent "counter-accounts" of the corporate activities with a view to expose an alternative form of corporate accountability of social and environmental impacts (Gray *et al.*, 2014a). One example here could be the accounts produced by the NGO—Friends of the Earth (FoE, http://www.foe.co.uk/sites/default/files/downloads/failing_challenge. pdf)—titled "Failing the Challenge: The Other Shell Report" and published in 2003. The accounts, prepared in response to Shell's 2002 report, capture the voices of communities around the world affected by the global operations of Shell. It paints a different picture to the one that can be found in Shell's own report. In this case, FoE acts as a surrogate of the communities affected by Shell's activities around the world and imposes a sanction on Shell via bad publicity and media exposure. The affected communities would otherwise have been unable, due to the power differential, to hold power wielders like Shell to account via direct standard accountability mechanisms. Gray *et al.* (2014b) provide several other examples of similar "counter-accounts".[4]

9.4 Brief reflections on accountability and development-oriented CSR

In the context of developing countries, the contributions of global corporations have been mainly limited to employment generation and tax revenues to the national coffer. However, given the diminished roles of governments in developing countries, modern businesses are urged to fulfil the developmental gaps left by such contractions of government roles. It is argued that a business cannot prosper in communities which fail due to widespread poverty (Pachauri, 2004, 2006). Business organizations tend to respond to this call by undertaking various community development activities in the areas of health, education and poverty alleviation (Eweje, 2006; Idemudia and Ite, 2006; Ite, 2004; Sharmin *et al.*, 2014). However,

---

4 See Gallhofer *et al.* (2006) for an example of "counter-accounts" in order to achieve the emancipatory potential of online reporting and Steiner (2010) for an alternative account of Shell's oil exploration activities in Nigeria and BP's oil spill in the Gulf of Mexico.

it should be borne in mind that these organizations are designed to maximize shareholders' wealth and whether they can ever fulfil the roles traditionally played by governments is a consideration beyond the scope of this chapter.

What we are seeing is that businesses are attempting to fulfil some of these contracted and retracted governmental roles via various development projects. This is normally done under the label of CSR. These CSR activities are often reported via CSR reports with the ambitious claims of promoting transparency and accountability. For example, the Bangladesh subsidiary of British American Tobacco made such claims in its Annual Report, 2002 (p. vi). However, the majority of researches on social and environmental accounting so far have found evidence that is quite contrary to the above claims leading to the conclusion that this reporting is anything but an exercise of transparency and accountability (Cooper and Owen, 2007). This necessarily brief reflection on development-oriented CSR shows that corporate potential to undertake CSR activities to help development agenda of the developing countries needs to be considered with caution and scepticism.

9.5 Summary and conclusion

To summarize, in this chapter I have argued that global corporate activities have created many benefits in the form of economic development of developing countries including employment generation and tax revenues for the state. However, social and environmental implications of these activities have not received adequate visibility in the corporate decision-making and policy-making arenas. I have provided some examples of these social and environmental consequences in this chapter from the context of a number of developing countries such as Bangladesh, Pakistan, Nigeria and Tanzania.

In conclusion, it can be noted that while social and environmental accounting has the potential to raise the visibility of the social and environmental impacts of corporate activities, it often fails to do so particularly under the current voluntary disclosure regime where corporations can choose what to report and how to report. I have argued for a possibility of "surrogate accountability" (Rubenstein, 2007) led by the civil societies to hold the corporations to account. This is necessary due to lack of strong state governance and powerlessness of vulnerable stakeholders in the developing countries. It could also be argued that, given the failure of current voluntary CSR reporting regimes, urgent steps are necessary to reform the existing corporate governance structures to empower the non-shareholder stakeholders, particularly the victims of global corporate activities. This can be achieved by giving them a voice in the corporate decision-making processes which affect these vulnerable stakeholders. The "surrogate accountability" mechanism discussed above might be a way (but not the only one) to ensure that these voices are heard.

Bibliography

Belal, A.R. (2002). Stakeholder accountability or stakeholder management: a review of UK firms' social and ethical accounting, auditing and reporting (SEAAR). *Corporate Social Responsibility and Environmental Management*, 9(1), 8-25.

Belal, A.R. (2008). *Corporate Social Responsibility Reporting in Developing Countries: The Case of Bangladesh*. Aldershot: Ashgate.

Belal, A.R., & Cooper, S. (2011). The absence of corporate social responsibility reporting in Bangladesh. *Critical Perspectives on Accounting*, 22(7), 654-667.

Belal, A.R., Cooper, S., & Khan, N.A. (2015). Corporate environmental responsibility and accountability: what chance in vulnerable Bangladesh? *Critical Perspectives on Accounting*, Forthcoming.

Belal, A.R., Cooper, S.M., & Roberts, R.W. (2013). Vulnerable and exploitable: the need for organizational accountability and transparency in emerging and less developed economies. *Accounting Forum*, 37(2), 81-91.

Belal, A.R., & Owen, D. (2007). The views of corporate managers on the current state of, and future prospects for, social reporting in Bangladesh: an engagement based study. *Accounting, Auditing & Accountability Journal*, 20(3), 472-494.

Cho, C.H. (2009). Legitimation strategies used in response to environmental disaster: A French case study of total S.A.'s erika and AZF incidents. *European Accounting Review*, 18(1), 33-62.

Cho, C.H., & Patten, D.M. (2007). The role of environmental disclosures as tools of legitimacy: a research note. *Accounting, Organizations and Society*, 32(7-8), 639-647.

Cooper, S.M., & Owen, D.L. (2007). Corporate social reporting and stakeholder accountability: the missing link. *Accounting, Organizations and Society*, 32(7-8), 649-667.

Deegan, C. (2002). The legitimizing effect of social and environmental disclosures—a theoretical foundation. *Accounting, Auditing and Accountability Journal*, 15(3), 282-311.

Deegan, C., Rankin, M., & Tobin, J. (2002). An examination of the corporate social and environmental disclosures of BHP from 1983–1997: a test of legitimacy theory. *Accounting, Auditing and Accountability Journal*, 15(3), 312-343.

Derry, R. (2012). Reclaiming marginalized stakeholders. *Journal of Business Ethics*, 111(2), 253-264.

EC (2001). Green paper: Promoting European framework for corporate social responsibility. Brussels: European Commission (EC).

Eden, L., & Lenway, S. (2001). Introduction to the symposium: multinationals: the Janus face of globalization. *Journal of International Business Studies*, 32(3), 383-400.

EIU. (2012, 27 October). Ship breaking in Bangladesh: Hard to break up.

Epstein, M.J., & Buhovac, A.R. (2014). *Making Sustainability Work: Best Practices in Managing and Measuring Corporate Social, Environmental, and Economic Impacts*. Sheffield: Greenleaf Publishing.

Eweje, G. (2006). The role of MNEs in community development initiatives in developing countries. *Business & Society*, 45(2), 93-129.

Gallhofer, S., Haslam, J., Monk, E., & Roberts, C. (2006). The emancipatory potential of online reporting: the case of counter accounting. *Accounting, Auditing & Accountability Journal*, 19(5), 681-718.

Gardner, K., Ahmed, Z., Bashir, F., & Rana, M. (2012). Elusive partnerships: gas extraction and CSR in Bangladesh. *Resources Policy*, 37(2), 168-174.

Gifford, B., Kestler, A., & Anand, S. (2010). Building local legitimacy into corporate social responsibility: gold mining firms in developing nations. *Journal of World Business*, 45(3), 304-311.

Gray, R., Adams, C., & Owen, D. (2014a). *Accountability, Social Responsibility and Sustainability: Accounting for Society and the Environment.* Hemel Hempstead: Pearson Publishers.

Gray, R., Brennan, A., & Malpas, J. (2014b). New accounts: towards a reframing of social accounting. *Accounting Forum*, 38(4), 258-273.

Hossain, M., & Islam, M. (2006). Ship breaking activities and its impact on the coastal zone of Chittagong, Bangladesh: towards sustainable management. Chittagong: Young Power in Social Action (YPSA)

Idemudia, U., & Ite, U.E. (2006). Corporate–community relations in Nigeria's oil industry: challenges and imperatives. *Corporate Social Responsibility and Environmental Management*, 13(4), 194-206.

Islam, M.A., & Islam, M.A. (2011). Environmental incidents in a developing country and corporate environmental disclosures. *Society and Business Review*, 6(3), 229-248.

Ite, U. (2004). Multinationals and corporate social responsibility in developing countries: a case study of Nigeria. *Corporate Social Responsibility and Environmental Management*, 11(1), 1-11.

Jamali, D. (2010). The CSR of MNC subsidiaries in developing countries: global, local, substantive or diluted? *Journal of Business Ethics*, 93(2), 181-200.

Jamali, D., & Mirshak, R. (2006). Corporate social responsibility (CSR): theory and practice in a developing country context. *Journal of Business Ethics*, 72(3), 243-262.

Kamal, Y., & Deegan, C. (2013). Corporate social and environment-related governance disclosure practices in the textile and garment industry: evidence from a developing country. *Australian Accounting Review*, 23(2), 117-134.

Khavul, S., & Bruton, G.D. (2013). Harnessing innovation for change: sustainability and poverty in developing countries. *Journal of Management Studies*, 50(2), 285-306.

KPMG (2013). KPMG International Survey of Corporate Responsibility Reporting 2013. Amsterdam: KPMG.

Lauwo, S., & Otusanya, O.J. (2014). Corporate accountability and human rights disclosures: a case study of Barrick Gold Mine in Tanzania. *Accounting Forum*, 38(2), 91-108.

Matin, M. (1995). Environmental pollution and its control in Bangladesh. *TrAC Trends in Analytical Chemistry*, 14(10), 468-473.

Maurice, J. (2001). Tannery pollution threatens health of half-million Bangladesh residents. *Bulletin of the World Health Organization*, 79(1), 78-79. Retrieved from http://www.scielosp.org/scielo.php?script=sci_arttext&pid=S0042-96862001000100018&lng=en&tlng=en.10.1590/S0042-96862001000100018.

McKinsey. (2011). Bangladesh's ready-made garments landscape: the challenge of growth. Germany: McKinsey and Company.

Medawar, C. (1976). The social audit: A political view. *Accounting, Organizations and Society*, 1(4), 389-394.

Miller, D. (2013, May 14). World's biggest ship graveyard—where huge tankers and cruise liners are scrapped on the shorefront and workers toil for £2 a day. Mail Online. Retrieved from http://www.dailymail.co.uk/news/article-2324339/Worlds-biggest-ship-graveyard--huge-tankers-cruise-liners-scrapped-shorefront-workers-toil-2-day.html#ixzz30NQx5hKK

Motlagh, J. (2013, September 3). Hell for Leather: Bangladesh's Toxic Tanneries Ravage Lives and Environment. *Time Magazine.*

Nasreen, M., Mokaddem Hossain, K., & Kumar Kundu, D. (2006). The interrelationship between poverty, environment and sustainable development in Bangladesh: an overview. *Bangladesh e-Journal of Sociology*, 3(2), 1-21.

Newenham-Kahindi, A. (2011). A global mining corporation and local communities in the Lake Victoria zone: the case of Barrick Gold multinational in Tanzania. *Journal of Business Ethics*, 99(2), 253-282.

Pachauri, R.K. (2004, December 22). The rationale for corporate social responsibility in India. *The Financial Express*. Retrieved from http://www.teriin.org/upfiles/pub/articles/art46.pdf.

Pachauri, R.K. (2006, April 28). CSR in new dimensions. *The Economic Times*. Retrieved from http://www.teriin.org/upfiles/pub/articles/art271.pdf.

Renton, A. (2012, December 13). Bangladesh's toxic tanneries turning a profit at an intolerable human price. *The Guardian*.

Rubenstein, J. (2007). Accountability in an unequal world. *Journal of Politics*, 69(3), 616-632.

Saha, P.S. (2014, March 10). Pollution affected neighbourhood. *Prothom Alo*.

Sharmin, S., Khan, N.A., & Belal, A.R. (2014). Corporate community involvement in Bangladesh: an empirical study. *Corporate Social Responsibility and Environmental Management*, 21(1), 41-51.

Siddiqui, J. (2001). Environmental non-accountability in Bangladesh?: the striking case of the Magurchara gas field disaster. *Social and Environmental Accountability Journal*, 21(2), 12-13.

Sikka, P. (2008). Globalization and its discontents. *Accounting, Auditing & Accountability Journal*, 21(3), 398-426.

Sikka, P. (2011). Accounting for human rights: the challenge of globalization and foreign investment agreements. *Critical Perspectives on Accounting*, 22(8), 811-827.

Steiner, R. (2010). Double standard: Shell practices in Nigeria compared with international standards to prevent and control pipeline oil spills and the deepwater horizon oil spill. Amsterdam: Friends of the Earth.

Unerman, J. (2003). Enhancing organizational global hegemony with narrative accounting disclosures: an early example. *Accounting Forum*, 27(4), 425-448.

Yardley, J. (2013, 14 July). Bangladesh pollution, told in colors and smells. *New York Times*.

10

CSR practices in Turkey
Examining CSR reports

Bilge Uyan-Atay
Bahçeşehir University, Turkey

Asli Tuncay-Celikel
Işık University, Turkey

This study examines the private companies that publish CSR reports in Turkey. Turkey has a growing economy, located in an international arena with an increasing number of global brands starting to export their products from Turkey with even more multinational enterprises (MNEs) planning to locate in the country. Now, some Turkish companies and subsidiaries of MNEs have started to publish CSR reports. Our findings show that strong Turkish conglomerates are playing a constructive role in macro-level development and governance in Turkey. They are also addressing local problems such as education, human rights, environmental protection and workers' rights. Besides, subsidiaries of MNEs are also having an impact with respect to the application of their headquarters' community programs in Turkish society.

The economic and historical roots of Turkey combined with its unique geography have resulted in considerable diversity in its economic, social and cultural dimensions. The aim here is to analyse economics, corporate governance, human capital, environment and community giving by examining CSR reports. We focus on whether and if so how companies explain and share information about these dimensions in their CSR reports.

A review of Turkey's history reveals that a corporate culture of paying attention to the needs of society and allocating resources for their fulfilment dates back to the Ottoman Empire. In those times, "vakıf" were the only social institutions which the religious establishment had formed for humanitarian purposes. Nowadays, companies set up what are called foundations rather than "vakıf" consisting of an institutionalized charity approach in the fields of education, health, and social security (Bikmen, 2003, p. 2). As a legacy from those days, many conglomerate family businesses in Turkey still own a foundation, which they use to channel their social contributions (Bugra, 1994). Moreover, much of the wider society in Turkey perceives socially responsible behaviour by companies, corporate donations, and charity activities as a part of this "foundation culture", believing that firms should conduct charity work so as to improve the welfare of the general population.

By 1980, the Turkish government realized that it would not be possible for it to deliver sustainable development, given the nation's legacy of high inflation, economic crises and military interventions in the preceding era, unless it made significant changes to ensure a stable economy. Hence, from that time onwards, policy changes were made aimed at reducing the state's role in the economy, liberalizing the markets, and competing with the economies of developed countries (Ararat and Ugur, 2003, p. 58). More specifically, increases in exports, liberalization of import regulations, growth of foreign capital investment, flexibility in the exchange rate policy, and privatization were among the most important components of the reforms launched during this period. In 2001, the country went through a serious economic crisis which led to a significant devaluation of its currency and created thousands of unemployed people, particularly in the banking sector, as well as leading to hundreds of small and medium-sized companies going bankrupt (Akyüz and Boratav, 2002). However, the Turkish economy did not go into complete melt down owing to the Central Bank, The Treasury and the Finance Ministry working together to put Turkey back on track.

The Turkish stock exchange is relatively small in absolute terms in comparison with more developed countries, but, perhaps surprisingly, the ratio of the size of its stock market to its GDP is comparable to some European countries, including Germany. This suggests that amongst the developing countries, Turkey has a relatively well developed financial system. Furthermore, in parallel with the growth of the Turkish economy, the capitalization of the Istanbul Stock Exchange National Index increased from US$163 billion to US$240 billion dollars between 2006 and 2013 (Turkish Statistical Institute, 2014). The success of the Turkish economy in recent years has led to very substantial fortunes being made by leading industrialists. In fact, the economic growth in recent years has resulted in Turkish businessmen enlarging their businesses on an international scale, with increasing numbers of global brands starting to outsource their products from Turkey as well as more MNEs deciding to locate in the country. The association of Turkish companies with global brands and the exporting of products to the developed countries has enhanced the need to ensure that these companies are behaving as expected, legally and ethically, as demonstrated by their CSR activities. To this end, some Turkish companies and subsidiaries of MNEs have started to publish CSR reports using the global reporting initiative (GRI) criteria.

The ever-growing participation of Turkey in international agreements like the UN Global Compact as well as its involvement in social and cultural campaigns such as the UNDP private companies community programs has played an important role in increasing awareness and consciousness of CSR and other associated issues throughout the country (UNDP, 2014a). The proliferation of such developments has affected civil society, the business world, the state, and other social stakeholder groups. Moreover, recently the alignment of Turkish legislation on associations and foundations with the "EU acquis" has also accelerated the positive evolution of civil society organizations, by generating a more appropriate environment in the country for civil participation. In sum, Turkey's historical culture in relation to the foundations, its growing voice in the international arena, as well as its economic evolution has led to the business community being effective in terms of its contributions to society. For example, Enka Holding donates 6% of net profit to its foundation, which it uses to open or renovate schools in the countries where it operates.

10.1 Literature review

Why companies decided to adopt CSR can be analysed under the lens of institutional theory. Scott (2001) defined the institutions that can have an impact by shaping the rules within an organization and hence its structure as governments, activists, trade associations, local communities, investors and customers. That is, institutional theorists argue that a society's rules, laws, certification, accreditation, social norms and values drive companies to act with consideration of this external environment so as to optimize their performance (Jepperson, 1991, p. 143; Scott, 1992). Turning to the reasons why companies engage in CSR: first, the literature holds that companies do so in response to institutional pressure to make profit (McWilliams and Siegel, 2000, p. 603; Waddock and Graves, 1997, p. 303). Similarly, Miller and Guthrie (2007) have pointed out that companies adopt CSR strategies in response to the pressures that corporations face in the local institutional environment as they are embedded in its rules.

Second, Werber and Carter (2002) showed that corporations act in socially responsible ways if CEOs have board membership of non-profit organizations and when this is not the case, the connection is lessened, but not eliminated all together. In a similar vein, Galaskiewicz (1997) stressed that when corporations or their managers are members of professional associations that are dedicated to charitable giving, their companies are more likely to invest in charity. Third, in developing countries, companies involve themselves in CSR activities in order to play a pioneering role in helping improve the economic and social system. For example, according to Uyan-Atay's (2012) case study in Turkey, many Turkish holdings mentioned that they have a high responsibility to develop the cultural, economic and social environments. Fourthly, the literature indicates that companies undertake CSR in order to please their stakeholders (Pfeffer and Salancik, 1978, p. 258). For example, the decision to contribute funds to charities and community projects demonstrates that managers are seeking to improve customer and/or investor goodwill (Adams and Hardwick, 1998, p. 641). Accordingly, under this lens, the preferences and expectations of stakeholders shape the way in which companies react to their environment and their CSR is rooted in a strategy aimed at gaining financial and utility benefits.

In sum, taking the institutional and stakeholder theories optics together, whether firms choose to change their policy about their governance structure is influenced by the pressures to copy the arrangements of institutions in order to make a profit, membership of NGOs, philanthropic orientation towards society, and the rearranging of strategies according to the stakeholder's interests.

10.2 Methodology

Qualitative research was used to present the pattern of CSR decisions of companies situated in Turkey with CSR reports representing the main source. In addition, supporting documents were obtained from companies, their websites and various databases. Our sample of interest included companies that publish CSR reports. Examination of the 100 biggest companies situated in Turkey elicited that 16 of them produce a CSR report, two of which are MNE subsidiaries with the rest being Turkish-based companies and 14 of them publish their CSR reports according to GRI criteria. We analysed the CSR reports of 16 companies according to the contribution of the companies in Turkish society based on five major areas, which are economic, corporate governance, human capital, environment and community involvement. The sectorial distribution of the companies is as follows: one pharmaceutical, one beverage, one finance, three petroleum and gas, two technology, one white goods, two construction, one furniture, one consumer goods and three conglomerate companies. Participation of companies from different industries and with different ownership status was required for this research in order to show a wide range of CSR patterns.

10.3 Economic development

Turkey has a growing economy with a $1.358 trillion GDP in 2012. Although there has been a tremendous increase in total GDP since 2006, with Turkey now ranked 15th in the world, when GDP per capita is considered, because of the country's large population, it is ranked 54th across the globe (World Bank, 2012). Moreover, as there is a high wealth inequality, many of its citizens have not benefited from the growth of the last three decades with the wealthiest 10% owning more than 70% of the wealth. Turkey comes fourth in the list of countries which have seen the most rapid rise in wealth inequality since 2000 (Research Credit Suisse, 2014). Turkey's economy started to expand in the 1980s, after the reforms designed by the government to change the economy from an export substitution based model to a more private-sector, market-based open-economy growth model (Saatcioğlu & Karaca, 1994, p. 30).

The success of the economy in recent years has led to very substantial fortunes being made by leading industrialists. Moreover, the economic growth has resulted in many in the Turkish private sector enlarging their businesses on an international scale, with increasing numbers of global brands starting to outsource their products from the nation as well as increasing the numbers of MNEs deciding to locate in the country. Although Turkey has been in the European Union Customs Union since 1995, it is still waiting to be granted full EU membership. In fact, it has been a candidate country undertaking formal accession negotiations with the EU since 2005. In order to bolster its chances of membership, the association of Turkish companies with global brands and the exporting of products to the developed countries have increased the need to ensure that these companies are providing the expected behaviours legally and ethically, as demonstrated by their CSR activities. To this end, some Turkish companies and subsidiaries of MNEs have started to publish CSR reports, in particular using GRI criteria.

Among our sample, profitability was reported by companies as being an important factor that determined whether they felt able to add economic value to society as a whole. All the companies declared their profitability in their CSR reports, with the most influential ones declaring high profits, market share growth and net cash flow. Koç Holding, which has a C+ level GRI report, is the largest conglomerate among the sample with high scores on all these three parameters; in particular, it has the most profitable strategic business units. This firm is in fact Turkey's highest exporting conglomerate company within the automotive, durables, energy and finance industries. In the case of the durables industry, Arçelik is a leading profitable company listed as belonging to Koç Holding and having a B+ level GRI report.

If companies are able to take advantage of government incentives, their economic structure will improve. In particular, if they are helped in having product development or R&D departments, this aids economic profitability and growth. Under Turkey's R&D law, companies can apply to the Scientific and Technological Council of Turkey (TÜBİTAK) for government support if they form an R&D department, which obviously fosters innovation. To date, more than 50% of the R&D projects have been funded by the government. For example, Bilim İlaç (Pharmaceuticals) has an R&D department consisting of 110 engineers, graded as having an A+ level GRI report and they invest 5% of their total budget in their R&D projects. They have developed more than 150 medicines, most of them being generic medicines, hence representing incremental innovations rather than radical ones.

Other companies with R&D departments that have availed themselves of government incentives and showed their R&D subsidies on their balance sheet are from the energy sector, Aygaz, which belongs to Koç Holding; banking sector, Akbank; cement industry, Akçansa and Çimsa, coming under Sabancı Holding and Dogu Holding, respectively; communication industry, Turkcell and Turk Telekom; and from the crude oil refinery sector, Tüpraş, which was initially a state-owned company but today belongs to Koç Holding. Coca Cola and Unilever as MNEs have placed special emphasis on innovation in Turkey, but have centralized R&D departments at their headquarters outside Turkey and hence, do not qualify for government R&D incentives. However, these two MNEs do have product development facilities in Turkey; for example, in their CSR reports Coca Cola undertakes marketing and sales related initiatives along with bottling innovation activities, whilst Unilever has innovation management teams of experts.

10.4 Corporate governance

The Corporate Governance Principles in Turkey are written in the Turkish Trade Act and Capital Markets Law (CMB, 2003) and they parallel world arrangements, primarily the "OECD Governance Principles" of 1999, covering four key aspects: shareholders, public disclosure and transparency, stakeholders and board of directors (CMB, 2003). As such, the principles mainly apply to publicly held joint stock companies, but the implementation is optional. However, conflicts arising from their inadequate implementation and information on whether there is a plan for change in the company's governance practices in the future, should all be included in the annual report and disclosed to the public (Aksoy, 2013, p. 1). Within the framework of the regulations to be enforced by the CMB (Capital Market Boards), the rating institutions conducting the rating of corporate governance are tasked with determining the implementation status of the principals by each firm.

National economic growth is dependent on good and effective company management (Plessis and Luttermann, 2007, p. 215) and firms have to be governed independently. However, this freedom principle has to be limited in the interests of accountability, which is the foundation of corporate governance principles, for these bond the representatives of the company with their stakeholders (Önder, 2003). Well-organized administrative boards help to overcome any problem which may appear and also protect the rights of the stakeholders (Kula, 2006). For this reason, the structure of the administrative board and the level of transparency in the corporate governance rating have to be given in CSR reports (Plessis and Luttermann, 2007, p. 215). In addition, the companies try to arrange their relationship with their stakeholders as part of their CSR policy. For, in order to avoid conflict of interest between the shareholders and corporate management, a good corporate governance principle's adaptation is required. How this adaptation is undertaken has to be explained in the CSR reports. That is, as part of the right to information of stakeholders about the company's transparency policy, CSR's influence on corporate governance has to be underlined in a company's CSR reports.

According to the above, CSR reports in Turkey address two key issues in respect of their governance mechanisms. The first is the degree to which independent members are on the board, whilst the second is the capacity for providing information to the company's stakeholders. In relation to the first matter, we present information regarding the number of independent members in listed and unlisted companies. Among the 12 listed companies, Coca Cola and Arçelik have four independent board members, whilst most of the others have three. However, Akbank has only one and there are three companies (one listed) which do not even have an independent board member. Regarding the other unlisted companies, Opet which has a C level GRI report and Boydaş, which does not apply any criterion in its CSR report, have no independent members. By contrast, Bilim İlaç, which is also unlisted, but published an A+ level GRI report, has a total of four independent members. That is, although this firm is not listed, it recognizes the importance of CSR reporting criteria; in particular, in relation to internalizing their corporate governance rules. It is also important to note that none of the companies have any employee representatives on the board. As a summary, the results show that the application of high criteria of CSR is also associated with an increase in the number of independent directors.

In relation to the second issue about "giving information to stakeholders", we consider two important criteria in the CSR reports. The first is how they explain their "company's transparency policy" and the second is the way they describe their stakeholders. Eight out of the 16 companies turned out not to make any mention of their transparency policy in their CSR report, whereas 12 listed companies in our sample published corporate governance reports in which this information was provided. With respect to those companies that do refer to their transparency policy in their CSR report, they also provide their corporate governance compliance rating for their transparency policy. We observed that companies with the highest score in respect of transparency share their policy regarding this in the CSR report. Regarding the stakeholder policy of our sample, apart from three, all companies list stakeholders in the CSR report as well as underlining their goals in terms of explaining what type of communication strategy they have created in order to ensure that they are meeting the requirements of their stakeholders. The remaining three only gave limited information pertaining to the types of stakeholders such as customers, community, employees and shareholders. However, in respect of the measurement of stakeholder's expectations, only Dogus Holding has carried out an investigation into stakeholder expectations, with its CSR report specifically stating that it has analysed the data for the three stakeholders which are customers, suppliers and employees.

10.5 Human capital

In the latest Human Development Report of 2013, the Human Development Index (HDI) indicates that with a value of 0.722, Turkey is listed in the "High Human Development" category, ranking 90th out of 187 countries. This ranking puts the country behind all EU member states and also below the OECD average. However, Turkey has made a lot of progress with its Millennium Development Goals since 2000. According to the data, extreme poverty below the income level of one dollar per day does not exist anymore. The percentage of poor in 2011 was 2.79% while it was 2.27% in 2012. The unemployment rate was 9.7% in 2014 (UNDP, 2014b) data as compared with 10.8% in France (Eurostat) and 7.1% in the UK (National statistics). OECD data shows that in 2013, there was an increase in the employment rate; especially between the age of 25 and 54, with the rate rising by 5.3% since 2005. We observed an upward trend in employment in Turkey, with respect to working conditions, with private companies taking a lead in the development of human capital, in particular, those who are applying CSR practices.

Information regarding labour force and improvement of HR practices can be found generally in statistical databases, the International Labour Organization (ILO) and in some association's publications. However, the GRI requires comprehensive information regarding human resources at the company level and it transpires that only those firms producing CSR reports share such detailed information. CSR reports encourage companies to act more ethically as well as be transparent and fair towards their employees. In our sample, 13 companies out of 16 stated that employees were their primary and most important stakeholders. Those three companies that did not have GRI application criteria in their CSR reports also did not have much information about their employees. We also observed that companies that experienced the highest level of GRI have more practices geared towards improvements in respect of the HR dimensions than their counterparts. Moreover, all the reviewed companies that published C, B or A level GRI reports provided statistics about the diversity of their workforce. That is, they gave information about such matters as gender, age, turnover rate as well as the number of blue or white collar employees. Three of the firms explicitly mentioned their diversity policy and how they were working to increase equality. Although none of the companies reported salary scales, seven did explain their salary policy. All of these 13 companies emphasizes their security and health policies. In fact, many attempted to provide robust security and health mechanisms that go beyond what is required in occupational health and security law.

Additionally, information regarding recruitment, job enhancement/enrichment, performance appraisal, compensation plans was provided by all 13 companies. However, it was Bilim İlaç with an A+ GRI level CSR report that provided the most comprehensive human resources policy with 104 pages which was half of the total CSR report. The other 12 companies provided such information only at the policy level and not in the form of exact data. When we analysed the given information about human value in the CSR reports, we observed that it was more comprehensive than legal principles as drawn up by the Ministry of Labour and Social Security. Thus, we conclude that companies that have adopted CSR policies have a more ethical approach to human resources than what is required by law.

10.6 Environmental factors

Our climate is changing and, as accepted in the Kyoto Protocol (1997), there is an urgent agenda for governments to be proactive in order to prevent the most important environmental threat of global warming. From transportation to housing, even in people's daily life routines, there are ways to decrease carbon emissions. In fact, climate change and global warming currently represent the world's most important environmental challenges and companies throughout our list declared that they were placing special emphasis on this matter. According to the CSR literature, MNEs operating in emerging markets may choose to respond to local environmental problems as a CSR strategy (Gnyawali, 1996, p. 251) and this is clearly the case when we consider Coca Cola and Unilever's policies in Turkey. For example, Coca Cola stresses the nation's drought problem and highlights its commitment to water management as a beverage company. Moreover, both Coca Cola and Unilever's CSR reports aim to protect the environment by using fewer chemicals, emitting less pollution, and generating alternative cleaner solutions to the extant technologies in Turkey.

Domestic firms also emphasize their being environmentally friendly and the actions they have been taking to address this matter in their CSR reports. For example, Aygaz, which maintains, stocks and fills liquid petroleum gas (LPG) as well as producing pressurized containers, has introduced Aygaz Euro LPG+, which consumes less fuel and is a cleaner energy. Akçansa declares its aim to lower carbon and dust emissions as well as to make investment in alternative fuels, which Çimsa has also pledged. Moreover, Akbank's environmental value added to Turkey is in relation to less usage of water, energy, paper and fewer carbon emissions, for which they have developed the carbon disclosure project (CDP). Arçelik (known as Beko globally) is one of the distinguished examples that has produced energy saving and greener products as well as being an environmentally friendly plant. All of its washing machines, dishwashers, refrigerators and small appliances have A class energy consumption, washing and drying performance. In fact, it produces the world's lowest water consuming machines and the maximum energy efficiency. Bilim İlaç has a well-established environmental plan including management of the environment, waste management, and control of gas emissions and such examples are found across the sample, with every sector reporting applications that can be used for energy saving products or services.

Some firms publish sustainability reports and their environmental concern is highly underlined in these. In particular, Akbank has received the Gold Prize for its reported sustainability policy and was selected as the "most socially and environmentally responsible company of the year" at the Best in Biz Awards, EMEA, 2012. Its substantial efforts have been geared towards decreasing carbon emissions, saving paper and technological waste. In addition, it provides energy-friendly loans that are used for the financing of heating, cooling, renewal of lighting systems, insulation of facades and conversion to environment friendly energy sources of commercial real estate, such as in the case of factories. Moreover, Akbank grants credit to customers who want to buy hybrid cars in Turkey. Waste management and recycling is also an important concern and Akfen Holding has a waste management plan for İzmir airport, with different kinds of waste (medical, cables, food, paper, etc.) being separated and stored for recycling. Similarly, Akçansa has a renewable energy investment project where each day one ton of waste (every kind of waste from plastics to rubber or oil) is processed at its environment and quality laboratories and consequently returned to the economy. This information shows that these companies pursue higher environmental standards than government expectations.

Moreover, firms collaborate with NGOs and universities in order to find ways to protect the environment. Regarding this, given the high threat of earthquake in Turkey, Akçansa facilitates meetings with the Search and Rescue Association (AKUT) with the goal of addressing safety and health concerns at work. In addition, this company holds meetings with the World Wildlife Fund (WWF) Turkey to improve its environmental reputation as its daily production activities cause pollution. Finally, Arçelik collaborates with a Turkish foundation, Combating Soil Erosion for Reforestation and the Protection of Natural Habitats (TEMA), with the aim of extending the nation's forest coverage.

10.7 Community involvement

The most comprehensive research about company's community involvement in Turkey is found in the book "Corporate Community Involvement: A Visible Face of CSR in Practice" (Uyan-Atay, 2013). From the types of corporate community involvement (CCI) as presented in Table 10.1, we can see the degree of motivation for its application in that it is for philanthropic and strategic reasons. It is quite clear that large Turkish holdings have been acting as the pioneers in involving businesses in communities, being spurred on by their highly philanthropic motivation. In our sample, we analysed all the reported community projects and found consistency with Uyan-Atay's contention. In particular, Turkish companies that publish CSR reports with GRI criteria have a high philanthropic motivation. The two multinational companies have, however, a high strategic motivation and prefer to carry out projects in collaboration with their overseas headquarters; Turkish companies that do not have any GRI policy would appear have low strategic and philanthropic motivation. Additionally, the companies that are highly visible (e.g. banks,

Table 10.1 **Companies' GRI levels and corporate community involvement projects**

Company name and level of GRI	Prominent project description	Types of CCI	NGOs	Motivation	Areas
Akbank (C level GRI criteria)	Aims to take a pioneering role in the development of contemporary arts in Turkey. Organizing sustainable projects with universities.	Sponsorship, cause-related marketing, gift-in-kind, philanthropy	Make a Wish (sustainable project), REC (regional environmental centre), Turmepa (Turkish Marine Foundation) and Kagider (Women's Entrepreneur Association of Turkey), TOG (Community Volunteers Foundation)	High strategic, low philanthropic	Culture and art, education and youth, entrepreneurship and environment
Akçansa (B level GRI criteria)	Have sustainable projects; however, they aim to invest in areas where they have operations.	Sponsorship, philanthropy	None	Low strategic, low philanthropic	Education and investment in their own sector
Akfen (none)	Establish art galleries at airports.	Philanthropy, gift-in-kind, sponsorship	UNICEF, TOFD (the Spinal Cord Paralytics Association of Turkey)	Low strategic, low philanthropic	Culture and art, education and sports
Arçelik (B+ level GRI criteria)	Reached 200,000 students studying at 300 regional primary boarding Schools across 60 cities with the Standing United for Education. Granted 275 students scholarships in the reporting period, adding up to 1,283 scholarships in total since the onset of the Vocational Education: A Crucial Matter for the Nation project initiated by Koç Holding.	Corporate volunteerism, philanthropy, gift-in-kind, sponsorship	AYDER (Alternative Life Association), Turmepa (Turkish Marine Foundation), REC (regional environmental centre), GETEM (Assistive Technology and Education Laboratory for Individuals with Visual Disabilities), TEMA (Foundation for Combating Soil Erosion, Reforestation and Protection of Natural Habitats), IKSV (Istanbul Foundation for Culture and Arts)	High philanthropic, high strategic	Education, sports and health

Company name and level of GRI	Prominent project description	Types of CCI	NGOs	Motivation	Areas
Aygaz (C level GRI criteria)	Renovates regional health centres. Organizes "The cautious child-creating awareness against accidents" campaign.		ÇADD (the Child and Adolescent Diabetic Association), TAP (the Family Health and Planning Foundation), IKSV (Istanbul Foundation for Culture and Arts)	High philanthropic, high strategic	Education, culture and arts, health and sports
Bilim İlaç (A+ level GRI criteria)	1,051 employees out of 1,950 are community volunteers. To date, Bilim İlaç with 26,614 hours of employees' volunteerism touches 37,911 people's lives in the Turkish community.	Corporate volunteerism, philanthropy, sponsorship	Diabetic Foundation, TEMA (Foundation for Combating Soil Erosion, Reforestation and Protection of Natural Habitats, REC (regional environmental centre), Alzheimer's Foundation	High philanthropic, low strategic	Environment, education, children, sports and health
Boytaş (none)	Have completed 20 projects with high schools/universities in order to satisfy their needs and, using employee knowledge, they have given lectures.	Corporate volunteerism, philanthropy	None	Low strategic, low philanthropic	Education and health

Coca-Cola (A+ level GRI criteria)	Transferred 3% of pre-tax profit, TL 1,600,000 to the Coca-Cola Life Plus Foundation and Anadolu Education and Social Aid Foundation. Donated $100,000 to the Employee Donations Contribution Fund. They launched the "1 TL Us, 2 TL CCI" campaign, aimed at increasing employee donations to natural disaster relief implementations following the earthquake in the Van region. With a similar campaign, the aim is to expand employee donations as part of an aid campaign to combat starvation in Africa. Coca-Cola's "Resetting the Indus" initiative instigated the building of schools, homes and a sewage system, with a donation of $28,000.	Sponsorship, philanthropy corporate volunteerism, gift-in-kind,	Coca-Cola Life Plus Foundation, Active Life Foundation, YADA Foundation, Anadolu Foundation, Aegean Foundation, WWF, ecodosd	High strategic, low philanthropic	Sports, health, environment and education
Çimsa (B level GRI criteria)	Five volunteer teams in five plants started the journey by adding their signatures to many projects carried out in cooperation with different civil society organizations. For example, after determining the needs of Çimsa Cement employee families and the region community they devoted time and money to social and cultural development. More than 200 Çimsa volunteers reached more than 1,500 people.	Philanthropy, sponsorship	Turkish Education Volunteers Foundation, ÇEDBİK (Turkish Green Building Council), SKD (sustainable development association), TURMEPA (Turkish Marine Foundation)	Low strategic, low philanthropic	Environment, education, arts and health

Company name and level of GRI	Prominent project description	Types of CCI	NGOs	Motivation	Areas
Dogus Group (none)	Para Durumu (first financial literacy initiative of Turkey that reaches out to the masses).	Philanthropy, sponsorship, corporate volunteerism	KAGIDER (Women's Entrepreneurs Association of Turkey), TOBB (The Union of Chambers and Commodity Exchanges of Turkey), AÇEV (The Mother Child Education Foundation), TURMEPA (Turkish Marine Environment Protection Association)	High strategic, high philanthropic	Art, music, education, children, environment, entrepreneurship, health and sports
Koc holding (B level GRI criteria)	Approximately 16 projects related to education, health and culture are undertaken under Vehbi Koc Foundation.	Philanthropy, sponsorship, corporate volunteerism, gift-in-kind	TEV (Turkish Educational Foundation) – Koc Holding has been providing support for education since the 1960s. TEGEV (Educational Volunteers)	High strategic, high philanthropic	Art, music, education, children, environment, health and sports
Opet (B level GRI criteria)	Under the name of "Conscious Society Projects" Opet has undertaken: Respect for the History Project, Green Road Project, Exemplary. Village Project and Clean Toilet Campaign.	Sponsorship, cause-related marketing	None	High strategic, low philanthropic	Sport, culture and arts, environment and education

Turkcell (C level GRI criteria)	The "Snowdrops", developed by Turkcell jointly with the Association in Support of Contemporary Living in 2000, is a scholarship project aimed at providing equal opportunities in education for underprivileged girls mainly in rural areas of Turkey. With Snowdrops, Turkcell's long-term goal is to decrease female illiteracy in Turkey by providing social, financial and moral support to 10,000 young Turkish women each year.	Philanthropy, sponsorship, corporate volunteerism, cause-related marketing	ÇYDD (The association supporting contemporary life)	High strategic, high philanthropic	Education, sport, entrepreneurship, employability and career, culture and art and support for disadvantaged groups
Turk Telekom (none)	Turk Telekom adds value to social life with "Value To Turkey" social responsibility projects implemented throughout the country, in addition to investments in technology, infrastructure and human resources, such as book on the phone, which is the first telephone library in Turkey for visually impaired people.	Sponsorship, gift-in-kind, philanthropy	GETEM (Bogaziçi University Technology and Education Laboratory for the Visually Impaired)	Low strategic, high philanthropic	Education, internet, support for deaf people, environment, sports, awareness for earthquakes and health
Tüpraş (C level criteria)	Umbrella movement: 100 smiling faces in Batman project aimed at reaching students facing social integration challenges due to financial problems, illiteracy and insufficient parental care as well as families who are unable to provide for their children. Moreover, it is geared towards teachers who have limited access to resources in order to raise awareness in areas such as personal and professional development as well as adolescent psychology.	Gift-in-kind, philanthropy, sponsorship	TEMA (Foundation for Combating Soil Erosion, Reforestation and Protection of Natural Habitats)	Low strategic, high philanthropic	Education, health, environment, sports, disabled people and art and culture

Company name and level of GRI	Prominent project description	Types of CCI	NGOs	Motivation	Areas
Unilever **(none)**	The "fun, learn, hygiene" project aims to educate 225,000 children and touch over 1,000,000 people within 3 years. Improving oral health and nutrition advancement programs are other projects.	Cause-related marketing, gift-in-kind, sponsorship.	TGEV (Educational Volunteers), WWF, KETEM (cancer early diagnosis screening and training centre	High strategic, low philanthropic	Health, education and environment

manufacturers or white goods and automobiles and oil and petroleum producers), besides their highly benevolent motivation would also appear to be acting strategically when carrying out their projects. Table 10.1 summarizes the issues of interest in CSR, covering types, areas, sources and motivation of involvement as well as providing examples of good practice. It can be observed that eight companies have developed sustainable projects, which are well thought through and organized. Some companies that have allocated employee time resources have a preference for undertaking collaboration projects with NGOs. In addition, some have established websites for their projects, which show how they want to address as many people's needs as possible by getting whole communities involved.

All the firms in our sample are providing sponsorship in one way or another to society. Even if they do not publish a CSR report, they give relief money for sudden events like earthquakes or donate old equipment or their products for schools, which appears to be a much-favoured form of involvement. We also observed companies mostly work with a very limited number of NGOs, some of which were established by Turkish holdings. However, willingness to participate in NGOs amongst the Turkish population as a whole is very low, with 87% of them expressing the opinion that people are not interested in supporting their activities (Directorate General of Foundations, 2014). Additionally, research has shown that only 9.7% of Turkish citizens are members of NGOs and only 7.1% are volunteers (Third Sector Foundation of Turkey, 2013). We observed that when a company's community project is overlapping with the main activities of an NGO, they often opt to undertake their projects jointly. In addition, we would argue that private companies' community projects have a positive influence on society in terms of improving public perception. It has also been contended that associations established by Turkish holding companies working collaboratively with NGOs tend to have more professional management teams (Uyan-Atay, 2014). Multinational companies mostly prefer to carry out projects either with multinational NGOs or Turkish subsidiaries of those NGOs or alternatively, in order to continue headquarters' community projects, they may act as pioneers by establishing a new NGO and working with it.

Areas for donations is another important factor regarding our sample companies with all 16 stating that they prefer to do so within their sector. This is especially the case for multinational companies who strategically invest in the areas where they see the necessity to invest in order to increase the knowledge of their brand. However, most of the local firms are investing in education, with some of the larger ones in particular, undertaking sustainable projects in this sphere. Sports sponsorship, whereby companies invest in sports teams is also on the increase, but none of these companies is investing in sports or sportsmen/women in a sustainable manner. Another important factor worth mentioning concerns those companies that have CSR reports without GRI criteria. These companies do not have any structured community projects, they have no long-term projects and they do not invest large amounts of resources.

10.8 Reflections on development-oriented CSR

From the 1980s onwards, Turkey shifted to being an export-led growth economy and through a range of liberalization programs during which many reforms were carried out. This led to a marked increase in the number of private companies, entrance of the subsidiaries of MNEs into the country and improved trade in the international marketplace. These changes resulted in imports outstripping exports, that is, there was a trade deficit. Moreover, although the economy grew rapidly, short-term debt rose sharply and Turkey had to be bailed out by strict IMF economic programs, which accelerated privatization of state economic enterprises and consequently significantly reduced governmental influence in health, education and culture spheres. In its place, private companies and MNEs began to play an extensive role in the areas of education, health, culture, sports, art, and development of youth programs among others. For example, General Electric's president in Turkey at an innovation conference in 2014 declared that their company has been investing in collaborations with universities and local companies in order to increase the employment rate with the aim of boosting production in Turkey. She also said that the private sector could not wait for government intervention and that it had to take up the responsibility of investing in innovation. For, by so doing, Turkey could increase its export level and hence this awareness had to be instilled in private companies.

Other private companies have been acting as social agents in areas where government resources are very limited, such as Borusan Holding, which has supported the arts by establishing the Borusan Philharmonic Orchestra and Enka Holding sponsored Şahika Ercüment, who broke the world record for diving. In fact, almost all large private companies sponsor various students in the educational area and some have opened universities. Sabancı and Koç Holding, through their foundations, have opened museums that exhibit international artists. However, the influence of the private sector on Turkish society is being hindered by the government, which has recently increasingly clamped down on freedom of speech and refused to support progressive legislation in a number of areas. According to Freedom House reports, the press in Turkey is "not free" (BBC News, 2014) and the Gezi Park protests in June 2013, resulted in growing censorship of the Turkish media. Moreover, social media has been clamped down and for more than two years the government has banned YouTube (Freedom House Turkey Report, 2014). Last year, a clamp down began on freedom of speech with the government increasingly intransigent when it comes to addressing social, environmental and political concerns. For instance, various NGOs have been putting in a lot of work on animal rights in collaboration with private companies but the government is refusing to pass protective animal laws. The same can be said of social security law and women's rights. Regarding health and safety at work, many people have attributed the disastrous explosion at the Soma mine to the Turkish government's refusal to sign the International Labour Organization agreement on worker's rights. This reflects the situation that there are tremendous gaps in the government's approach to addressing social needs learning and tremendous scope and leeway for private companies to intervene with development-oriented CSR. Some companies, because they work internationally, carry out CSR reporting and apply the social security law found at the international level. Given these circumstances, it would appear that Turkish conglomerates, listed Turkish companies and MNE subsidiaries are well ahead of the law and are lobbying for the modernization of Turkish legislation so that it conforms with international norms and values.

10.9 Conclusion

This chapter has investigated CSR practices in Turkey. Our findings reveal the uniqueness of Turkey being an amalgam of a Westernized and Middle Eastern society, which influences its CSR practices. That is, our data shows that Turkish companies have started to compile CSR reports because developed Western counterparts do so and it is perceived as a requirement to be accepted in the international arena. However, the domestic Turkish institutional environment does not put any pressure on companies to publish CSR reports and so only the biggest firms who wish to expand beyond Turkey's borders have an incentive to do so. Foreign MNEs only focus on developing community projects such as sponsorship or cause-related marketing. These projects are geared towards increasing market share and hence profits, rather than for pure philanthropic reasons. By contrast, Turkish companies, sometimes working with NGOs, recognize they have a responsibility to provide investment and support for the less fortunate as the government has yet to develop a welfare system that provides for all. That is, many domestic firms not only pursue economic and reputational benefits through their CSR activities, but accept they have a philanthropic duty to help in the building of the nation as a whole. This study has revealed serious shortcomings in CSR reporting in Turkey. Although we have observed that the biggest companies are showing increasing concern regarding aspects of CSR, very few of them are publishing CSR reports and even those that are do not generally do so on an annual basis. Moreover, the data in this study shows that CSR in Turkey is in a transition stage. It is important that Turkish companies wanting to operate in developed countries are aware that practices in those countries are at a more mature stage. For instance, they should look to publishing a CSR report every year based on one or more of the frameworks that have been developed according to various reporting guidelines such as Global Reporting Initiatives, The Fair Labour Association, Good Corporation's Standard and the United Nations Global Compact.

10.10 Policy implications

The government needs to play a constructive role in the development of CSR practices. Although the Turkish stock exchange is encouraging companies to publish corporate governance reports, the guidelines for CSR practices are not obligatory and in our view the government should make them so. To this end, it should instruct the stock exchange to employ indices similar to FTSE4GOOD, the Dow Jones Sustainability Group, and AccountAbility, which use GRI criteria, thereby increasing the transparency of the activities of Turkish firms both domestically and internationally. This will raise the profile of CSR and hopefully, lead to Turkish stakeholders becoming more actively engaged in ensuring that firms are meeting their responsibilities to society.

10.11 Proposals for further research

Although there are existing CSR studies in developing countries, this is one of the few that have investigated CSR reports and consequently, there needs to be further research of this type. In particular, it would prove beneficial to carry out a comparative study with other developing countries to identify the similarities and differences in their CSR reporting and activities. Second, the data used in this study only covers a single accounting period and therefore can only reflect time-specific effects, which do not capture the dynamics of CSR in Turkey today nor changes in the country's economic fortune. Therefore, a longitudinal study is needed to redress this.

Bibliography

Adams, M., & Hardwick, P. (1998). An analysis of corporate donations: United Kingdom evidence. *Journal of Management Studies*, 35(5), 641-654.

Aksoy, M.A. (2013). Under Turkish corporate governance regulations, capital marked board of directors, Gazi University. *Journal of Law Faculty*, 17(1-2). Retrieved from http://webftp.gazi.edu.tr/hukuk/dergi/17_1-2_3.pdf.

Akyüz, Y., & Boratav, K. (2002). The Making of the Turkish Financial Crisis. Discussion presented at the United Nations Conference on Trade and Development, No. 158. Retrieved from http://content.csbs.utah.edu/~ehrbar/erc2002/pdf/i049.pdf.

Ararat, M., & Ugur, M. (2003). Corporate governance in Turkey: an overview and some policy recommendations. *Corporate Governance: International Journal of Business in Society*, 3(1), 58-75.

BBC News (2014). Press is Not Free in Turkey. Retrieved from http://www.bbc.co.uk/turkce/haberler/2014/05/140501_freedom_house.

Bikmen, F. (2003). Corporate philanthropy in Turkey: Building on tradition, adapting to change. *SEAL—Social Economy and Law Project Journal*, Autumn, 2.

Bugra, A. (1994). *State and Business in Modern Turkey: A Comparative Study*, New York, US: State University of New York Press.

CMB (Capital Markets Board of Turkey) (2003). Turkish Trade Act and Capital Markets Law, Corporate Governance Principles of Turkey. Retrieved from http://www.cmb.gov.tr/ displayfile.aspx?action=displayfile&pageid=84&fn=84.pdf&submenuheader=-1.

Directorate General of Foundations (2014). Statistics on Associations. Retrieved from http:// www.dernekler.gov.tr/index.php?option=com_content&view=article&id=148%3Ayllara-goere-faal-dernek-saylar-adet&catid=52%3Agrafikler&Itemid=67&lang=tr, last accessed 30th April 2014.

European Commission Eurostat (2014). Unemployment Statistics. Retrieved from http:// epp.eurostat.ec.europa.eu/statistics_explained/index.php/Unemployment_statistics.

Freedom House (2014). Freedom of Press and Internet in Turkey. Retrieved from http://www. freedomhouse.org/country/turkey#.VCkjmOAcTIU.

Galaskiewicz, J. (1997). An urban grants economy revisited: corporate charitable contributions in the twin cities 1979–81, 1987–89. *Administrative Science Quarterly*, 42, 445-471.

Gnyawali, D.R. (1996). Corporate social performance: an international perspective. In S.B. Prasad & B.K. Boyd (Eds.), *Advances in International Comparative Management* (pp. 251–273). Greenwich: JAI Press.

Jepperson, R.L. (1991). Institutions, institutional effects and institutionalism. In W.W. Powell, & P.J. DiMaggio (Eds.), *The New Institutionalism in Organizational Analysis* (pp. 143-163). Chicago: University of Chicago Press.

Kula, V. (2006). *Kurumsal Yönetim: Hissedarların Korunması Uygulamaları ve Türkiye Örneği.* (Istanbul, Turkey: Papatya Publishing.

Kyoto Protocol (1997). United Nations Framework Convention on Climate Change. Retrieved from https://unfccc.int/kyoto_protocol/items/2830.php.

McWilliams, A., & Siegel, D. (2000). Research notes and communications corporate social responsibility and financial performance: correlation or misspecification. *Strategic Management Journal*, 21, 603-609.

Miller, J.I., & Guthrie, D. (2007). The Rise of Corporate Social Responsibility: An Institutional Response to Labor, Legal and Shareholder Environments. *Social Science Research Council.* Retrieved from http://pages.stern.nyu.edu/~dguthrie/papers/csr/2007-institutionalresponse.pdf, last accessed 12th October 2009.

OECD (2014). Statistical Profile Turkey, Employment Data. Retrieved from http://www.oecd-ilibrary.org/economics/country-statistical-profile-turkey_20752288-table-tur.

Önder, Z. (2003). Türkiye'de Sermaye Piyasaları ve Kurumsal Şirket yönetimi, kurumsal Şirket Yönetimi. Paper Presented at the Corporate Governance Conference, Ankara, Turkey, 14–18 April.

Pfeffer, J., & Salancik, G.R. (1978). *The External Control of Organizations: A Resource Dependence Perspective*. New York, US: Harper & Row Publishers.

Plessis, J.D., & Luttermann C. (2007). *German Corporate Governance in International and European Context*. Berlin, Germany: Springer.

Research Credit Suisse (2014). Retrieved from http://www.hurriyetdailynews.com/wealth-inequality-deepens-in-emerging-world-including-turkey.aspx?pageID=238&nID=73029 &NewsCatID=344.

Saatcioğlu C., & Karaca, O. (1994). Causality relationship between Exports and Growth in Turkey: Effect of transformation in 1980, Yönetim. Retrieved from http://isletmeiktisadi. istanbul.edu.tr/wp-content/uploads/2013/04/Yonetim-49-2004-3.pdf.

Scott, W.R. (1992). *Organizations: Rational, Natural and Open systems* (3rd Edition). Englewood Cliffs, NJ: Prentice-Hall.

Scott, W.R. (2001). *Institutions and Organizations*. Thousand Oaks: Sage Publications.

Third Sector Foundation of Turkey. (2013). State of Civil Society Report. Retrieved from http://socs.civicus.org/?p=3552.

Turkish Statistical Institute (2014). Statistical Data About Turkey's Stock Exchange. Received from http://www.tuik.gov.tr/PreTablo.do?alt_id=1064.

United Nations Development Programme (UNDP) (2014a). Human Development Index (HDI). Retrieved from http://hdr.undp.org/en/content/human-development-index-hdi.

United Nations Development Programme (UNDP) (2014b). Unemployment Rate. Retrieved from http://unstats.un.org/unsd/demographic/products/socind.

Uyan-Atay, B. (2013). *Corporate Community Involvement: A Visible Face of CSR in Practice.* UK: Gower Publishing Limited.

Uyan-Atay, B. (2014). The role of NGOs in the improvement of the Turkish labour market. In R. Blanpain (Ed.), *Readings on Labour and Employment Relations.* The Netherlands: Wolters Kluwer.

Waddock, S., & Graves, S. (1997). The corporate social performance-financial performance link. *Strategic Management Journal,* 18(4), 303-319.

Werber, J.D., & Carter, S.M. (2002). The CEO`s influence on corporate foundation giving. *Journal of Business Ethics,* 40, 47-60.

World Bank (2012). Data about Turkey. Retrieved from http://data.worldbank.org/country/turkey.

11

CSR and sexual and reproductive health

A case study among women workers in the football manufacturing industry of Sialkot, Pakistan

Sara Husain
The Aga Khan University Hospital, Pakistan

Peter Lund-Thomsen
Copenhagen Business School, Denmark

In this chapter, we address an under-explored issue in the literature on corporate social responsibility (CSR) in developing countries; namely, the extent to which local suppliers that are integrated into global value chains pay attention to the sexual and reproductive health of female workers employed in export-oriented industries. Using the high-profile football manufacturing industry in Sialkot, Pakistan as our case study, we explore whether, and if so, how CSR initiatives in this industry have addressed sexual and reproductive health needs of female football stitchers labouring at the base of the global football manufacturing value chain.

Football is a global sport enjoyed by millions of supporters around the world (FIFA, 2012). Football manufacturing was concentrated in the northern hemisphere until the early 1970s when mass production of footballs was relocated to sites in Asia including India, Pakistan, Thailand and China (UNComtrade, 2011). In the area of handstitched footballs, Pakistan emerged as a major exporter accounting for almost 80% of global production at the turn of the millennium (Khan, 2004). The Pakistani football manufacturing industry is located in the city of Sialkot in the province of Punjab. Today the industry is home to approximately 390 football manufacturers, most of which are small and medium-sized enterprises that sell footballs to Europe, North America, Africa, Latin America, Russia, and the Middle East (Lund-Thomsen and Nadvi, 2009). From a development perspective, the industry is interesting, because it has been the subject of various interventions aimed at eradicating child labour and improving the rights of workers within the industry. Some of these have involved multistakeholder initiatives including agencies such as the International Labour Organization (ILO), the United Nations Children Fund (UNICEF), local industry bodies such as the Sialkot Chamber of Commerce of Industry, and NGOs such as Save the Children (Lund-Thomsen and Nadvi, 2010a).

In this chapter, we describe initiatives that are aimed at integrating economic, social, or environmental considerations into the core business practices of companies as corporate social responsibility (CSR) initiatives (Lund-Thomsen, 2004). In the case of Sialkot, these have been extensively documented in earlier writings on the industry. For example, some work has explored the individual CSR efforts of corporate brands such as Nike in its supply chain in Sialkot (Lund-Thomsen, 2013; Lund-Thomsen and Coe, 2013). Within this literature, a particular theme of interest has been the effect of CSR interventions on women workers, especially how some female football stitchers have been excluded from the football manufacturing process as a result of the introduction of centralized production facilities (in the form of factories and village-based stitching centres). In fact, many female football stitchers were not allowed by their male family members to venture outside their homes in the villages surrounding Sialkot in search of continued employment within the industry. This happened when the football stitching process was being concentrated within centralized village-based stitching centres or factories with the aim of facilitating the monitoring of the absence/presence of child labour within the industry in the late 1990s (Khan, 2007; Lund-Thomsen, 2013; Lund-Thomsen and Nadvi, 2010a; Lund-Thomsen and Nadvi, 2010b).

In this chapter, we add to this literature on CSR in the Sialkot football manufacturing cluster by focusing on the unexplored issue of the sexual and reproductive health of female football stitchers. In doing so, we also contribute to the broader literature on critical perspectives on CSR in developing countries that has mostly highlighted the difference between the intended and the actual outcomes of CSR interventions for companies, workers, and communities in developing countries, the types of issues that CSR initiatives addressed and/or largely ignored, and the broader structural limitations embedded in managerialist approaches to working with CSR in developing countries (Blowfield and Frynas, 2005; Newell and Frynas,

2007). As a contribution to this literature, our chapter examines the extent to which CSR initiatives in the football manufacturing industry of Pakistan address or overlook the sexual and reproductive health concerns of female football stitchers. We focus on this issue in relation to female stitchers as football stitching is the most labour-intensive part of the football manufacturing process (Lund-Thomsen, 2013). To the best of our knowledge, this issue has so far not been discussed in the literature on critical perspectives on CSR in developing countries.

In the first section of the chapter, we establish an analytical framework for understanding how the sexual and reproductive health challenges faced by female football stitchers are shaped by the interaction between broader global forces (global value chains in the football manufacturing industry) and a particular national socio-economic and socio-cultural context in the developing world (i.e. Pakistan). We then outline the context and methodology used for this study before analysing our empirical data in the light of our analytical framework. Finally, the conclusion outlines our main findings, the research, and policy implications flowing from our analysis.

11.1 The context of football manufacturing in Pakistan

Concentrated in Sialkot, a relatively small district located along the north-eastern border of Punjab province near India, the Pakistani football manufacturing industry is mostly comprised of small family-owned businesses established in the late 19th and early 20th centuries (Nadvi *et al.*, 2011). The early 1970s witnessed a large increase in football orders in the industry at a time when nationalist and labour movements were gaining popularity in Pakistan under the populist leadership of Prime Minister Zulfiqar Ali Bhutto. At that time, football stitching used to take place inside the factories in the central part of Sialkot. However, fearing that labour unions would disrupt production and demand increased wages, the football entrepreneurs decided to outsource the process of football stitching to home-based locations in the villages surrounding the city (Khan, 2007). This arrangement allowed for lowering the cost of production as the labour management function was transferred to subcontractors who could call upon a flexible, non-unionized workforce in Sialkot's villages to stitch footballs in accordance with the changing patterns of international demand. With the outsourcing of the stitching process, what was once a factory-based profession became a cottage industry, involving all family members including women and children in villages surrounding the city (Khan, 2004).

In the mid-1990s, international media reports highlighted the widespread use of child labour within home-based football stitching in Pakistan (ILRF, 2010). In response to these developments, a multistakeholder initiative known as the

"Atlanta Agreement" was signed in 1997 with the aim of eradicating child labour from the industry. This initiative involved international brands, NGOs, the Sialkot Chamber of Commerce and Industry, International Labour Organization (ILO) and the United Nations Children Fund (UNICEF).

The Atlanta Agreement envisaged a re-organization of the football stitching value chain in Sialkot. Changes included shifting football stitching out of home-based locations to designated village-based stitching centres, enrolment of children engaged in football stitching in local NGO operated schools and the provision of income-generation alternatives for families losing the money earned by their children through football stitching (Lund-Thomsen and Nadvi, 2010a).

Today the geography of global football production is determined by a small number of leading global brands which determine the kinds of footballs to be produced, the location of production, the quantity, and the price (Nadvi *et al.*, 2011). Local suppliers in Sialkot dealing directly with large international brands have altered their value chains to meet the CSR guidelines promoted by brands as they risk losing business from customers in Europe and North America if they fail to comply with these demands. Smaller industrial units catering for non-branded football production have fewer incentives to re-centralize operational set-up and have continued to out-source football stitching to home-based workers (Lund-Thomsen and Nadvi, 2010a).

The Atlanta Agreement, the CSR demands of international buyers, and the introduction of machine-stitching in the football manufacturing industry of Sialkot has now resulted in a three-tier football stitching value chain in the cluster (see Figure 11.1). Factories either undertake all stages of football production in-house in the city centre (including the stitching process) or have factory-owned stitching centres and/or centres managed by subcontractors in the villages surrounding Sialkot. Factories are subject to rules of national labour laws and the CSR requirements of international brands including the right to receive a minimum wage, over-time payment, social insurance (health and safety as well as pension insurance) and other worker benefits (Lund-Thomsen, 2013).

Small and medium-sized factories have adopted a more piece-meal approach to outsourcing to registered stitching centres, retaining quality checks, lamination, branding and packing of final products in-house. Whereas some stitching centres were registered and factory-owned, many are operated independently by supervisors or "makers" (subcontractors). Housing a smaller number of workers than larger production units, these centres lack formal contracts with specific football manufacturers and take on orders from different companies while recruiting and supervising stitchers on a piece rate basis. There is often a hierarchy of middle-men involved in the football manufacturing value chain from the factory to the individual worker (Khan, 2007). Home-based workers are mostly linked to independent contractors who accept job work from football manufacturing units that tend to sell into the local Pakistani market. Centre-based and home-based stitchers labour on piece rates, with monthly incomes declining noticeably from factory to centre-based and then home-based work. Lacking a formalized working relationship with their

Figure 11.1 **Production structure of Pakistan's football industry**
Source: Adapted from Lund Thomsen (2013)

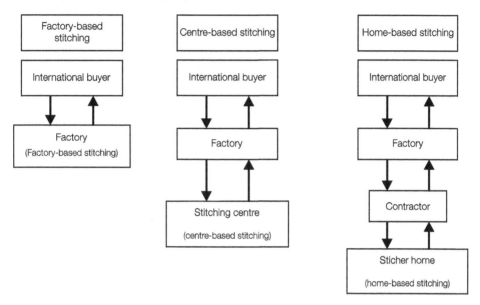

employers, home-based and centre-based football stitchers negotiate with contractors who in-turn have limited authority and incentives to grant benefits or represent workers to negotiate better rates with factory owners (Lund-Thomsen, 2013). Figure 11.1 presents an overview of the football stitching value chain in Sialkot.

11.2 Methodology

We used a qualitative methodology to understand the extent to which CSR initiatives of local football manufacturers addressed the sexual and reproductive health concerns of female football stitchers in Sialkot. We undertook a longitudinal study, with our fieldwork stretching from 2008 to 2013. Data collection involved a total of 132 interviews with a range of stakeholders including international buyers, their local sourcing offices/partners in Pakistan, supplier firms in Sialkot, contractors, workers, government representatives, staff from United Nations agencies, NGOs, and trade unions with a field-based presence in Sialkot. Our interviews with male and female football stitchers included factory-based, centre-based, and home-based stitchers and were undertaken as both individual and focus group interviews.

The interviews with local manufacturers touched upon a range of issues including the sourcing and CSR relationships of international buyers and local suppliers in Sialkot. We also attempted to understand whether the CSR policies implemented

Table 11.1 **Primary data collected in Sialkot, 2008–2013**

International sports buyers	5
Local sourcing offices	2
Donors, government officials, and NGOs	15
Managers of football production units	14
Academia and researchers	2
Contractors	8
IMAC and SCCI	3
Healthcare providers	3
Factory-based stitchers	14
Centre-based stitchers	19
Home-based stitchers	17
Focus group discussions	15
Males	9
Females	6
Total	132

by different manufactures in factory, centre or home-based settings addressed the sexual and reproductive health concerns of female stitchers (Table 11.1). In our conversations with government officials, United Nations representatives, NGO staff, and local health care providers, we discussed the priorities, policies, and field-level support activities of these actors that were present in the cluster. Finally, our worker interviews touched upon topics such as wages, work hours, overtime payments, freedom of association, collective bargaining, and social insurance, as well as the sexual and reproductive health challenges faced by both male and female football stitchers in Sialkot.

Information sought on the sexual and reproductive health of workers included their choice of and access to care providers, care during pregnancy, delivery and post-natal services, uptake of family planning methods, occurrence and management of sexually transmitted infections and access to information on sexual and reproductive health. In this chapter, we thus draw mainly upon information collected through 15 focus group interviews with male and female football stitchers[1] (11 in 2008, 4 in 2013) to identify currently prevailing sexual and reproductive

1   Keeping in view cultural sensitivities, separate focus group discussions were conducted among male and female workers. Additionally, the difference of experiences between married and unmarried participants, led participant groups to be further sub-divided depending on marital status. Ages of unmarried participants ranged between 17–25 years, while married participants tended to be older, with ages ranging between 25–40 years.

health issues in the industry. These focus group interviews were conducted on holidays, when the football factories were closed and football stitchers were invited to join with the assistance of a local NGO. Attending stitchers came from all stitching sites, including home-based stitchers and those engaged in more formal stitching at stitching centres and factory settings. A break-down of the interviews carried out as part of the study is contained in Table 11.1.

Interview guides were developed on the basis of our pre-existing knowledge of the football manufacturing industry in Pakistan and the sexual and reproductive health challenges facing women in Punjab province, Pakistan. These interview guides were pre-tested in Sialkot and translated into Urdu[2] before undertaking data collection for the project. Transcripts and field notes were written in Urdu/Punjabi by the lead author of this chapter. Field notes were later transcribed in InPage, analysed for content and translated at the time of analysis. Initial themes evolving from the notes were identified as "sub-nodes" and with progressive analysis, categories tying together experiences were linked to form "nodes". As a final step, nodes were used to develop themes for discussion and presentation of field data. Secondary sources of information included journal articles, reports of United Nations agencies, and local NGOs involved in CSR reporting and monitoring in Pakistan. In the next section, we go on to conceptualize how many of the Sialkot-based actors that we interviewed for the study were integrated into global value chains linking international consumers, buyers, suppliers, contractors, and workers in the global football manufacturing value chains.

11.3 Towards an analytical framework

The literature on global value chains focuses on how the design, manufacturing, distributing, marketing, and consumption of goods and services takes place in global value chains that link consumers and international retailers/supermarkets in so-called developed countries with suppliers, contractors, and workers in the developing world (Rossi, 2014). This literature sees global value chains as being controlled by multinational corporations headquartered in Europe or North America that determine the profile and quantity of products, technical inputs and social/environmental conditions under which production takes place in the lower ties of the value chain in the developing world (Cattaneo *et al.*, 2013). From this point of view, suppliers from developing countries are often described in the literature as occupying inferior, lesser-value added roles than those of international retailers/supermarkets that drive global value chains. Hence, developing country suppliers are often competing with firms in other developing nations with the aim of attracting orders from Western buyers(Schmitz 2006).

---

2 The national and most widely spoken and understood language in Pakistan

In order to survive in this immensely competitive environment, local firms face strategic choices. On the one hand, they can choose a path of industrial upgrading (i.e. improving the quality of their products, production processes, moving into higher value added functions or transferring skills learned in one industry to gain competitive advantage in another industry). This literature describes this path of industrial development as a prerequisite for improving wages and work conditions in export-oriented industries in developing countries. On the other hand, local firms can also pursue a so-called downgrading strategy; (i.e. producing inferior products, using out-dated production technologies and squeezing wages and worker's conditions with the aim of gaining an edge in highly competitive international markets) (Schmitz, 2004). Within this broader context, the participation of women workers in global value chains might provide them with more income generation opportunities, thereby offering greater possibilities for influencing key choices in their lives (Said-Allsopp and Tallontire, 2014). However, the Achilles heel of women's participation in global value chains is that they are often more exposed to job insecurity, flexibilization of labour practises, and precarious work conditions than men. Whereas men tend to occupy more stable, full-time jobs at the base of global value chains, women are sometimes more likely to be employed in part-time positions that allow them to combine their work in the sphere of production (i.e. the workplace) with that of social reproduction (child rearing and domestic household work) (Barrientos, 2003).

It is within this broader context of the gendering of global value chains that we must analyse the sexual and reproductive health challenges faced by women workers. By sexual and reproductive health, we mean a range of concerns from family planning and safe motherhood to prevention of sexually transmitted infections and gender violence which could set the stage for rapid gains in human development. In fact, global value chains are not only "global" in nature, but they are also "touch down" in place-bound socio-economic contexts of work and employment in the developing world (Carswella and Neveb, 2013; Neilson and Pritchard, 2009). In other words, male and female workers at the base of global value chains are not labouring in isolation from the broader social networks and the informal norms and values that guide their participation in both the spheres of production and social reproduction (Coe and Jordhus-Lier, 2011).

In this regard, sexual and reproductive health is an important aspect of an individual's life that is influenced by gendered norms, roles and responsibilities (Sagarra et al., 2007). In fact, sexual health and reproductive needs evolve over time, moving from good nutrition and hygiene in the formative years to the ability and freedom of making choices over the course of the reproductive years; impacting human development, health, poverty, acquisition of skills and life opportunities. Cultural practices of male domination place women at risk of proxy decision-making, restrictive behavioural norms and at worst, sexual exploitation and violence at home and the workplace, all of which negatively impact their health (Kabeer et al., 2008; Sagarra et al., 2007).

Women's health and productive capacity is also intricately linked with their social status (Kandiyoti, 1998). For instance, Pakistan is part of the "classic patriarchy belt" running through most of the Middle East and South Asia, characterized by a firm belief in the traditional extended family model where the male head of the household is the obligatory provider, protector and decision-maker of all family members, particularly women and children. Statistics reveal the systematic exclusion of girls and women from decision-making spaces which is reflected in their relatively poor health and economic status. Moreover, Pakistan has lower rates of childhood immunization (NIPS, 2013), poor decision-making authority resulting in early and frequent child bearing, and one of the lowest rates of deliveries by skilled birth attendants in the world (Khan *et al.,* 2009; UNICEF, 2008), all of which are reflected in the high rates of reproductive morbidity and mortality (NIPS, 2012–2013; UNICEF, 2011). Thus, pregnant women in Pakistan currently face the highest risk of mortality when compared to women in other countries in South Asia (WHO, 2010).

Data suggest that more women are joining the workforce in Pakistan but that they are also labouring in vulnerable circumstances with little bargaining power over their working conditions or wages (PBS, 2010). Although unionization of workers is legally mandated, there has been no cohesive trade union movement in Pakistan, and less than 3% of the labour force is organized (Khattak and Sayeed, 2000).

In this context, CSR initiatives are gaining momentum and provides a potential avenue to improve the sexual and reproductive health conditions of female workers, in addition to their "usual" focus on improving labour and environmental conditions more broadly at the base of the global value chain (UNESCAP, 2009). CSR is often understood in the Pakistani context as an extension of the ubiquitous religious and cultural philanthropy of the region although the effects of such corporate philanthropy are yet to be systematically documented in the Pakistani context (Waheed, 2005). Yet the question of how CSR activities might address the sexual and reproductive health of female workers is one that remains virtually unaddressed in the literature on CSR in the Pakistani context. In the next section, we move onto exploring how the CSR initiatives of local suppliers in the Pakistani football manufacturing industry address (or overlook) the sexual and reproductive health concerns of female football stitchers.

11.4 Empirical findings

11.4.1 CSR initiatives and the sexual and reproductive health of women football stitchers in Sialkot

Our stakeholder interviews in Sialkot in 2013 revealed that CSR initiatives rarely address the sexual and reproductive health concerns of stitchers within the industry. Clearly, the ability of CSR initiatives to address such concerns was linked to the work forms that football stitchers participated in. Most factory-based workers were provided medical benefits through social security hospitals which were operated and managed by the Pakistani government. In addition, two different CSR models, "the home-grown CSR model" and a "stitching centre" model, were identified as having the potential for providing sexual and reproductive health services (Lund-Thomsen and Nadvi, 2010a). Operating mostly through stitching centres, one manufacturer had adopted what Lund-Thomsen and Nadvi (2010a) called the home-grown CSR model. This manufacturer had developed a local project that provided healthcare cover for the male and female football stitchers that were integrated into its stitching value chain. Workers with a history of stitching footballs for more than a year were eligible for medical benefits through a health card. In this indigenous model, football stitchers obtained access to subsidized, skilled service providers at local private and missionary hospitals operating in Sialkot and Lahore. For married stitchers, health cover included the stitcher, his/her spouse, and their children while unmarried stitchers received medical benefits only for themselves. Additionally, outreach staff conducted regular health education training sessions with workers at stitching centres on issues such as hygiene, women/child health and family planning. Additional benefits for women working in the home-grown CSR model included paid maternity leave and facilitation for bringing newborns to the work place (an informal day-care system). However, although football stitchers taking part in this CSR model wished to know more about sexual health and sexually transmitted diseases, neither the male nor the female educators employed by the local manufacturer were trained in providing information on this topic.

Other manufacturers operated with what Lund-Thomsen and Nadvi (2010a) called a more traditional stitching centre model. Adherents to this model were suppliers that had adopted CSR policies—which were partly determined by their international buyers and partly adopted in response to the implementation of the Atlanta Agreement that required them to centralize the process of football stitching within clearly demarcated stitching centres. As stitching centres tended not to be directly owned by the local manufacturers, their suppliers were not directly legally liable for paying social insurance (including health insurance) to football stitchers at these centres. Hence, there was a significant difference in the health facilities and health insurance available to workers in different work forms (whether factory or stitching centres).

Factory workers were hired on annual contracts and had access to medical benefits after three months of probation including onsite care and access to a local social security hospital (a public sector facility for blue-collar workers). One manufacturer provided emergency transport from factory to hospital, while a second exporter cited proximity to the social security hospital as a reason for the lack of on-site medical facilities. Football stitchers employed at stitching centres of these production houses had a less structured work environment but were provided with first-aid boxes, which workers reported were empty "most of time" and replenished only before an "official visit from factory inspectors or from monitoring agencies". In both work forms, there were no health promotion/education programs, and sexual and reproductive health did not receive attention within the larger package of care provided at healthcare facilities on factory sites.

Poverty was described by health workers in Sialkot as a major barrier that prevented female football stitchers from accessing better care offered by private sector health providers. As a health worker put it, "(poor people can) only avail free public healthcare, regardless of how bad the service may be". The physical distance to better equipped care centres in the public sector and associated travel costs meant that many football stitchers decided to seek private healthcare closer to home regardless of the quality of the facilities and the advice given there. Piece-rate remuneration to stitchers employed in stitching centres limited their capacity to absorb financial losses associated with sick leave. Factory-based workers faced deductions in income for leaves of absence beyond the allowed single sick day in a month, sometimes causing workers to delay seeking medical assistance. Piece-rate remuneration to stitchers employed in stitching centres limited their capacity to absorb financial losses associated with sick leave, with workers taking loans to cover healthcare costs. For workers employed in factories and stitching centres operating under the "homegrown model of CSR", subsidized healthcare offered a measure of monetary relief.

Menstrual irregularities, menstrual cramping, and heavy menstruation were among the commonly reported reproductive morbidities among unmarried female football stitchers. Despite being fairly common complaints, very few female stitchers sought trained medical assistance for the symptoms because of socio-cultural constraints. While close family members such as mothers and married sisters were largely relied upon for advice, these relations often formed the first barrier to obtaining care from trained practitioners, resorting instead to traditional care givers including homeopaths and *hakims* (local self-proclaimed doctors). Stitchers employed at factories reported facilities to assist during menstruation, including stocking of "cottons" (sanitary napkins). However, these were stored in a separate room and could be accessed only through permission of the concerned line supervisors. Women working from home or at stitching centres had no assistance provided by employers for such occasions.

Most married women football stitchers worked till the last week of pregnancy and rejoined soon after delivery, as they were not provided with paid maternity leave, and loss of income was ill-afforded by their families. Owing to a lack of day care facilities, care of newborns was often done by surrogate care-takers as infants were not allowed within factory or stitching centre premises. Thus, women resorted to either bottle feed their infants or would visit their homes regularly to nurse their infants. This was possible for those employed at stitching centres as most centres were located near homes. Owing to a lack of workplace support, some female stitchers left work once they delivered a child. Only women employed at stitching centres adopting the "home-grown CSR model" were allowed to bring children to the centres, enabling continued employment and child care.

Despite deaths associated with closely spaced, unwanted or ill-timed pregnancies, contraception use amongst married football stitchers was poor. Although male stitchers tended to be more knowledgeable about the use of modern contraceptives, they often considered it an unimportant issue. As a male stitcher put it, "we get only a Sunday [off], and we don't have time to think about these things". None of the football stitchers we interviewed identified the workplace as a source of information on family planning or access to birth spacing products. Antenatal care during pregnancy formed the first point of contact between expectant mothers and healthcare providers. While none of the female stitchers planned their pregnancies, some younger women did seek obstetric care from trained healthcare providers and delivered their babies at health facilities instead of engaging in home-based deliveries supervised by traditional birth attendants. Decisions on delivery place were based on numerous factors, such as estimated expenditures related to using health clinics, distance to healthcare providers, previous experiences, perception of complications, family norms, and employee benefits that influenced the cost of care.

Although induced abortions were considered "sinful" by both male and female stitchers, they were described as a fairly common practice by married women. As this act was not culturally sanctioned, women would turn to untrained traditional birth attendants (*dais*) for help; resorting to trained care providers only in the case of complications. As a local health care provider explained, "sometimes girls come to us in a very bad shape, we know they had an abortion (which is illegal), but what can be do? We can't refuse to offer them care". This statement leads us to the conclusion of our chapter.

11.5 Conclusion

In this chapter, we sought to extend the literature on critical perspectives on CSR in developing countries by focusing on a largely unexplored topic in this body of knowledge. Namely, whether the CSR initiatives undertaken in export-oriented industries in developing countries can play a meaningful role in addressing sexual and reproductive health concerns of female workers. In our study of CSR interventions undertaken in the football manufacturing industry of Sialkot, Pakistan, our conclusion was that existing CSR interventions have done very little to systematically address this issue with the exception of one CSR initiative initiated by a single manufacturer. Hence, for the female stitchers working in the value chain of this particular manufacturer, there were clear benefits accruing from their participation in this program. However, in our view, this is barely a drop in the ocean.

To some extent these findings remind us of the earlier work of Frynas (Blowfield and Frynas, 2005), who—in his study of the CSR interventions sponsored by oil corporations in Africa—concluded that such projects were often adopted in a piecemeal, haphazard fashion, with little coordination among the sponsoring companies, often leading to a duplication of existing efforts. In the context of our study, however, our findings point to very limited awareness of sexual and repro-ductive health issues among football stitchers, and very few CSR interventions appear to have taken this issue onboard in Sialkot. Yet, given the large number of women workers that are employed in export-oriented industries in developing countries, we believe that this is an issue that requires increased focus—not only in the CSR approaches of international supermarkets/retailers and local suppliers, but also in future research on CSR in the developing world. From a policy perspec-tive, we believe that a first step would simply be to raise the awareness of managers and (fe)male football stitchers through systematic training on this issue so that this could become part of broader efforts aimed at creating better factories and work-places in export-oriented industries in developing countries.

Bibliography

Barrientos, S. (2003). A gendered value chain approach to codes of conduct in African horticulture. *World Development*, 31(9), 1511-1526.

Blowfield, M., & Frynas, J.G. (2005). Editorial. Setting new agendas: critical perspectives on corporate social responsibility in the developing world. *International Affairs*, 81(3), 499-513.

Carswella, G., & Neveb, G.D. (2013). Labouring for global markets: conceptualizing labour agency in global production networks. *Geoforum*, 44, 62-70.

Cattaneo, O., Gereffi, G., Miroudot, S., & Taglioni, D. (2013). Joining, Upgrading and Being Competitive in Global Value Chains: A Strategic Framework. World Bank Policy Research Working Paper No. 6406.

Coe, N.M., & Jordhus-Lier, D.C. (2011). Constrained agency? Re-evaluating the geographies of labour. *Progress in Human Geography*, 35, 211-233.

FIFA (2012). Financial Report 2011. 62nd FIFA Conference. Budapest: FIFA.

ILRF (2010). Missed the Goal for Workers: The Reality of Soccer Ball Stitchers in Pakistan, India, China and Thailand. International Labour Rights Forum (ILRF).

Kabeer, N., Starl, A., & Magnus, E. (2008). Global Perspectives on Gender Equality: Reversing the Gaze. New York: Routledge.

Kandiyoti, D. (1998). Gender, power and contestation: "rethinking bargaining with patriar-chy". In C. Jackson, & R. Pearson (Eds.), *Feminist Visions of Development: Gender, Analysis and Policy*. London/New York: Routledge.

Khan, A. (2007). *Representing Children: Power, Policy and the Discourse on Child Labour in the Football Manufacturing Industry of Pakistan*. Karachi: Oxford University Press.

Khan, F.R. (2004). Hard times recalled: the child labour controversy in Pakistan's soccer ball industry. In F. Bird, E. Raufflet, & J. Smucker (Eds.), *International Business and the Dilemmas of Development: Case Studies in South Africa, Madagascar, Pakistan, South Korea, Mexico, and Columbia* (pp. 132-155). London: Palgrave-MacMillan.

Khan, Y.P., Bhutta, S.Z., Munim, S., & Bhutta, Z.A. (2009). Maternal health and survival in Pakistan. Issues and options. *Journal of Obstetricians and Gynaecologists Canada*, 31(10), 920-929.

Khattak, S.G., & Sayeed, A. (2000). Subcontracted Women Workers in the World Economy: The Case of Pakistan. Islamabad: Sustainable Development Policy Institute (SDPI).

Lund-Thomsen, P. (2004). Towards a critical framework on corporate social and environmen-tal responsibility in the south: the case of Pakistan. *Development*, 47(3), 106-113.

Lund-Thomsen, P. (2013). Labor agency in the football manufacturing industry of Sialkot, Pakistan. *Geoforum*, 44, 71-78.

Lund-Thomsen, P., & Coe, N.M. (2015). Corporate social responsibility and labor agency: the case of Nike in Pakistan. *Journal of Economic Geography*, 15(2), 275-296.

Lund-Thomsen, P., & Nadvi, K. (2009). Global Value Chains, Local Clusters, and Corporate Social Responsibility: A Comparative Assessment of the Sports Goods Clusters in Sialkot, Pakistan and Jalandhar, India. Technical Paper 17, Industrial Policy and Private Sector Development Branch. Vienna, United Nations Industrial Development Organization.

Lund-Thomsen, P., & Nadvia, K. (2010a). Clusters, chains and compliance: corporate social responsibility and governance in football manufacturing in South Asia. *Journal of Business Ethics*, 93, 201-222.

Lund-Thomsen, P., & Nadvi, K. (2010b). Global value chains, local collective action and corporate social responsibility: a review of empirical evidence. *Business Strategy and the Environment*, 19(1), 1-13.

Nadvi, K., Lund-Thomsen, P., Xue, H., & Khara, N. (2011). Playing against China: global value chains and labour standards in the international sports goods industry. *Global Networks*, 11(3), 334-354.

Neilson, J., & Pritchard, B. (2009). *Value Chain Struggles: Institutions and Governance in the Plantation Districts of South India*. New York: John Wiley & Sons.

Newell, P., & Frynas, J.G. (2007). Beyond CSR? Business, poverty and social justice: an introduction. *Third World Quarterly*, 28(4).

NIPS (2012–2013). Pakistan Demographic and Health Survey. Islamabad: National Institute of Population Studies.

NIPS (2013). Pakistan Demographic and Health Survey. Islamabad: National Institute of Population Studies.

PBS (2010). *Pakistan Employment Trends*. Islamabad: Pakistan Bureau of Statistics.

Rossi, A. (2014). Does economic upgrading lead to social upgrading in global production networks? Evidence from Morocco. *World Development*, 46, 223-233.

Sagarra, A., Stancher, A., & Clara, M. (2007). Better Access to Growth: Mainstreaming Gender in Cluster Development. Technical Working Paper Series. Vienna: UNIDO.

Said-Allsopp, M., & Tallontire, A. (2014). Enhancing fairtrade for women workers on plantations: insights from Kenyan agriculture. *Food Chain*, 4(1).

Schmitz, H. (2004). Local Upgrading in Global Chains: Recent Findings. DRUID Summer Conference. Elsinore, Denmark. Institute of Development Studies, University of Sussex.

Schmitz, H. (2006). Learning and earning in global garment chains. *European Journal of Development Research*, 18(4), 546-571.

UNComtrade. (2011). United Nations Commodity Trade Statistics Database, 28th November, 2012. Retrieved from http://comtrade.un.org.

UNESCAP (2009). Creating Business and Social Value: The Asian Way to Integrate CSR into Business Strategies. Studies in Trade & Investment. Bangkok, Thailand, United Nations.

UNICEF. (2008). Progress for children: *A Report Card on Maternal Mortality*. November 12th, 2013. Retrieved from www.childinfo.org/files/progress_for_children_maternalmortality.pdf.

UNICEF (2011). Multiple indicator cluster survey (MICS). Islamabad: UNICEF.

Waheed, A. (2005). Corporate Social Responsibility in Pakistan and a Strategy for Implementation. Securities and Exchange Commission of Pakistan.

WHO (2010). Trends in maternal mortality: 1990 to 2008. Estimates developed by WHO, UNICEF, UNFPA and the World Bank. Geneva: World Health Organization.

12

CSR and firm performance
New evidence from developing countries

Chiara Amini and Silvia Dal Bianco
London Metropolitan University, UK

We empirically explore whether corporate social responsibility (CSR) might operate as an effective development tool as well as whether the goals of private enterprises can be aligned with the ones of sustainable development. In particular, we take advantage of the 2006 World Bank Enterprise Survey on Argentina, Bolivia, Chile, Colombia, Ecuador and Mexico and we analyse the CSR–revenues nexus in six Latin American economies. In order to tackle the likely endogeneity of CSR adoption, our empirical strategy relies on the two-step maximum likelihood estimator. Our results show that firms that engage in socially responsible projects do not underperform firms that do not adopt such practices. Thus, our study highlights that social responsibility has a twofold positive developmental impact. On the one hand, social and environmental practices are compatible with greater production and, on the other, CSR adopters engage in activities that are compatible with the notion of sustainable development.

In the last decade, both business practitioners and policy-makers have placed increasing attention on firms' socially responsible practices as these are of interest not only to firms but also to society as a whole (Margolis and Walsh, 2003; McWilliams and Siegel, 2000; Orlitzky *et al.*, 2003).

Traditionally, research efforts on corporate social responsibility (CSR) were concentrated on developed countries (Bird *et al.*, 2007; Jamali, 2008; Orlitzky, 2003). This was primarily because CSR originated in western companies and information on such firms' practices was mainly available for developed countries. Over the last decade, there has been a considerable diffusion of CSR practices, and those policies are increasingly adopted by emerging and developing country firms. However, one of the hottest topics in this field is the "global credibility" of CSR and the integration of social and environmental concerns into ordinary business in developing countries. In particular, one of the most intriguing and relatively under-explored research questions is whether CSR can serve as an effective development tool.

The link between socially responsible business' practices and economic development is multifaceted. It is evident, for example, that business activities and economic growth are having a dramatic impact on both the society and the environment of developing countries. Thus, the pressure to adopt CSR practices has promptly increased in the last decade (Visser, 2008). Socially responsible businesses are now considered by many scholars to be intertwined with poverty alleviation and sustainable development (Blowfield, 2005; Moon, 2007). However, firms in developing (and developed) countries have had a mixed reaction to the increasing popularity of CSR. While some companies have devoted more resources to social and environmental activities, others have resisted such a trend because of the concern that growing expenditure in this area may negatively affect the economic viability of the business. This issue is particularly relevant to developing countries firms' exporters. In this instance, firms are faced with having to meet the social and environmental requirement of global buyers while maintaining competitiveness in international markets (Luken and Stares, 2005). If the firm is vertically integrated, the lead firm may be able to offer technical assistance, but small and medium enterprises, often lack the know-how and resources needed to adopt the environmental and global standard required by global buyers (Luken and Stares, 2005).

Thus, a better understanding of the effects of CSR in developing countries appears of great policy relevance. In particular, it is crucial to understand whether the goals of private enterprises can be aligned with those of sustainable development in underdeveloped economies (Newell and Frynas, 2007).

Existing empirical research on developed countries has analysed the impact of CSR on firm performance but results have been mixed. While conflicting evidence may be related to differences in samples and methodologies employed, a crucial issue that has been overlooked by most of the existing literature is that the adoption of CSR may be endogenously determined. This implies that firms with better performance or with certain characteristics tend to engage in CSR. So in a regression where performance depends on CSR and a set of controls, CSR is endogenous (Chen and Shang, 2009).

The present chapter aims at narrowing the knowledge gap on CSR and firm performance in developing countries[1]. In particular, our work analyses the CSR-revenues nexus in six developing Latin American countries, taking into account the likely endogeneity of socially responsible practices. In particular, we take advantage of the 2006 World Bank Enterprise Surveys (WBES) on Argentina, Bolivia, Chile, Colombia, Ecuador and Mexico.

Our aim is twofold. First, we analyse the prevalence of CSR and various aspects of it, and we also investigate the characteristics of firms engaged in such practices. Second, our work will reassess and extend the empirical evidence on the impact of CSR on firms' performance. With the use of the appropriate econometrics technique, the analysis aims to unveil specific causal mechanisms and, thus, it is informative to policy-makers.

The results show that most companies do engage in some CSR activities, although there is a higher share of firms adopting environmental programs relative to labour practices or community projects. In all countries, firms that engage in CSR tend to have higher sales and sales per employee, and this difference although small is significant. However, we also observe systematic differences in firms' characteristics between two groups of firms, at least on average. Firms that engage in CSR tend to be foreign, larger, older and engaged in research and development (R&D). Because of the observed differences, we cannot attribute the better performance of CSR firms to engaging in social and environmental activities.

To investigate the impact of CSR on firms' performance, we employ the two-step likelihood procedure to contemporaneously estimate an extended production function as well as a selection model. Our results show that firms that engage in environmental or community projects are no less efficient than firms that do not adopt such practices. Thus, they suggest that corporate goals, such as revenue maximization, are compatible with conscious operations.

The remainder of this chapter is organized as follows. Section 12.1 reviews the main theoretical hypotheses linking CSR and firm performance and it provides an overview of the existing empirical evidence in both advanced and developing economies. Section 12.2 discusses the econometric methodology adopted. Section 12.3 provides details on the data employed together with some descriptive statistics. Section 12.4 discusses the results obtained from the empirical exercise. Section 12.5 concludes.

---

1 Here we define CSR as a multidimensional construct which entails a firm in such a way that it can be "economically profitable, law abiding, ethical and socially supportive" (Carroll, 1999: p. 286),

12.1 Literature review

12.1.1 CSR and firm performance: theoretical background and empirical strategies

The impact of CSR on firm performance has been theoretically and empirically analysed under the spectrum of two alternative hypotheses, namely: "the social impact" and "the shift of focus" hypothesis (Chen and Shang, 2009).

According to the social impact hypothesis, CSR has a positive effect on firm performance and such a positive link can be explained through three channels. First, CSR can improve employees' productivity by providing a better working environment (Turban and Greening, 1997). Second, CSR should increase managerial know-how and thus enhance organizational efficiency (Orlitzky et al., 2003). Finally, CSR might foster a firm's social reputation and trust (Bowman and Haire, 1975) as well as a firm's brand image and product competitiveness (Porter and Van der Linde, 1995). Chen and Shang (2009) show that the social reputation-channel works principally through the media, which make firms responsible to stockholders and consumers.

Contrary to the social impact hypothesis, the shift of focus view argues that CSR activities, such as building employee and community relationship as well as providing environmental protection, are detrimental to firm performance. This is because such socially responsible activities cause a "shift of focus" from the maximization of stockholders' value to the interests of a wider-set of stakeholders and thereby increases the firm's costs (Becchetti et al., 2007). Other studies argue that corporations engaged in CSR activities have lower market competitiveness and worse performance because they either limit products' development (Bragdon and Marlin, 1972) or they engage in non-profitable social activities (Aupperle et al., 1985; Ullmann, 1985; Vance, 1975).

Turning now to the empirical investigation of the link between CSR and firm performance, the bulk of the existing applied literature has examined the relationship between some measure of CSR and the long-term firm performance, which has been proxied either by accounting or financial measures of profitability (Margolis et al., 2007). These studies estimate the effect of CSR by regressing firm performance on corporate social performance and several control variables. Firm performance has usually been measured as price per share and returns on asset or on equity (Orlitzky et al., 2003). Moreover, the four most common ways to measure CSR have been based upon: (a) disclosures, which consist of annual reports, letters to shareholders and other corporate disclosures to the public; (b) reputation ratings; (c) social audits; and (d) managerial principles and values (Orlitzky et al., 2003).

12.1.2 CSR and firm performance: empirical results from developed countries

The research on CSR is mainly focused on developed economies' experiences or on the activities of western multinational companies (MNC) in emerging markets (Muller and Kolk, 2009).

The empirical investigation of the CSR–firm performance nexus has shown mixed results. Among the most comprehensive studies in the field, Newgren *et al.* (1985) and Brammer *et al.* (2012) found that firms that engage with environment protection and community relationship have significantly lower stock returns. In contrast, Cochran and Wood (1984), Tsoutsourz (2004), Waddock and Graves (1997) have shown that CSR reputation index positively affects a firm's performance. Moreover, the meta-analysis conducted by Orlitzky *et al.* (2003) on 52 previous studies highlight that social responsibility and, to a lesser extent, environmental responsibility is likely to have a positive effect on a firm's performance.

At this point, it is worth underlining the results of Chen and Shang (2009), which are particularly important for the present analysis. To the best of our knowledge, this is the only study in the literature that takes into account the likely endogenous nature of CSR. In more detail, Chen and Shang (2009) used quarterly data on Taiwanese firms from 2005 to 2006 and employed propensity score matching to investigate the relationship between CSR and financial performance.[2] Their findings showed that firms engaging in CSR activities obtain significantly higher values of pre-tax income and profit margin, but there is no significant difference on returns on investment and earnings per share. Even if their results might be sensitive to the set of conditioning factors employed to calculate the propensity score and to the matching method employed, the main conclusion of their study is that CSR does not deteriorate firms' performance, in the sense that it never has a significant and negative effect on performance.

12.1.3 CSR and firm performance: empirical results from developed countries

Although initially the greatest efforts have been concentrated on advanced economies, the recent literature shows some attempts to document and analyse CSR practices in developing countries.

In terms of regional coverage, several studies have focused on Asia (Visser, 2008).[3] For instance, Luken and Stares (2005) used information from a United Nations Industrial Development Organization (UNIDO) project with 22 small

---

2 Chen and Shang (2009) measure for CSR is the rating of one of Taiwan's leading commercial magazines, the *Global View Monthly* (GMV), while firm performance has been proxied through different indicators such as the return on investment and on equity, the pre-tax income to net sales, the gross profit to net sales and the earnings per share.

3 See, for instance, Blowfield (2004) on Indonesia, Kaufman *et al.* (2004) on Thailand, Lund-Thomsen (2004) on Pakistan and Zhuang and Wheale (2004) on China.

and medium-sized enterprises in four Asian developing economies. Their analysis shows that environmental and social practices are correlated to financial savings, environmental, social and product improvement. A comparative analysis by Welford (2005) shows, perhaps unsurprisingly, that Asian countries, such as Hong Kong, Malaysia and Thailand, consistently under-perform developed countries in both internal and external elements of CSR.[4] Nevertheless, the regions show some variations in CSR reporting with 75% of large Indian companies having some CSR policies compared to 30% in the Philippines and 32% in Malaysia.

There are some studies on CSR in Africa, mainly on South Africa and Nigeria, and most of them focus on critical sectors such as agriculture (Blowfield, 2003), mining (Kapelus, 2002), and petrochemicals (Acutt *et al.*, 2004). In contrast to other developing countries where social and environmental concerns have been at the centre of CSR, debates in the region have been centred on ethical issues related to apartheid, colonialism and corruption.

In the case of Latin America, Visser (2008) points out that with regard to CSR research, this is the least covered of all developing regions. So far, most studies have focused on Argentina (Newell and Muro, 2006), Brazil (Vivarta and Canela, 2006) and Mexico (Weyzig, 2006). The literature reports that CSR in these regions is increasing with 34% of large companies publishing a report on sustainability (Araya, 2006). Vives (2006) provides some insights on the importance of specific CSR activities in small and medium-sized enterprises (SMEs) in eight Latin American countries. He finds that most CSR by SMEs is focused on internal activities, especially employee welfare, whereas philanthropic and environmental activities are less common.

12.2 Methodology

In order to assess the extent to which CSR practices affect firm performance, our methodological framework is designed to face a typical evaluation problem. Our research question poses two methodological issues. First, the unobserved counter-factual cannot be estimated. This means that we have information on firm performance for CSR adopters and non-adopters only but there is no information on the counter-factual (i.e. CSR adopters performance in the case of non-adoption and vice-versa). And, second, the decision of adopting responsible practices might systematically depend on firms' characteristics and this in turns implies that such a decision is non-random. Thus, CSR adopters and non-adopters might systematically differ and, hence, the risk of selection bias arises (see Blundell and Costa Dias (2002), Heckman (1979), and Vella and Verbeek (1999) for reviews on these points).

---

4 For what concerns internal aspects, Welford (2005) investigates written policies of non-discrimination, equal opportunities, staff development and working conditions. While external elements are defined as human rights protection, labour standards, code of ethics and commitment to local communities.

Our empirical assessment strategy relies on the two-step maximum likelihood estimation approach and it is built upon two main blocks. The first one is an extended Cobb-Douglas production function, which allows us to analyse how efficiently firms generate sales revenue, taking into account not only capital and labour inputs but also controlling for firms' characteristics as well as for measures of the business environment (see Equation 12.1). The second part of our framework is, instead, the evaluation problem itself, that is the formal way to assess the CSR impact on firm performance, taking into account the previously explained issues (i.e. absence of unobserved counter-factual and CSR endogeneity). This refers to Equations 12.2 to 12.4.

Formally, the production function is written as:

$$\ln y_i = \beta_0 + \beta_1 \ln k_i + \beta_2 \ln l_i + \beta_3 CRS_i + \beta_4 X_i + \beta_5 I_i + \varepsilon_i \tag{12.1}$$

where i indexes the ith firm; y represents firms' revenues; k and l represent, respectively, the capital and labour inputs; CSR is a dummy variable that indicates whether the firm adopts socially and/or environmentally responsible practices; X_i is a vector of firms' characteristics as well as business environments' variables; I_i is a vector collecting industries' dummies and it is the idiosyncratic error term. As noticed by De Rosa *et al.* (2010), controlling for observable aspects of firms' heterogeneity, and thus including the observables in vector X_i, is fundamental in order to identify the effects of CSR on firm productivity. More specifically, following the existing literature, the set of controls included in our analysis are: ownership, export orientation, innovativeness, firms' age and size and the perceived degree of business obstacles (Commander and Svejnar, 2011).

Turning to the evaluation problem, we follow Bolwig *et al.* (2009) and we formulate it as a system of equations involving an outcome of interest (i.e. firm revenue in the present case, labelled as y_i), selected covariates (i.e. the aforementioned firm's revenues determinants such as capital and labour inputs, ownership, industries dummies, labelled as X_i) and a selection equation for treatment (i.e. indicator function which states the condition for participating into the treatment that is adopting CSR practices in the present case, labelled as t_i). Over observations i, the system of equations representing the evaluation problem can be formally written as:

$$y_{1i} = x'_i \beta_1 + \mu_{1i} \tag{12.2}$$

$$y_{0i} = x'_i \beta_0 + \mu_{0i} \tag{12.3}$$

$$t_i = 1(z'_i \beta_1 + v_i > 0) \tag{12.4}$$

Starting with Equation 12.4, it formally describes the treatment variable, which is adopting CSR practices. Such an equation is an indicator function, taking the value of 1 in the firm engaged in CSR and 0 otherwise. In particular, variable z_i is a latent variable that captures the propensity to participate in the treatment above a certain threshold and v_i is the choice equation error term. Then, turning to Equations 12.2 and 12.3, y_{1i} is the outcome for the treated respondents (i.e. CSR adopters or more formally $t_i = 1$); y_{0i} is the outcome for the control group (i.e. CSR non-adopters or $t_i = 0$); x'_i is a raw vector of firm's i characteristics; μ_{0i} and μ_{1i} are the error terms.

As previously explained, Equations 12.2 and 12.3 cannot be directly estimated as we cannot know the unobserved counter-factual, that is the outcome of the counter-factual y_{0i}. The solution to such a problem is to estimate the following switching equation:

$$y_i = x'_i\beta_0 + tx'_i(\beta_1 - \beta_0) + u_{0i} + t(u_{1i} - u_{0i}) \tag{12.5}$$

The second term of the above equation gives the impact of the treatment. Assuming that in Equations 12.2 and 12.3 all the parameters except the intercepts are the same, so $\beta_1 = \beta_0 = \beta$, then Equation 12.5 can be transformed in an equation of the outcome on participation and the covariates (Ravallion, 2005):

$$y_i = x'_i\beta_0 + t_i\alpha + u_{0i} + t_i(u_{1i} - u_{0i}) \tag{12.6}$$

where α captures the treatment effect given by the difference in the intercepts of Equations 12.2 and 12.3.

Then, recalling that our data is not generated by an experiment and, thus, we cannot assume that the choice to adopt CSR practices is purely random, we have to tackle such an endogenous selection issue. In our case, we can either employ instrumental variables (IV) or Heckman selection models (Heckman, 1979). Here, we employ the Heckman selection model since it is more robust compared to IV, particularly for small samples (Bolwig et al., 2009). A drawback of such a methodology is that models are sensitive to both specification and distributional assumptions (Blundell and Costa Dias, 2000). To address this issue, it is advisable to place an exclusion restriction on vector x, analogous to an IV identification strategy. This requires to augment vector z with exogenous predictors that do not enter the outcome equation. Thus, the vector of selection variables z is partitioned as such: $z' = [1\ x_1\ z_1]$, where z_1 refers to the exogenous determinants of participation that do not enter the outcome equation. In the present case, we augment z with a measure of external pressures for adopting CSR, that is a dummy variable that takes value 1 when the firms receive external pressures to adopt CSR practices and 0 otherwise. It is worth clarifying that, in our empirical exercise, vector x in Equation 12.6 includes all the covariates specified in Equation 12.1.

Finally, two technical points are worth mentioning. First, the two-step maximum likelihood estimation approach differs from the original two-step approach as the selection and outcome equations (i.e. Equations 12.6 and 12.4) are estimated jointly, thereby enhancing asymptotic efficiency (Puhani, 2000). Second, in this instance, we follow the standard approach and assume that the effect of treatment is homogeneous. This implies that there is no correlation between the decision to participate in the treatment and the individual treatment effects (Bolwig et al., 2009).

12.3 Data and descriptive statistics

The data employed in this chapter is drawn from the World Bank Enterprise Surveys (WBES). WBES have been used for investigating firms' performances by many well-known scholars such as Beck *et al.* (2005a, b) and Djankov *et al.* (2008). However, to the best of our knowledge, the present study is the first one that employs the information on CSR, which is available for six developing Latin American countries, namely: Argentina, Bolivia, Chile, Colombia, Ecuador and Mexico.[5]

The 2006 WBES contained 10 questions on CSR which gave the opportunity to explore three different dimensions of CSR, namely: environmental, social and labour. The surveys also contain information on firm performance, business sector, export intensity, ownership, R&D and perception of the business environment.

The descriptive statistics presented here provide evidence on the diffusion of CSR across countries (Table 12.1); the spectrum of CSR activities within firms (Table 12.2) and finally, the characteristics of CSR adopters (Table 12.3).

12.3.1 The diffusion of CSR practices within firms across countries

Table 12.1 summarizes the CSR questions contained in the WBES for the six countries analysed. The results are presented to clearly show the prevalence of certain CSR activities, which are grouped along three dimensions, namely environment, labour, and community. There are four questions related to environmental practices, two to the labour one and one to the social one. The table contains the percentage of firms that responded positively to the questions reported in the first column.

The first row shows that between 44.38% and 78.59% of the firms surveyed have some oral or written CSR policies with Mexico being the country with the lowest share and Ecuador with the highest.

For what concerns environmental practices, the surveys contain information on the adoption of energy or water optimization programs, recycling programs and the use of standard water/air pollution control systems. To summarize the questions, we generate a variable "CSR_env" which takes value 1 if the establishment has at least of one of these practices and 0 otherwise. The majority of the establishments appear to adopt some CSR practices. The minimum value of "CSR_env" is 67% in Argentina and the maximum is 87% in Ecuador.

WBES contains one question on the adoption of community support programs, hence this allows for investigating the prevalence of CSR in the social dimension. In all countries the frequency of community projects seems lower with respect to

5 In 2013, the World Bank income-classification for these six countries had Bolivia as a lower–middle-income country; Argentina, Colombia, Ecuador and Mexico are upper middle-income and Chile was high income. It is worth noting that Chile entered the high-income group between 2012 and 2013.

Table 12.1 **World Bank Enterprise Surveys, CSR questions**

	Argentina	Bolivia	Chile	Colombia	Ecuador	Mexico
The firm has written/oral CSR policies	65.83	77.84	75.12	63.69	78.59	44.38
Environmental CSR						
The firm has an energy use optimization program	39.07	47.53	47.32	45.81	63.16	56.94
The firm has a water use optimization program	33.75	52.88	39.81	50.4	64.54	48.38
The firm has a recycling program	33.28	38.95	43.06	63.03	59.62	36.47
Use any standardized water and air pollution control system?	53.2	46.69	48.89	40.63	63.97	39.43
CSR_env*	67.45	77.26	73.23	79.78	87.26	70.15
Community CSR						
The firm has a community support program	46.39	53.95	45.37	39.65	55.52	22.54
Labour CSR						
Have an explicit policy about hiring women or handicapped persons	6.34	13.7	7.13	6.8	18.01	12.71
Have programs supporting balance between family and work	11.2	23.22	15.61	20.48	28.89	11.32
CSR_labour**	14.29	29.32	18.82	24.13	37.22	20.49
Receive pressure to be socially/ environmentally responsible	13.34	23.16	18.08	11.85	25.14	5.7
Being socially responsible has a positive effect on the firm's competitiveness	59.95	78.21	67.9	81.33	81.72	86.34
Observations	641	361	623	633	355	1,105

*CSR_env takes value 1 if the firms engage in one of the environmental practices surveyed.

**CSR_labour takes value 1 if the firms have answered yes to one of the two questions on labour practices.

Table 12.2 CSR simultaneous practices

	Argentina				Bolivia			
	CSR_labour		CSR_soc		CSR_labour		CSR_soc	
CSR_env	0	1	0	1	0	1	0	1
0	142	57	4	6	45	22	12	4
%	45.81	24.36	13.33	10	33.58	17.89	35.29	5.56
1	168	177	26	54	89	101	22	68
%	54.19	75.64	86.67	90	66.42	82.11	64.71	94.44
Total	310	234	30	60	134	123	34	72

	Chile				Colombia			
	CSR_labour		CSR_soc		CSR_labour		CSR_soc	
CSR_env	0	1	0	1	0	1	0	1
0	112	40	7	9	92	17	9	7
%	37.58	19.51	16.28	12%	29.77	10.12	12.86	8.64
1	186	165.0	36	66	217	151	61	74
%	62.42	80.49	83.72	88%	70.23	89.88	87.14	91.36
Total	298	205	43	75	309	168	70	81

	Ecuador				Mexico			
	CSR_labour		CSR_soc		CSR_labour		CSR_soc	
CSR_env	0	1	0	1	0	1	0	1
0	18	17	7	3	261	16	36	3
%	14.88	16.19	17.95	3.16	38.33	9.58	25.35	3.9
1	103	88	32	92	420	151	106	74
%	85.12	83.81	82.05	96.84	61.67	90.42	74.65	96.1
Total	121	105	39	95	681	167	142	77

Csr_env takes value 1 if the firms engage in at least in one of the environmental practices listed in Table 12.1; Csr_soc takes value 1 if the firms have a community support project; Csr_labour takes value 1 if the firms engage in at least one of the labour practices listed in Table 12.1.

Table12.3 Firm characteristics and CSR adoption

	Argentina			Bolivia			Chile		
	CSR	No CSR	Proportion/ t-test (p-value)	CSR	No CSR	Proportion/ t-test (p-value)	CSR	No CSR	Proportion/ t-test (p-value)
Sales per employee	11.65	11.46	0.0479	11.26	10.86	0.096	16.88	16.62	0.072
Sales	4.75e+07	3775833	0.022	1.91e+07	1749839	0.0821	6.25e+11		0.647
Foreign	0.123	0.028	0.001	0.102	0.088	0.776	0.091	0.017	0.008
Export	14.6	6.68	0.002	11.65	16.82	0.239	10.39	3.919	0.005
R&D	0.561	0.288	0.000	0.476	0.177	0.002	0.365	0.205	0.001
Age	33.74	26.02	0.001	22.61	15.86	0.010	30.55	25.9	0.036
Size 1	0.361	0.605	0.000	0.496	0.6	0.195	0.257	0.482	0.000
Size 2	0.416	0.336	0.279	0.347	0.333	0.848	0.465	0.428	0.474
Size 3	0.222	0.028	0.000	0.155	0.066	0.113	0.276	0.089	0.000
Capital	1.79e+07	633459	0.079	1.60e+07	2281942	0.342	4.32e+09		0.272
Labour	192	26.3	0.0320	54.51	22.64	0.071	136.33	37.95	0.013
Female owners	0.341	0.366	0.586	0.436	0.511	0.347	0.375	0.432	0.276
Skilled/unskilled L	2.46	2.12	0.74	1.57	1.80	0.616	1.40	2.11	0.032
Food	0.303	0.077	0.000	0.354	0.2	0.040	0.261	0.187	0.100
Clothes	0.138	0.33	0.000	0.282	0.666	0.000	0.099	0.169	0.031
Textile	0.174	0.204	0.4182	0.180	0.022	0.006	0.059	0.160	0.003
Machinery	0.178	0.225	0.2084	0.059	0.022	0.308	0.055	0.035	0.395

	Argentina			Bolivia			Chile		
	CSR	No CSR	Proportion/t-test (p-value)	CSR	No CSR	Proportion/t-test (p-value)	CSR	No CSR	Proportion/t-test (p-value)
Chemical	0.109	0.007	0.0001	0.124	0.088	0.494	0.129	0.053	0.022
Other Manufacturing	0.0952	0.1549	0.043	n/a	n/a	n/a	n/a	n/a	n/a

	Colombia			Ecuador			Mexico		
	CSR	No CSR	Proportion/t-test (p-value)	CSR	No CSR	Proportion/t-test (p-value)	CSR	No CSR	Proportion/t-test (p-value)
Sales per employee	17.57	17.24	0.003	10.28	9.34	0.0026	12.38	12.04	0.001
Sales	8.53e+09	1.01e+09	0.087	5661819	413601.1	0.092	3.41e+08	8463577	0.052
Foreign	0.0241	0.010	0.425	0.125	0.166	0.608	0.104	0.026	0.001
Export	9.24	8.68	0.806	8.57	1.11	0.077	8.42	0.498	0.000
R&D	0.4935	0.1648	0.000	0.504	0.222	0.019	0.268	0.022	0.000
Age	19.13	11.38	0.000	24.39	17.94	0.069	20.8	15.5	0.000
Size 1	0.491	0.663	0.002	0.402	0.666	0.026	0.408	0.716	0.000
Size 2	0.402	0.293	0.047	0.277	0.341	0.579	0.326	0.237	0.006
Size 3	0.105	0.043	0.061	0.256	0.055	0.053	0.264	0.045	0.000
Capital	4.06e+09	4.96e+08	0.279	1544289	283688.5	0.320	2.79e+07	7533565	0.041
Labour	69.48	18.47	0.057	80.75	20.94	0.126	125	23	0.000
Female owners	0.532	0.510	0.824	0.342	0.277	0.573	0.248	0.235	0.663
Skilled/unskilled L	1.35	1.20	0.700	1.69	01.19	0.555	442	103	0.056
Food	0.257	0.163	0.050	0.294	0.222	0.510	0.135	0.145	0.689
Clothes	0.256	0.358	0.040	0.072	0.055	0.781	0.120	0.210	0.003

Textile	0.207	0.358	0.001	0.064	0.055	0.884	0.135	0.157	0.338
Machinery	0.276	0.119	0.001	0.005	0	0.745	0.230	149	0.005
Chemical	0.001	0	0.679	0.274	0.111	0.127	0.180	0.065	0.000
Other Manufacturing	n/a	n/a	n/a	0.5	0.265	0.030	n/a	n/a	n/a

*There is no convergence for Ecuador so the results are not reported. Foreign takes value 1 if the foreign ownership is greater than 10% and 0 otherwise. Export is the percentage of sales exported directly and indirectly. R&D takes value 1 if the firm invested in R&D within the firm's age in 2006. Polstab and Corruption takes value 1 if the firm perceives political instability or corruption to be major obstacles to business. Robust standard errors in parentheses.

environmental practices. Ecuador again has the highest share of firms that adopt community programs, with 55%, while Mexico has lowest share at 22.54%.

The questions related to the labour dimension of CSR give information on whether firms have an explicit policy about hiring women or handicapped persons or have programs supporting the balance between family and work. In all countries, the prevalence of labour related practices is even lower than the adoption of community programs. Argentina is the country with the lowest share of such firms, 14%, while Ecuador is again the best performing country with a share of 37.2% of firms.

Overall the data shows that in all Latin American countries surveyed, there is a high share of firms engaged in some type of CSR. This is in line with Visser (2008) who reports a trend of increasing CSR for Latin American countries. However, our data shows that there is large variation in terms of the prevalence of various types of CSR. Environmental practices are the most common one, while social and labour practices are less diffuse. This finding is in line with Baskin's (2006) analysis which notes that emerging markets lag behind the OECD with regard to business ethics and equal opportunities, but are roughly on a par for environmental reporting.

Concerning the prevalence of CSR in the countries analysed, Ecuador is the country that has the highest share of firms engaged in CSR, for all the CSR dimensions considered. Large countries such as Mexico and Argentina perform poorly; for instance, Mexico has the lowest share of firms with some kind of CSR and has a very low share of firms with community support projects, in particular.

In all countries, most firms agree that CSR has a positive impact on competitiveness. As much as 87% of Mexican firms believe that being socially responsible has a positive effect on the firm's competitiveness.

It is striking that the external pressures to adopt CSR practices are extremely low in all countries. Only 5% of Mexican firms receive pressure to be socially/environmentally responsible, with the highest being in Bolivia (23%) and Ecuador (25%).

12.3.2 The spectrum of CSR activities within firms

As Muller and Kolk (2009) note it is important to assess not only the prevalence of the various CSR aspects, but also the degree to which companies engage in them simultaneously. Table 12.2 shows the number of firms that are engaged in more than one type of CSR and, in particular, it takes environmental practices as a baseline group and it shows whether the firm is engaged either in labour or social practices or both. The data highlights that firms tend to adopt one or more aspect of CSR simultaneously; so, for example, the majority of firms that have some environmental programs also have some labour policies or community projects. For instance, in Argentina only 10% of firms that have a community project do not have any environmental program, while 24.36% of firms which have some labour policies do not have any environmental CSR. Similarly, in Colombia, 89.88% of firms with CSR_labour also have CRS_env, while 91.36% of firms with CRS_soc also have CRS_env. This pattern holds for all countries examined.

In line with what discussed above, there is a greater correlation between environmental and social practices, compared to labour practices and the other two dimensions.

12.3.3 The characteristics of CSR adopters

Table 12.3 summarizes, for each country, relevant firms' characteristics for two groups of establishments: firms that adopt at least one of the social, environmental or labour practices defined above (see Table 12.1), and those who do not adopt any of those practices. The table also reports if there is a significant difference between the two groups of firms. To this end, we use the *t*-test for continuous variables and proportion test for dummy variables.

Within the CSR group, there is a higher percentage of foreign, larger, older firms and engaged in R&D. For instance, in Argentina, 12% of CSR firms are foreign-owned against 2% of non-CSR ones. Ownership does not appear to be significantly different in Colombia, Ecuador and Bolivia. Export intensity is usually higher for CSR firms, again this characteristic is not significantly different for Bolivia and Colombia. It is interesting to note that across all countries, there is a quite high share of small firms engaged in CSR, this share is the highest in Colombia and Bolivia at 49%. There are also some differences across sectors. CSR practices are more prevalent in the food industry and in the chemical sector, but less so in clothing and textile companies.

We have also analysed the type of CSR activities by the firms' size and we find that all dimensions of CSR are more common in medium and large firms. This is in contrast with Vives (2006) that CSR by SMEs is focused on internal activities and where external and environmental activities are less common.

Because of the observed differences, we cannot attribute the better performance of CSR firms to engaging to philanthropic activities. Moreover, it could be that more productive firms may likely to engage in such activities because, for example, they may have larger resources available. These observations provide support to our methodological choice, which is aimed at tackling this issue and, thus, at getting a purer identifiable effect of CSR on firm performance.

12.4 Results

The top part of Table 12.4 reports the maximum likelihood estimation (MLE) of the production function specified in Equation 12.6, while its bottom part shows the results of the selection model as in Equation 12.4. Overall, our estimates allow

Table 12.4 **MLE estimation***

Variables	Argentina log sale	Bolivia log sale	Chile log sale	Colombia log sale	Mexico log sale
Log emp	0.907***	0.706***	0.712***	0.816***	0.874***
	(0.0818)	(0.137)	(0.0981)	(0.0845)	(0.104)
Log capital	0.0983**	0.341***	0.133***	0.195***	0.220***
	(0.0430)	(0.0390)	(0.0341)	(0.0277)	(0.0396)
Firm age	0.00163	0.00703*	−0.00330	0.00415	0.00518
	(0.00219)	(0.00409)	(0.00230)	(0.00333)	(0.00375)
Foreign	0.0668	0.808**	0.596**	0.249	0.280*
	(0.220)	(0.329)	(0.274)	(0.233)	(0.150)
Export	0.00530**	0.00246	−0.000289	0.00232	0.00444*
	(0.00257)	(0.00322)	(0.00308)	(0.00261)	(0.00234)
R&D	−0.0269	−0.0972	0.351***	0.419***	−0.117
	(0.130)	(0.157)	(0.130)	(0.111)	(0.125)
Polstab	0.192	0.209	−0.214	−0.156	−0.100
	(0.134)	(0.198)	(0.154)	(0.0980)	(0.0921)
Corruption	−0.296**	−0.145	−0.0590	0.0908	0.123
	(0.139)	(0.198)	(0.197)	(0.0913)	(0.100)
Small firm	−0.1000	−0.507	−0.893***	−0.199	0.315
	(0.240)	(0.481)	(0.320)	(0.259)	(0.292)
Medium firm	−0.0886	−0.522	−0.509**	−0.138	0.210
	(0.175)	(0.358)	(0.213)	(0.189)	(0.174)
CSR	1.201***	1.269***	0.892	−0.628	0.921***
	(0.310)	(0.397)	(0.825)	(0.412)	(0.282)
Constant	9.765***	9.239***	15.44***	15.21***	8.601***
	(0.553)	(0.813)	(1.135)	(0.615)	(0.627)
Selection equation					
Log employment	0.122	0.356*	0.142	0.397***	0.0106
	(0.113)	(0.211)	(0.166)	(0.147)	(0.124)
Log capital	0.0822	0.0439	−0.0435	−0.0103	−0.00467
	(0.0513)	(0.0551)	(0.0537)	(0.0525)	(0.0294)
Firm age	0.00213	4.55e-05	0.00643	0.0200***	0.00769
	(0.00328)	(0.00658)	(0.00449)	(0.00758)	(0.00528)
Foreign	0.439	0.0659	0.600	0.388	0.0532
	(0.298)	(0.440)	(0.550)	(0.509)	(0.279)
Export	−0.00152	0.00274	0.0272**	−0.00433	0.00984**
	(0.00351)	(0.00538)	(0.0121)	(0.00417)	(0.00452)

Variables	Argentina log sale	Bolivia log sale	Chile log sale	Colombia log sale	Mexico log sale
R&D	0.399**	0.151	0.0160	0.835***	1.248***
	(0.184)	(0.207)	(0.205)	(0.170)	(0.233)
Polstab	−0.388**	0.0749	0.129	−0.0194	0.0548
	(0.177)	(0.280)	(0.220)	(0.195)	(0.125)
Corruption	0.320*	0.182	0.115	0.0578	0.00311
	(0.179)	(0.257)	(0.222)	(0.193)	(0.128)
Small firm	−0.312	0.987	−0.309	0.818*	−1.061**
	(0.375)	(0.664)	(0.484)	(0.464)	(0.427)
Medium firm	−0.299	0.602	−0.275	0.521	−0.762**
	(0.282)	(0.463)	(0.344)	(0.357)	(0.297)
Receive pressure to adopt CRS	0.181	0.365	0.231	1.097**	1.197***
	(0.241)	(0.295)	(0.279)	(0.431)	(0.372)
Constant	−0.675	−1.557	0.929	−0.856	0.488
	(0.826)	(1.210)	(1.232)	(1.114)	(0.710)
Observations	387	226	391.0	533	736
Chi-square	1,240	802.0	2,422	1,494	1,837
Rho	−0.816	0.798	−0.443	0.416	−0.536

*There is no convergence for Ecuador so the results are not reported. Foreign takes value 1 if the foreign ownership is greater than 10% and 0 otherwise. Export is the percentage of sales exported directly and indirectly. R&D takes value 1 if the firm invested in R&D within the establishment or through a third party and 0 otherwise. Age is the firm's age in 2006. Polstab and Corruption takes value 1 if the firm perceives political stability or corruption to be major obstacles to business. Robust standard errors in parentheses; *** $p<0.01$, ** $p<0.05$, * $p<0.1$.

investigation whether CSR firms are more or less productive in terms of the revenue that they generate from given inputs than non-CSR firms.

Considering the upper part of the table, it is worth clarifying that CSR is a dummy variable that takes value 1 when firms adopt either an environment or a social community program. Moreover, it should be noticed that the results for Ecuador have not been reported due to the lack of convergence in MLE estimates. This might be due to the documented similarities between CSR adopters and non-adopters (see Table 12.3 for details).

Looking to the upper part of Table 12.4, we focus on the coefficients of the treatment variable (adoption of CSR practices). The coefficient indicates the percentage increase in a firm's sales for the firms that adopt CSR relative to those that do not. There is a positive and significant effect from the adoption of CSR only for Argentina, Bolivia and Mexico, while the variable is not significant for Chile and Colombia. When we find a significant effect, the coefficient of range is in between 0.91 and 1.2.

The estimated coefficients of the control variables are highly comparable across countries, also running in the expected directions, although their significance changes across countries. For example, foreign ownership, export intensity and R&D are associated with greater productivity. This is in line with the existing literature on firms productivity based on WBES data.

Given the empirical strategy applied, these estimates control for other observed determinants of revenue and any unobserved (latent) selection bias.

There is goodness of fit of all models estimated given by the high χ^2 which is significant in all cases at 1% level. We report the adjusted ρ-statistic, which is the hyperbolic arctangent of the correlation (q) between the residuals in the selection and outcome equations. For all countries, the outcome and selection equations cannot be considered independent (at the 5% level). Thus, moderate selection bias exists and OLS results may not be reliable. Hence, this validates the econometric technique employed.

Passing to the bottom part of Table 12.4, it serves to assess whether the concerns regarding endogenous selection are warranted. This part of the table reveals the extent to which the adoption of CSR can be attributed to firms' characteristics and the chosen instruments. The results show that specific firms characteristics are significant predictors of participation. In particular larger firms that engage in export and R&D have an increased probability of adopting the CSR practices. The significance of these variables indicates the presence of selection bias and underscores the importance of considering selection when estimating the impact of CSR on firms' performance. The coefficient of the chosen "instrument" (i.e. "receive pressure to adopt CSR") is significant only for Colombia and Mexico. So, for Argentina, Bolivia and Chile, estimates should be interpreted with care. Overall the analysis of the selection equation suggests that, in most cases, the extent to which firms act responsibly is non-random and hence the use of an econometric technique that accounts for endogenous selection is relevant.

Overall our exercise shows that firms that engage in environmental or community projects are no less efficient than firms that do not adopt such practices. Thus, our results suggest that corporate goals, such as productivity, are compatible with conscious operations.

12.5 Conclusions

This chapter has analysed the impact of CSR on firms performance, defined here as firms' revenues, in six Latin American countries, addressing the likely endogeneity of CSR through the two-step MLE estimator applied to the system of simultaneous equations constituted by an extended production function and to a selection model. Our results have shown that firms that engage in environmental or community projects do not underperform firms that do not adopt such practices. The advocates of CSR claim that responsible firms' behaviour, toward both shareholders and stakeholders, is essential to compete in the global market. Our findings suggest that corporate goals, such as revenue maximization, are compatible with conscious operations. However, we should ask why, in some cases, CSR fails to have a clear positive impact on firms' performance. Scholars have suggested that the prevalence of CSR in the developing world may be related to prevailing social and cultural norms (Gao, 2009; Jamali and Neville, 2011), or the presence socio-economic needs (Frynas, 2005). If firms have non-pecuniary motives for improving the welfare of interest groups, it is possible that CSR may not have any effect on sales and profit maximizations. Thus, common frameworks drawn in the developed world may not be suitable for analysing CSR developing countries and so new theories will need to be employed to fully understand the characteristics that CSR manifests in emerging markets (Kolk and Lenfant, 2010; Kolk and Van Tulder, 2010). This is left for future research.

Another promising line of further investigation relies on the synergies between different types of management practices. For instance, whether business integrity in term of social and environmental practices has any impact on corruption and, thus, exploring the link between CSR and corruption seems particularly relevant to developing countries.

12.5.1 CSR and development

This chapter has discussed the prevalence of CSR activities across six Latin American countries and the impact on a selected measure of firms' performance, namely their revenues. The econometrics analysis shows that CSR has a positive, although at times insignificant, effect on the outcome variable analysed. We conclude that firms that engage in environmental, social and/or labour policies produce no less compared to those firms that do not adopt those practices. Given the focus of this book, it is worth mentioning how, and to what extent, our findings provide an example of development-oriented CSR.

It is well known that a firm's production is the engine of economic growth. Endogenous growth theory has provided an explanation on the engines of economic growth, which are all related to increasing returns (Aghion and Howitt, 1998). Greater output can lead to increased investment and productivity, which in turn generates further employment and, thus, this creates a virtuous circle. So our example stresses that certain business practices are conducive to output generation and, thus, to economic growth. This clearly shows how businesses that engage in CSR can be a catalyst for economic development. In today's world, the focus of governments and international organizations is no longer limited to economic growth; rather, they embrace the idea of sustainable development. This notion reflects the idea that economic growth in order to build prosperity for today and future generations must respect the environment and communities that are affected by such a process. Firms are increasingly considered key contributors to poverty reduction and sustainable development goals (Clifford *et al.*, 2013). CSR is inherently linked to the concept of sustainable development. In fact, it may be defined as "the commitment of business to contribute to sustainable economic development in ways that are both good for business and good for development" (Ward, 2004).

Although our empirical analysis focuses on a measurable impact of CSR (the revenue), the activities of the firms discussed in our study have a broader but, in this case, not quantifiable impact on the environment and the communities. Given the prevalence of CSR among the firms surveyed, our study shows that companies in the Latin American countries analysed are likely to act as development agents. The development-oriented approach of firms is particularly important for developing countries (Fox, 2004). In many countries, in particular developing ones, governments have shown little ability and/or willingness to improve social, economic and (environmental) well-being. This leaves greater scope for the involvement of corporations in the society and the environment (Moon, 2007). Moreover, the role of firms in the society has increased as a result of greater liberalization and globalization of markets (Kolk and Van Tulder, 2006).

So civil society organizations can collaborate with market actors to promote development (Brugmann and Prahalad, 2007). This idea is at the heart of the 'co-creation approach' where different actors bring specific skills and resources to facilitate development and poverty reduction (Brugmann and Prahalad, 2007).

To conclude, our study shows that companies that engage in CSR contribute to development in two ways. First social and environmental practices are compatible with greater production. Second, firms largely engage in activities that are compatible with the notion of sustainable development.

One caveat to keep in mind is that our empirical analysis merely focuses on the impact of CSR on firms' revenue. This is by no means a perfect or complete measure of a firm's performance, hence our analysis provides a somehow narrow prospective on the relationship between CSR practices and traditional corporate goals. Future research on the countries here analysed will shed light on the broader effect of CSR activities on a variety of firms indicators (i.e. productivity, innovation, profitability etc ...). Moreover, because of the limitation of the data employed, our study does not assess the extent to which companies are successful in promoting sustainable development. For instance, we know that the majority of firms adopt some environmental program, but we have no means of evaluating the effectiveness of these practices.

Finally, in the spirit of Sen (1999), we should not forget that development is not only confined to income; there is also the non-monetary aspect of human life such as education, health, civil and political rights. Again, future data may help in the investigation of the impact of CSR activities on the environment, employees and relevant stakeholders (i.e. the community).

Bibliography

Acutt, N., Medina-Ross, V., & O'Riordan, T. (2004). Perspectives on corporate social responsibility in the chemical sector: a comparative analysis of the Mexican and South African cases. *Natural Resources Forum*, 28(4), 302-316.

Aghion, P., & Howitt, P. (1998). *Endogenous Growth Theory*. Cambridge, MA: MIT Press.

Araya, M. (2006). Exploring terra incognita: non-financial reporting in Latin America. *Journal of Corporate Citizenship*, 21(Spring) 25-38.

Aupperle, K. E., Carroll, A.B., & Hatfield, J.D. (1985). An empirical examination of the relationship between corporate social responsibility and profitability. *Academy of Management Journal*, 28(2), 446-463.

Baskin, J. (2006). Corporate responsibility in emerging markets. *Journal of Corporate Citizenship*, 24(24), 29-47.

Becchetti, L., Ciciretti, R., & Hasan, I. (2007). Corporate social responsibility and shareholder's value: an event study analysis. Working paper, Federal Reserve Bank of Atlanta.

Beck, T., Demirguc-Kunt, A., & Levine, R. (2005a). Law and firms access to finance. *American Law and Economics Review*, 7(1), 211-252.

Beck, T., Demirguc-Kunt, A., & Maksimovic, V. (2005b). Financial and legal constraints to growth: does firm size matter? *Journal of Finance*, 60, 137-177.

Bird, R., Momentè, F., & Reggiani, F. (2007). What corporate social responsibility activities are valued by the market? *Journal of Business Ethics*, 76(2), 189-206.

Blowfield, M. (2003). Ethical supply chains in the cocoa, coffee and tea industries. *Greener Management International*, 43(Autumn), 15-24.

Blowfield, M. (2004). Implementation deficits of ethical trade systems: lessons from the Indonesia cocoa and timber industries. *Journal of Corporate Citizenship*, 13(Spring), 77-90.

Blowfield, M. (2005). Corporate social responsibility: reinventing the meaning of development?. *International Affairs*, 81(3), 515-524.

Blundell, R., & Costa Dias, M. (2000). Evaluation methods for non-experimental data. *Fiscal Studies*, 21(4), 427-468.

Blundell, R., & Costa Dias, M. (2002). Alternative approaches to evaluation in empirical microeconomics. *Portuguese Economic Journal*, 1(2), 91-115.

Bolwig, S., Gibbon, P., & Jones, E.S. (2009). The economics of small-holder organic contract farming in tropical Africa. *World Development*, 37(6), 1094-1104.

Bragdon, J.H., & Marlin J. (1972). Is pollution profitable? *Risk Management*, 19(4).

Brammer, S., Jackson, G., & Matten, D. (2012). Corporate social responsibility and institutional theory: new perspectives on private governance. *Socio-Economic Review*, 10(1), 3-28.

Brugmann, J., & Prahalad, C.K. (2007). Cocreating business's new social compact. *Harvard Business Review*, February.

Bowman, E.H., & Haire, M. (1975). A strategic posture toward corporate social responsibility. *California Management Review*, 18(2), 49–58.

Carroll, A.B. (1999). Corporate social responsibility: evolution of a definitional construct. *Business and Society*, 38(3), 268-295.

Chen, C., & Shang, Y. (2009). Ambition versus conscience, does corporate social responsibility pay off? The application of matching methods. *Journal of Business Ethics*, 88(1), 133-153.

Clifford, M., Forbes, I., Sesan, T., & Sesan, R. (2013). Corporate-led sustainable development and energy poverty alleviation at the bottom of the pyramid: the case of the clean cook in Nigeria. *World Development*, 45, 137-146.

Cochran, P.L., & Wood, R.A. (1984). Corporate social responsibility and financial performance. *Academy of Management Journal*, 27(1), 42-56.

Commander, S., & Svejnar, J. (2011). Business environment, export, ownership and firm performance. *The Review of Economics and Statistics*, 93(1), 309-337.

De Rosa, D., Gooroochurn, N., & Gorg, H. (2010). Corruption and productivity: firm-level evidence from the BEEPS survey. World Bank Policy Research, Working Paper Series, No. 5348.

Djankov, S., La Porta, R., Lopez-de-Silanes, F., & Shliefer, A. (2008). The law and economics of self-dealing. *Journal of Financial Economics*, 88(3), 430-465.

Djankov, S., & Murrell, P. (2002) Enterprise restructuring in transition: a quantitative survey. World Bank Working Paper.

Estrin, S., Hanousek, J., Kocenda, E., & Svejnar, J. (2009). Effects of privatization and ownership in transition economies. *Journal of Economic Literature*, 47(3), 699-728.

Fox, T. (2004). Corporate social responsibility and development: in quest of an agenda. *Development*, 47(3), (29-36).

Frynas, J.G. (2005). The false developmental promise of corporate social responsibility: evidence from multinational oil companies. *International Affairs*, 81(3), 581-598.

Gao, Y. (2009). Corporate social performance in China: evidence from large companies. *Journal of Business Ethics*, 89, 23-35

Heckman, J. (1979). Sample selection bias as a specification error. *Econometrica*, 47(1), 153-161.

Heckman, J., LaLonde, R., & Smith, J. (1999). The economics and econometrics of active labour market programs. In O. Ashenfelter & D. Card (Eds.), *Handbook of Labor Economics* (1865-2097). London, UK: Elsevier.

Heckamn, J., Ichimura, H., Smith, J., & Todd, P. (1998), Characterizing selection bias using experimental data. *Econometrica*, 66(5), 1017-1098.

Jamali, D. (2008) Corporate governance and corporate social responsibility synergies and interrelationships. *Corporate Governance: An International Review*, 16(5), 443-459.

Jamali, D., & Mirshak, R. (2007). Corporate social responsibility: theory and practice in a developing country context. *Journal of Business Ethics*, 72(1), 243-262.

Jamali, D., & Neville, B. (2011). Convergence versus divergence of CSR in developing countries: an embedded multi-layered institutional lens, *Journal of Business Ethics*, 102(4), 599-621.

Jones, M.T. (1996). Missing the forest for the trees. A critique of the social responsibility concept and discourse. *Business and Society*, 35(1), 7-41.

Kapelus, P. (2002). Mining, corporate social responsibility and the case of Rio Tinto Richards Bay Minerals and the Mbonambi. *Journal of Business Ethics*, 39(3), 275-296.

Kaufman, A., Tiantubtim, E., Pussayapibul, N., & Davids, P. (2004). Implementing voluntary labour standards and codes of conduct in the Thai garment industry. *Journal of Corporate Citizenship*, 13(Spring), 91-99.

Kolk, A., & Lenfant, F. (2010). MNC reporting on CSR and conflict in Central Africa. *Journal of Business Ethics*, 93(2), 241-255.

Kolk, A., & Van Tulder, R. (2006). Poverty alleviation as business strategy?. Evaluating commitments of front-runner multinational corporations. *World Development*, 34(5), 789-801.

Kolk, A., & Van Tulder, R. (2010). International business, corporate social responsibility and sustainable development. *International Business Review*, 19(2), 119-125.

Luken, R., & Stares, R. (2005). Small business responsibility in developing countries: a threat or an opportunity? *Business Strategy and the Environment*, 14(1), 38-53.

Lund-Thomsen, P. (2004). Towards a critical framework on corporate social and environmental responsibility in the south: The case of Pakistan. *Development*, 47(3), 106-113.

Margolis, J.D., Elfenbein, H.A., & Walsh, J.P. (2007). Does it pay to be good? A meta-analysis and redirection of research on corporate social and financial performance, Working Paper, University of California at Berkeley.

Margolis, J.D., & Walsh, J.P. (2003) Misery loves companies: Whither social initiatives by business?. *Administrative Science Quarterly*, 48(2), 268-305.

McWilliams, A., & Siegel, D. (2000). Corporate social responsibility and financial performance: correlation or misspecification?. *Strategic Management Journal*, 21(5), 525-623.

Moon, J. (2007). The contribution of corporate social responsibility to sustainable development. *Sustainable Development*, 15(5), 296-306.

Muller, A., & Kolk, A. (2009). CSR performance in emerging markets: evidence from Mexico. *Journal of Business Ethics*, 85(2), 325-337.

Newell, P., & Muro, A. (2006). Corporate social and environmental responsibility in Argentina: the evolution of an agenda. *Journal of Corporate Citizenship*, 24(Winter), 49-68.

Newell, P., & Frynas, J.D. (2007). Beyond CSR? Business, poverty and social justice: an introduction. *Third World Quarterly*, 28(4), 669-681.

Newgren, K., Rasher, A., LaRoe, M., & Szabo, M. (1985). Environmental assessment and corporate performance: a longitudinal analysis using market determined performance measures. 7, 153-164.

Orlitzky, M., Rynes, F.L., & Schmidt, S.L. (2003). Corporate social and financial performance: A meta-analysis. *Organization Studies*, 24(3), 103-441.

Porter, M.E., & Van der Linde, C. (1995). Green and competitive. Ending the stalemate. *Harvard Business Review*, 73(5), 120-135.

Puhani, P. (2000). The Heckman correction for sample selection and its critique. *Journal of Economic Surveys*, 14(1), 53-68.

Ravallion, M. (2005). Evaluating anti-poverty programme. In T.P. Schultz & J. Strauss (Eds.), *Handbook of Development Economics* (Vol. 4). Amsterdam, North-Holland.

Sen, A. (1999). *Development as Freedom*. Oxford: Oxford University Press.

Tsoutsourz, M. (2004). Corporate Social Responsibility and Financial Performance (Applied Financial Project, Berkeley, California).

Turban, D.B., & Greening, D.W. (1997). Corporate social performance and organizational attractiveness to prospective employees. *Academy of Management Journal*, 40(3), 658-672.

Yong Y., & Mallick S., (2010). Export premium, self-selection and learning-by-exporting: evidence from Chinese matched firms. *The World Economy*, 33(10), 1218-1240.

Ullmann, A. (1985). Data in search of a theory: a critical examination of the relationship among social performance, social disclosure and economic performance of US firms. *Academy of Management Review*, 10(3), 540-557.

Vance, S.C. (1975). Are socially responsible corporations good investment risks? *Management Review*, 64, 18-24.

Vella, F., & Verbeek, M. (1999). Estimating and interpreting models with endogenous treatment effects. *Journal of Business & Economic Statistics*. 17(4), 473-478.

Visser, W. (2008).Corporate social responsibility in developing countries. In A. Crane, A. McWilliams, D. Matten, J. Moon, & D. Siegel (Eds.), *The Oxford Handbook of Corporate Social Responsibility* (pp. 473-479). Oxford, UK: Oxford University Press.

Vivarta, V., & Canela, G. (2006). Corporate social responsibility in Brazil: the role of the press as watchdog. *Journal of Corporate Citizenship*, 21(Spring), 95-106.

Vives, A. (2006). Social and environmental responsibility in small and medium enterprises in Latin America. *Journal of Corporate Citizenship*, 21, 39-50.

Waddock, S., & Graves, S. (1997). The corporate social performance—financial performance link. *Strategic Management Journal*, 18(4), 303–319.

Walsh, J.P., Weber, K., & Margolis, J.D. (2003). Social issues and management: our lost cause found. *Journal of Management*, 29(6), 859-882.

Ward, H. (2004). Public sector roles in strengthening corporate social responsibility: Taking stock, Washington, D.C: World Bank Group.

Welford, R. (2005). Corporate social responsibility in Europe, North America and Asia. *Journal of Corporate Citizenship*, 17(1), 33-52.

Weyzig, F. (2006). Local and global dimensions of Corporate Social Responsibility in Mexico. *Journal of Corporate Citizenship*, 24(Winter), 69-81.

Zhuang, C., & Wheale, P. (2004). Creating sustainable corporate value: a case study of stakeholder relationship management in China. *Business and Society Review*, 109(4), 507-547.

13

Political CSR and social development

Lessons from the Bangladesh garment industry

Kristin Huber and Dirk Ulrich Gilbert
University of Hamburg, Germany

In this chapter, we argue that viewing corporations as political actors in developing countries provides additional insights for understanding the relationship between CSR and social development. We introduce a framework from the "political" CSR literature that is geared towards evaluating multistakeholder initiatives (MSIs) from a normative point of view and suggest that this framework provides a solid theoretical basis for examining the potential of firms, through their engagement in MSIs, to contribute to social development. The introduced framework is then used to assess the implications for social development of a recently set-up MSI in the garment sector in Bangladesh. We conclude that while there are a number of issues associated with the analysed MSI, it has a chance to enhance social development in Bangladesh and can thus be perceived as an example of development-oriented CSR.

Although business activities in developing countries have substantially increased over the past years (UNCTAD, 2013), so far no agreement has been reached as to what constitutes businesses' responsibilities in development (Lenssen and van Wassenhove, 2012). However, given that production facilities collapse in countries like Bangladesh and that millions of people are still living in poverty, the question whether and to what extent business in general, and multinational corporations (MNCs) in particular, can foster or hinder progress in developing countries seems a highly relevant and timely one.

Both CSR and development are contested concepts. CSR today is usually defined as an umbrella term circumscribing the social and environmental responsibilities of corporations beyond legal compliance (Blowfield and Frynas, 2005). Development in recent years has come to be mainly associated with the notion of human development; that is, the aim of reducing poverty and fulfilling the millennium development goals (MDGs) (Sumner and Tribe, 2008). The MDGs represent eight international development goals that were established by the United Nations (UN) General Assembly at the turn of the millennium aiming, among other things, at halving extreme poverty, universal primary education or containing the spread of HIV/AIDS (United Nations, 2014). In this chapter, we focus on social development which, according to the UN, refers to a broad range of issues such as the eradication of poverty, the promotion of employment and the fostering of social integration in order to achieve just and stable societies (United Nations, 2002).

We suggest that a stream of research within the CSR literature, so called "political" CSR, holds the promise for a more nuanced understanding of the possibility of businesses to contribute to social development. The political turn in CSR research highlights that as businesses increasingly provide public goods and shape global regulation through their engagement in multistakeholder initiatives (MSIs), they are turning into political actors. MSIs have proliferated in recent years in number and scope and many of them address issues that directly relate to core dimensions of social development. Yet, as Utting (2012) notes, so far the implications of MSIs from a development perspective have only scarcely been addressed. We therefore focus on the question of whether and under which conditions firms can be expected to contribute to social development by participating in MSIs. Following a brief overview of (i) the debate on the role of CSR in development and (ii) the discussion on so-called "political" CSR, we use the introduced "political" CSR lens to assess the developmental implications of a recently set up MSI in the garment sector in Bangladesh. Finally, we critically reflect on the MSI from a development perspective and draw lessons from the case of the Bangladesh garment industry.

13.1 (Political) corporate social responsibility and development

Questions concerning the social responsibility of businesses have been discussed under the umbrella term CSR ever since the 1950s (Carroll, 2008). Initially, CSR was narrowly associated with corporate philanthropy (Carroll, 2008) and research on CSR focused on developed economies analysing the meaning, key features, explanations, applications and scope of the concept (Carroll, 2008; Garriga and Melé, 2004). In the recent CSR literature, however, two distinct streams of research have emerged that both go beyond the confines of developed economies. Writings on CSR have on the one hand taken a "developmental" turn while on the other hand, research has also taken a "political turn".

13.1.1 The developmental turn in CSR research

The responsibility of businesses in the transition towards a more sustainable development as well as the prospects and limitations of CSR of contributing to international development have received increased attention over the past two decades (Barkemeyer et al., 2011; Kolk and Van Buuse, 2012; Kolk and van Tulder, 2010; Lund-Thomsen, 2005). One reason for this turn in CSR research towards developmental issues relates to the changing views of development agencies and practitioners, on what the objectives of development should be and how they can best be achieved (Jenkins, 2005). Development theory has gone through a number of phases from the developmental state in the 1960s/1970s, to the neoliberal reform associated with the Washington Consensus in the 1980s, to the emphasis on partnerships with the private sector and CSR from the 1990s onwards (Jenkins, 2005; Pieterse, 2010; Reed and Reed, 2009; Utting and Zammit, 2009). Over the years, CSR has thus gained prominence with development practitioners as a means to mitigate the negative consequences of globalization (Marques and Utting, 2010).

However, CSR has been discussed controversially by authors addressing the role of MNCs in developing countries (see, for example, Barkemeyer, 2009; Blowfield, 2012; Jenkins, 2005; Kolk and van Tulder, 2006; Merino and Valor, 2011; Newell and Frynas, 2007; Utting and Marques, 2009). Regarding the developmental potential of CSR, two opposing views have emerged (Blowfield, 2012). One group of authors advocates that business with their CSR activities should take a proactive role in promoting development (see, for example, Brainard, 2006; Prahalad and Hart, 2002). These authors generally stress that corporations can potentially play an integral part in development through the provision of goods and services, capital, infrastructure, employment, innovation, technology or by promoting good governance. Another group of authors has voiced severe criticism and caution regarding the consequences of business taking on such roles and has thus called for a more critical research agenda (Blowfield and Frynas, 2005; Jeppesen and Lund-Thomsen, 2010; Newell and Frynas, 2007). Authors in favour of a critical perspective on CSR in developing countries have pointed out that the empirical evidence is lacking to support the win-win hypothesis (Jeppesen and Lund-Thomsen, 2010) and that the notion of the business case for CSR is incompatible with substantive contributions to development (Blowfield and Frynas, 2005; Frynas, 2005; Jenkins, 2005).

In recent years, academic interest in multistakeholder partnerships has gained momentum in the debate on CSR and development. The increased interest in partnerships for development can among other things be attributed to the launch of the UN Global Compact in 1999, which was established to foster corporate responsibility and to promote private sector partnerships with the UN for the benefit of developing countries (Reed and Reed, 2009). Partnerships usually represent collaborative arrangements involving actors from different spheres of society, that is, from the spheres of the state, the market or civil society and sometimes also from academia (Van Huijstee *et al.*, 2007). In the literature, depending on the particular actor constellation, various labels are used to refer to partnerships, such as public-private or tripartite partnerships (Kolk *et al.*, 2008; Reed and Reed, 2009), standardized ethics initiatives (Gilbert and Rasche, 2008), or MSIs (O'Rourke, 2006; Utting, 2002) to name but a few. In this chapter, we use MSI as an umbrella term to refer to collaborative arrangements involving business and civil society actors in setting standards for social and environmental issues. MSIs can certainly differ substantially in terms of the actors involved or the intensity, scale and intentions of activities. However, a characteristic feature of all MSIs is that they are primarily based on soft-law; that is, non-binding, voluntary regulation (Abbott and Snidal, 2000; Utting, 2002). Multistakeholder regulation has rapidly expanded across industries over the past decade (O'Rourke, 2006). Research so far has scrutinized the emergence and rise of MSIs as well as the potential and limitations of these new institutions (see, for example, O'Rourke, 2006; Utting, 2002, 2012; Vogel, 2008, 2010). Regarding the impact of MSIs on development, again two opposing views have emerged. While proponents argue that such initiatives represent an essential new way of engaging business, others fear that MSIs will "crowd-out" more effective forms of regulation and thus rather hinder development (O'Rourke, 2006; Reed and Reed, 2009; Vogel, 2008, 2010).

Research on CSR and development thus so far has produced inconclusive results regarding the question to what extent CSR can help address poverty, social exclusion and further developmental challenges. Against this background, Blowfield and Dolan (2014) propose that we need a more nuanced understanding of the business development relationship. Blowfield and Dolan (2014) suggest three criteria to evaluate businesses' potential to act as development agents, stating that firms can only be referred to as genuine development agents provided that they employ capital, exhibit a willingness to be held accountable for the development effort, and lastly give primacy to the development issue. Evaluating the engagement of businesses in development through "bottom of the pyramid" (BOP) initiatives, Blowfield and Dolan (2014) conclude that these initiatives are usually constructed in terms of what is material and instrumental for businesses without factual accountability for development outcomes.

We concur with Blowfield and Dolan (2014) that a more nuanced understanding of the possibilities and limitations of business acting as a development agent is essential for defining a future role of business in development. Yet, Blowfield and Dolan (2014) in their analysis exclusively focus on businesses' engagement in BOP initiatives. We suggest that analysing the possibilities and limitations of corporations to serve as development agents through their engagement in

MSIs is equally important. MSIs are usually aimed at filling institutional voids (Kolk *et al.*, 2008). Developing countries often exhibit such institutional gaps as they tend to be characterized by weak or limited statehood. Limited statehood refers to states being incapable of, or unwilling to implement or enforce central decisions either in parts of a country's territory or in certain policy areas (Risse, 2011). Thus, it can be argued that MSIs, as new forms of governance, are unfolding a particular relevance in developing countries. We therefore aim at understanding to what extent and under what circumstances corporations, through their engagement in MSIs, can act as development agents. In this regard, we propose that the stream of research that has been coined as "political" CSR holds the promise of a more nuanced understanding of businesses' relationship with social development.

13.1.2 The political turn in CSR research

"Political" CSR suggests that corporations increasingly assume responsibilities that were formerly regarded as genuine governmental responsibilities such as when businesses engage in the protection of human rights, draft regulation for social and environmental standards (e.g. through MSIs) (Palazzo and Scherer, 2006), or engage in the provision of public goods such as healthcare, education or security (Matten and Crane, 2005). This new political conception of CSR goes beyond the traditional understanding that businesses mainly influence politics via lobbying, stating that firms themselves can become political actors (Scherer *et al.*, 2006).

The political turn in CSR research is based on two interrelated observations (Whelan, 2012). First, according to Scherer and Palazzo (2007, 2011), the process of globalization has led to a "postnational constellation" (Habermas, 2001); that is, a post-Westphalian global order in which the traditional division of labour between political and business actors has eroded. In this new global order, MNCs through their global supply chains often operate in contexts lacking basic institutional structures. Moreover, national governments are increasingly subjected to externality problems with global causes and effects such as global warming or deforestation which they cannot solve on their own. Second, new forms of global governance operating above and beyond the state, partly compensate for the decline in governance capability of nation-states (Scherer and Palazzo, 2011). Businesses increasingly take part in these new voluntary regulatory governance forms to solve public goods problems and fill gaps in global regulation and are thereby gradually engaging in activities that were formerly regarded as genuine governmental roles. The reason why corporations assume such roles, according to Palazzo and Scherer (2006), lies in their need to secure their licence to operate as global civil society actors increasingly scrutinize and contest corporate activities.

Beyond this descriptive analysis, Scherer and Palazzo (2007; 2011), aim at a normative conception of "political" CSR to account for the growing political activities of corporations. Scherer *et al.* (2006) understand political in terms of Young (2004) as relating to activities,

[...] in which people organize collectively to regulate or transform some aspect of their shared social conditions, along with the communicative activities in which they try to persuade one another to join such collective action or decide what direction they wish to take it. (Young, 2004, p. 377)

Drawing on Habermas's theory of deliberative democracy (Habermas, 1996, 1998), Scherer and Palazzo (2007) translate the idea of political participation into the discursive interaction between corporations and civil society organizations. They emphasize that through deliberative interaction with civil society organizations (CSOs), businesses will enter into a process of argumentative "self-entrapment" (Risse, 1999, p. 542) and thus "increasingly contribute to an institutionalization of norms and the solution of political challenges" (Scherer and Palazzo, 2007, p. 1111). "Political" CSR is thus highlighted as a means through which MNCs can positively impact on societal problems and social rights of citizens (Whelan, 2012). Scherer and Palazzo (2011) present their new political approach to CSR as a means of overcoming the established and narrow instrumental view of CSR that generally highlights a "business case" logic. Contrasting "instrumental" with "political" CSR, they emphasize that once corporations cooperate with actors from other spheres of society to solve political problems, they turn into political actors (Scherer and Palazzo, 2011, p. 918). "Political" CSR ultimately suggests that corporations should proactively engage in overarching processes of public will formation (Palazzo and Scherer, 2006).

According to Mena and Palazzo (2012), MSIs represent an important manifestation of the idea of "political" CSR as they represent fora in which corporations can discursively engage with civil society. However, the intentional efforts of businesses to voluntarily contribute to the regulation of societal issues raises a number of questions regarding the legitimacy of such activities. Corporations and other actors participating in MSIs have neither been elected nor are controlled like democratic governments (Baumann-Pauly and Scherer, 2013). Yet, in a global context, democratic participation cannot result from a process of expressing preferences and a system of vote-aggregation (Scherer and Palazzo, 2011). Thus, the legitimacy of MSI regulation has to be conceptualized differently. Drawing on the work of Scharpf (1997; 1999), and building on the Habermasian concept of deliberative democracy, Mena and Palazzo (2012) argue that the democratic legitimacy of an MSI relates to questions concerning the inclusiveness and fairness of deliberation within MSIs as well as the ability of the issued regulation to effectively solve the problems that an MSI intends to deal with. To critically assess the democratic quality of MSIs, they introduce a set of criteria pertaining to the input and output dimension of MSIs (see Table 13.1).

According to Mena and Palazzo (2012), from the input perspective, the legitimacy of an MSI depends on (a) stakeholder inclusion, that is, to the question to what extent stakeholders who will be affected by the regulation are considered or incorporated in the process. It further relates to (b) procedural fairness of deliberations, which requires that all involved stakeholders in an MSI are able to exert the

Table 13.1 **Criteria of MSI democratic legitimacy**

Dimension	Criterion	Definition	Key questions
Input	Inclusion	Involvement of stakeholders affected by the issue in the structures and processes of the MSI	Are the involved stakeholders representative for the issue at stake? Are important stakeholders excluded from the process?
	Procedural fairness	Neutralization of power differences in decision-making structures	Does each of these categories of stakeholder have a valid voice in decision-making processes?
	Consensual orientation	Culture of cooperation and reasonable disagreement	To what extent does the MSI promote mutual agreement among participants?
	Transparency	Transparency of structures, processes and results	To what extent are decision-making and standard-setting processes transparent? To what extent are the performance of the participating corporations and the evaluation of that performance transparent?
Output	Coverage	Number of rule-targets following the rules	How many rule-targets are complying with the rules?
	Efficacy	Fit of the rules to the issue	To what extent do the rules address the issue at hand?
	Enforcement	Practical implementation of the rules and their verification procedures	Is compliance verified and non-compliance sanctioned?

Source: Mena and Palazzo (2012, p. 537)

same influence on the discussions within an MSI and that existing power imbalances between the participants are compensated or neutralized. Moreover, input legitimacy depends on (c) consensual orientation; that is, the extent to which decisions made by the MSI reflect a consensus among the participants. Consensual orientation may insofar enhance legitimacy as it indicates that proposals have stood up to "dialogical examination" (Young, 2000, p. 23). Whether or not a consensus is possible depends on the participants' willingness to accept the "forceless force of the better argument" (Habermas, 1999, p. 332). Mena and Palazzo (2012) further propose (d) the transparency of an MSI as a legitimacy criterion. It relates to the question whether and to what extent, the activities of an MSI as well as the decision procedures, distribution of voting rights, and so on, are known to all participants involved.

In contrast, the output dimension can be assessed through an MSI's (a) coverage, which refers to the number of actors considering the standards or rules issued by an MSI as binding, and (b) its efficacy, that is, the extent to which the rules and standards produced by the MSI are suited to solve the problem at hand. Ineffectiveness may be related to either the weakness of the rules or negative externalities arising along with the MSI. Finally, it also relates to questions of (c) enforcement, that is, the ability of an MSI to ensure that the involved actors abide by the rules and standards developed by the MSI.

13.2 Merging the two debates: understanding corporations as political actors in developing countries

The two streams of CSR research that have been sketched above so far have evolved in parallel with some, albeit little, cross-referencing. We contend that there is considerable overlap between the discussions on "political" CSR and the debate on CSR and development. First of all, both streams of research address the same actors (i.e. the focus of both research streams primarily lies on MNCs, and their problem solving capacity in areas of limited statehood). While the developmental CSR literature analyses MNCs' ability to generate solutions to development issues, the "political" CSR literature assesses their potential to generate solutions to problems emerging in the context of transnational governance which is often characterized by a regulatory vacuum. Second, both streams address and theorize the same kind of processes in which MNCs take part, namely MSIs. The two streams, however, differ in their focus. Whereas the CSR and development debate revolves around describing the effects of MNCs' CSR activities on developmental issues such as poverty (see, for example, Blowfield, 2012; Blowfield and Dolan, 2014) and critically evaluating these from a social justice perspective, "political" CSR as introduced by Scherer and Palazzo (2007, 2011) is intended as a normative concept. Although the engagement of corporations in new governance modes such as MSIs can be argued to have substantial implications for social development, the "political" CSR debate has so far only implicitly addressed this aspect. The CSR and development literature, in turn, has aimed at establishing links between MSIs and development. Yet, while there is a growing body of research that aims at analysing and assessing the potential and limitations of MSIs (see, for example, Bäckstrand, 2006; Kolk *et al.*,

2008; Lund-Thomsen, 2009; O'Rourke, 2006; Reed *et al.*, 2012; Utting, 2002; Utting and Zammit 2009), the implications of MSIs from a developmental perspective are far from being fully investigated.

By introducing the normative perspective of "political" CSR into the debate on CSR and development, we aim at a more nuanced understanding of the potential of firms to act as development agents. Scherer and Palazzo (2007, 2011) suggest that corporations need to proactively engage in continuous deliberations with civil society (e.g. through participating in MSIs). To normatively evaluate the political engagement of corporations in MSIs, Mena and Palazzo (2012) have introduced the above-mentioned input and output criteria pertaining to the democratic legitimacy of MSIs (Table 13.1). We argue that the criteria suggested by Mena and Palazzos (2012) also help to critically assess the potential of firms in an MSI to serve as development agents. We propose that there are three main reasons as to why the democratic legitimacy of an MSI matters for social development.

First, in multidimensional conceptions of human development, democratic participation in terms of "being able to participate effectively in political choices that govern ones' life" (Nussbaum, 2000, cited in Alkire, 2002, p. 188) is generally perceived as an integral dimension of development. For stakeholders from developing countries, receiving a voice in an MSI that issues regulation regarding matters of public concern consequently represents an end in itself. How inclusively MSIs are set up, as well as which measures are taken to counter power imbalances and how consensually an initiative is oriented will have direct implications for social development in terms of either allowing for, or hindering, parties aggrieved by a developmental issue to have a chance to effectively influence decisions that impact their lives.

Second, from democratically legitimate MSIs, rules and standards with positive development impact can be expected. Integrating voices of stakeholders from developing countries in MSIs is likely to produce policies that enhance social development because affected parties will have had a say in the set-up of the regulation. An MSI operating according to the ideals of deliberative democracy thus serves as a means to the end of social development (Crocker, 2008). However, it needs to be noted that the criteria suggested by Mena and Palazzo (2012) represent a procedural approach in which the outcome and impact of an MSI are not directly accounted for.

Third, we propose that the democratic legitimacy of an MSI indicates to what extent firms still act according to an instrumental rationale. Blowfield and Dolan (2014) conclude that businesses are hindered in serving as development agents due to their instrumental rationale. Scherer and Palazzo (2011) explicitly delineate their conception of "political" CSR by contrasting it with an instrumental understanding of CSR. Thus, if corporations "contain" themselves in civil society discourses, the likelihood of a more substantive contribution to social development increases.

For the reasons outlined above, we argue that social development is one effect of the increased democratic legitimacy of an MSI. The engagement of corporations in democratically legitimate MSIs not only implies a willingness to be held accountable and give due respect for the interest of other participating stakeholders and to devote time and resources but also a conscious decision to engage in an issue in need of development. Therefore, the suggested input and output legitimacy criteria can be argued to also reflect Blowfield and Dolans' (2014) notion of development agents and provide a more solid theoretical basis for assessment. However, legitimacy, as Scharpf (1999, p. 26) notes, "cannot be considered an all-or-nothing proposition". Therefore, MSIs can have various implications for social development, ranging from "enhancing" to "obstructing" social development as polar cases on a continuum. In the following section, we outline the practical application of the proposed "political" CSR lens at the example of a recent MSI in the garment industry in Bangladesh.

13.3 "Political" CSR and social development: the case of Bangladesh

On 24 April 2013, the factory complex Rana Plaza in Savar near Dhaka, the capital city of Bangladesh, collapsed killing over 1,100 textile workers and leaving more than 1,500 injured (Muller, 2014). The disaster at Rana Plaza, however, only constitutes the peak of a series of tragic events that have struck the garment industry of Bangladesh over the preceding years. In November 2012, for example, over 100 workers died in a fire at another factory (Tazreen), as they found themselves trapped behind locked doors (Passariello and Banjo, 2013). According to a report by two international NGOs, since 2005, hundreds of workers have died in Bangladesh in garment factory incidents (CCC and SOMO, 2013).

With 152 million inhabitants, Bangladesh counts as the eighth most populous country in the world (UNDP, 2014). While Bangladesh has experienced considerable GDP growth over the past thirty years and achieved some progress in human development, with about 47 million people living in poverty (World Bank, 2013a), it is still one of the poorest countries in South Asia (World Bank, 2013b). The ready made garment (RMG) industry has become Bangladesh's most important industry sector employing around 3.5 million people, the majority of which are young women (approximately 80%) (World Bank, 2013a). International investors are drawn to Bangladesh due to its low-cost manufacturing opportunities. Wages in Bangladesh are only half of those in India and Vietnam, and only one-fifth of China's (World Bank, 2013b).

In the aftermath of the Tazreen fire, a number of retailers agreed to meet with CSOs in order to debate possibilities of improving working conditions in the industry (Passariello and Banjo, 2013). These discussions, fuelled by the succeeding collapse of Rana Plaza, have ultimately led to two competing safety initiatives. The Accord on Fire and Building Safety in Bangladesh (hereafter "Accord") as well as the Alliance for Bangladesh Worker Safety ("Alliance"). The Accord was officially signed in May 2013 between a number of mainly European, retailers such as H&M, Inditex,

Benetton and Mango and two global as well as four Bangladeshi union federations and with four international labour rights NGOs as witnesses (Accord, 2013). In contrast, the Alliance for Bangladesh Worker Safety, which was also signed in May 2013, mainly by American retailers (e.g. Walmart and Gap Inc), is a sole business initiative (Alliance, 2013).

In the following, we will focus on the Accord instead of the Alliance, since the Accord represents an MSI in which actors from more than one sphere of society cooperate whereas the Alliance represents a purely business led initiative.

13.3.1 Content and governance structure of the Accord

The Accord provides a commitment by the signing parties to implement a comprehensive program over a period of five years to improve health and safety measures in the Bangladeshi RMG sector (Accord, 2013; Gearhart, 2013). Signing retailers and brands of the Accord are obliged to indicate all factories in Bangladesh from which they source, conduct independent inspections in these factories, publicly report the results and to implement corrective measures, if necessary. The signatories further commit to funding the program, with contributions ranging up to US$500,000 per company, per year, for the period of five years. The Accord also foresees special protection for factory workers. If a factory needs to close in order to conduct renovations, employment for the workers of that given factory needs to be ensured for a period of up to six months. In case workers lose their jobs due to loss of orders, signing companies need to "make reasonable efforts" to ensure that those workers receive employment at a safe factory. Moreover, the Accord requires that workers can refuse working if they believe that a factory is unsafe, without loss of pay. Trade unions are to be actively involved in factory trainings.

The Accord has a two-tier governance structure (Accord, 2013). A Steering Committee (SC) serves as the executive organ of the Accord. It is, for example, responsible for selecting safety inspectors and overseeing the budget of the Accord. The SC consists of three representatives from the trade unions and three signatory companies, as well as a neutral chairperson from the ILO. Moreover, the Accord has an Advisory Board (AB) which is supposed to enable deliberations among a wider range of participating parties and which is supposed to provide input to the SC. A distinctive feature of the Accord is that it is legally binding. The Accord explicitly outlines a dispute resolution process which is enforceable in the courts of the home countries of the respective signatory brands and retailers.

13.3.2 Input legitimacy of the Accord

The Accord was initiated by international non-governmental organizations but ultimately signed by 150 international companies and retailers, two global as well as numerous local Bangladeshi unions. The competing Alliance was only signed by 26 apparel companies and retailers. Thus, particularly in contrast to the alternative initiative, the Accord exhibits greater inclusion. Yet, in terms of inclusion, two issues remain. On the one hand, factory owners who have the primary obligation to improve the safety conditions in their factories, do not form part of the Accords' SC. On the other hand, representation of women's interests can be held in question as, although women form the lion's share of the work force in the RMG sector, so far they are vastly underrepresented in Bangladeshi unions (ILO, 2009). Regarding the criterion of procedural fairness, the Accord performs well. The SC consists in equal numbers of representatives from the corporate side and from the side of trade unions. Power imbalances are further neutralized through the dispute resolution process specified in the Accord. All participating stakeholders can thus be expected to have a valid voice in decision-making processes. The degree of consensual orientation is more difficult to assess. The provisions of the Accord mainly build on an earlier Memorandum of Understanding (MoU), which was negotiated between international NGOs and two retailers. In the aftermath of the Rana Plaza disaster, the MoU was adapted to take into account suggestions for alterations particularly from the company side (CCC, 2013). While the modifications of the Accord could be interpreted as some sort of bargaining by the retailers, the fact that the Accord goes beyond the previous practice of voluntary self-regulation reflects that a compromise has been reached beyond the smallest common denominator. Furthermore, as the Accord requires a considerable financial commitment from the signing corporations, through, for example, the co-funding of corrective safety measures in factories in Bangladesh, and given that the Accord is legally binding, some form of arguing and reason giving must have taken place among the parties involved. In terms of transparency, the Accord improves on previous standards. Safety inspectors will be appointed by the SC and must not be currently employed by companies. Moreover, in order to put an end to multiple inspections, all reports of factory inspections will be publicly reported and industry compliance will be monitored. These measures go much further than those installed by the competing Alliance. In the latter case, inspections will not necessarily be independent and the companies retain control over inspection results. All in all, the input legitimacy of the Accord can be considered as being higher than that of the Alliance. Assessing the input legitimacy in absolute terms is more difficult. Yet, as the Accord contains a number of distinctive features in that it provides, for example, that the parties' commitments are legally enforceable and transparency requirements go much further than in past agreements, one may argue that the Accord altogether performs well in terms of input legitimacy.

13.3.3 Output legitimacy of the Accord

The Accord is rolling out an inspection program to around 1,700 supplier factories in the upcoming months. In these factories, approximately 2.1 million workers are employed (Accord, 2014). Considering the total amount of workers (3.5 million), this constitutes a considerable share. With 150 signatories on the part of business including many large retailers—such as H&M (the largest buyer from Bangladesh), Inditex (the world's largest fashion retailer) and Carrefour and Tesco (two of the world's three largest retailers) (ILRF, 2013)—coverage of the Accord regarding participation from the business side can be regarded as being high. However, the focus of the inspections through the Accord, lies on Tier 1 and 2 factories; that is, on those factories which form the primary and long-term suppliers of the signatory brands. While these factories are certainly in need of inspection, it can be held in doubt whether this approach adequately captures and covers the common practice of subcontracting that has become established in the Bangladeshi RMG sector (Labowitz and Baumann-Pauly, 2014). The efficacy of the Accord is more difficult to assess as it is still in its initial phase. Given the fact that the Accord involves local stakeholders and strengthens the role of unions within factories, the Accord may trigger further processes of social development. Moreover, as the Accord integrates with the governmental efforts to improve conditions in the RMG sector, and as it is set up as a legally enforceable contract, it is an interesting hybrid governance mechanism between soft and hard law. The fact that the Accord resides on the "harder" side of the soft–hard law continuum seems to be more "fit to the issue" of changing the current fatal long-standing practices in the Bangladeshi RMG sector. Enforcement of the Accord can be expected to be high for two reasons (ILRF, 2013). First, workers' representatives are part of the SC of the Accord. They have a strong interest in enforcing the companies' commitments. Moreover, as four international NGOs signed as witnesses to the Accord, one may expect that they will closely monitor the enforcement of the Accords' provisions. Second, the Accord constitutes a legally binding contract providing a dispute resolution process and arbitration in courts of a company's home country. Therefore, it is likely that companies will indeed be held accountable for their promise to improve safety in the factories from which they source. Unlike with the Alliance, from which parties can drop out of at any time, the Accord stipulates the participation of signing companies for a period of five years (ILRF, 2013). Therefore, the output legitimacy of the Accord can altogether be assessed as being higher than that of the Alliance. In absolute terms, as of today, the overall output of the Accord is more difficult to determine. Whether the Accords' signatories actually fulfil their obligations remains to be seen.

13.3.4 Implications of the Accord for social development in Bangladesh

Our analysis of the input and output legitimacy of the Accord implies that all in all, despite the mentioned issues in terms of inclusion and coverage, the Accord performs well in both dimensions and can thus be evaluated as having relatively high democratic legitimacy. We therefore conjecture that the Accord will have a positive impact on social development. In our view, there are two main implications of the Accord for social development in Bangladesh.

First, the Accord improves the democratic participation of workers in matters affecting their lives which can in and of itself be regarded as social development. The fact that local unions have been involved in the Accord has not only led to the interests of workers being represented in the Accord but also enhanced the status of unions in Bangladesh. The number of registered unions has grown from three in 2012 to more than 120 today (Muller, 2014). The strengthening of the role of unions in the aftermath of Rana Plaza is certainly also related to a new labour law adopted by the Bangladeshi government. The inclusion of numerous local unions in the Accord, however, means that they are now also considered as relevant negotiating parties, which further enhances their status. The strengthened role of unions has already led to an increase in the minimum wage in Bangladesh in December 2013 (BBC, 2013) and in the long run may lead to further improvements in social development in terms of workers' rights and wages.

Second, the discursive interaction of relevant stakeholders in a democratically legitimate MSI is likely to yield standards and policies enhancing social development. The Accord aims at new standards in terms of safety, transparency and enforcement. If the corporations involved in the Accord fulfil their obligations, the envisioned higher standards in the workplace will improve the quality of life of workers. Said safety improvements are also needed to restore the attractiveness of the Bangladeshi RMG sector in order to preserve jobs in the industry.

13.4 Reflections on development-oriented CSR

Despite the rather positive picture that our analysis so far has drawn of the Accord, we want to stress that many challenges remain. There are a number of issues that call into question whether the corporations that have signed the Accord can be considered as agents of social development.

First of all, the Accord appears to be a reactive instead of a proactive initiative. Tragically, only after the collapse of Rana Plaza were international retailers and brands willing to sign the Accord for improvements in the industry. While the Accord now seems promising, the example of the Bangladeshi RMG sector highlights the ambivalent role of businesses in development. The Accord was initiated and propagated by international NGOs and global unions. Scherer and Palazzo (2007, 2011), in their concept of political CSR, explicitly highlight that corporations are supposed to proactively engage in dialogues with civil society. For Scherer and Palazzo (2007, 2011) a proactive engagement of corporations in democratic will formation represents a moral obligation and an important aspect of setting political CSR apart from an instrumental understanding of CSR. The emergence of the Accord could thus just as well be read as "the same old story" of how businesses have tried to avoid responsibility.

Second, it remains questionable whether signing the Accord means that corporations have fully overcome the instrumental rationale that Scherer and Palazzo (2011) associate with "old" CSR. Besides the Accord, a remedy fund has been installed by the ILO and NGOs to compensate victims of the Rana Plaza disaster. Yet, many of the retailers which demonstrably produced at Rana Plaza and also signed the Accord are not willing to contribute to this fund (BBC, 2014). Thus, it remains questionable whether those corporations are now actually operating "with an enlarged understanding of responsibility" (Scherer and Palazzo, 2011, p. 918) or whether their engagement represents mere window-dressing. This also shows that the suggested input and output legitimacy criteria only helps to evaluate the possibility of corporations to serve as development agents through their particular role as participants in MSIs. It does not provide insight into the overall authenticity and coherence of corporations in their role as development agents.

Third, whether the Accord actually contributes to developing the RMG sector of Bangladesh remains to be seen, as the initiative still has to deliver on its promise and implement its program. The legally binding element of the Accord reflects a transition from political corporate social responsibility to corporate legal responsibility. Yet, whether and to what extent workers will ultimately be able to enforce their claims against international retailers and brands remains to be seen. Furthermore, it is uncertain whether the Accord will have an adverse impact on other CSR activities and community programs of the signatory corporations; that is, whether the Accord will lead to a crowding out of other engagements.

Finally, due to the limited scope of the Accord, the development orientation of the signing companies can be called into question. The Accord is only geared towards the RMG sector in Bangladesh; neither other sectors nor other countries with similar safety issues such as Pakistan, India or Cambodia will profit from the negotiated efforts of corporations. Time will tell whether the Accord companies will proactively extend their engagement to other countries and sectors.

Nonetheless, we contend that the Accord, due to its comparatively high democratic legitimacy and due to the fact that it represents a legally binding contract, outperforms previous and simultaneous initiatives (e.g. the Alliance). Despite its existing weaknesses, we argue that the Accord represents a progress in terms of the discursive interaction between MNCs and relevant stakeholders and that it has the potential to substantively improve the safety of workers in the Bangladeshi RMG sector. The concept of "political" CSR with the legitimacy criteria of Mena and Palazzo (2012) provides, in our view, a solid theoretical basis and normative framework for how corporations can and should engage themselves in developing countries. Due to its high democratic legitimacy, the Accord, in our view, can be considered as an example of development-oriented CSR.

13.5 Conclusion

This chapter examined the political role of businesses in developing countries. We have argued for the value of integrating two streams of CSR research, the debate on CSR and development and research on "political" CSR, since corporations operating in the weak regulatory environment of developing countries often exert regulatory functions (e.g. through their engagement in MSIs). Our analysis of the Accord on Fire and Building Safety in Bangladesh has indicated that this MSI performs relatively well both in terms of input and output legitimacy and can thus be judged to be democratically legitimate. As a democratically legitimate MSI, the Accord has the chance to enhance social development in Bangladesh. However, the case of the Bangladeshi RMG sector after all highlights the ambivalent role of business in development. It took the deaths of those 1,100 workers before major retailers and brands were finally willing to agree on a program for safety improvements in the industry. The Bangladesh case study also emphasizes that strong CSOs are needed to embed corporations in public deliberations. While the Accord program only applies to Bangladesh, there is certainly an urgent need for businesses to proactively enter into CSO discourses in order to also enhance social development in other countries such as Pakistan, Cambodia or India which have all experienced similar fatal factory disasters.

Our analysis of the implications of firms' political engagement in MSIs is based on the input and output dimensions, with only indirect reference to the outcome and impact dimension. This deficiency needs to be remedied by future research. Future research thus needs to empirically validate the relation between democratic legitimacy of MSIs and social development with outcome and impact variables. Future research is also needed to address the "hardening" of soft law, as in the case of the Accord, and the emergence of corporate "legal" responsibility as a new accountability regime for politically engaged corporations. Finally, the controversy which sparked around the concept of "political" CSR highlights that further research is needed to deal with the normative question concerning the scope and content of corporate responsibility in developing countries.

Bibliography

Abbott, K.W., & Snidal, D. (2000). Hard and soft law in international governance. *International Organization*, 54(3), 421-456.

Accord (Accord on Fire and Building Safety in Bangladesh) (2013). Accord on fire and building safety in Bangladesh. Retrieved from http://www.bangladeshaccord.org/wp-content/uploads/2013/10/the_accord.pdf.

Accord (Accord on Fire and Building Safety in Bangladesh) (2014). Public disclosure report 1. Retrieved from http://www.bangladeshaccord.org/wp-content/uploads/Accord-Public-Disclosure-Report-1-April-2014.pdf.

Alkire, S. (2002). Dimensions of human development. *World development*, 30(2), 181-205.

Alliance (Alliance for Bangladesh Worker Safety) (2013). About the Alliance for Bangladesh worker safety. Retrieved from http://www.bangladeshworkersafety.org/about.

Bäckstrand, K. (2006). Multi-stakeholder partnerships for sustainable development: rethinking legitimacy, accountability and effectiveness, *European Environment*, 16(5), 290-306.

Barkemeyer, R. (2009). Beyond compliance—below expectations? CSR in the context of international development. *Business Ethics: A European Review*, 18(3), 273-289.

Barkemeyer, R., Holt, D., Preuss, L., & Tsang, S. (2011). What happened to the development in sustainable development? Business guidelines two decades after Brundtland. *Sustainable Development*, doi:10.1002/sd.521.

Baumann-Pauly, D., & Scherer, A.G. (2013). The organizational implementation of corporate citizenship: an assessment tool and its application at UN Global Compact participants. *Journal of Business Ethics*, 117(1), 1-17.

BBC (British Broadcasting Corporation) (2013). Bangladesh seeks 77% rise in wage for garment workers. Retrieved from http://www.bbc.com/news/business-24800279.

BBC (British Broadcasting Corporation) (2014). Survivors of Rana Plaza collapse wait for compensation. Retrieved from http://www.bbc.com/news/world-south-asia-27141385.

Blowfield, M. (2012). Business and development: making sense of business as a development agent. *Corporate Governance*, 12(4), 414-426.

Blowfield, M., & Dolan, C.S. (2014). Business as a development agent: evidence of possibility and improbability. *Third World Quarterly*, 35(1), 22-42.

Blowfield, M., & Frynas, J.G. (2005). Setting new agendas: critical perspectives on corporate social responsibility in the developing world. *International Affairs*, 81(3), 499-513.

Brainard, L. (2006). *Transforming the Development Landscape. The Role of the Private Sector*, Washington, DC: Brookings Institution Press.

Carroll, A.B. (2008). A history of corporate social responsibility: concepts and practices. In A. Crane, A. McWilliams, D. Matten, J. Moon & D.S. Siegel (Eds.), *The Oxford Handbook of Corporate Social Responsibility* (pp. 19-46). Oxford, New York: Oxford University Press.

CCC (Clean Clothes Campaign) (2013). The History behind the Bangladesh Fire and Safety Accord. Retrieved from http://www.cleanclothes.org/resources/background/history-bangladesh-safety-accord/view.

CCC & SOMO (2013). Fatal Fashion. Analysis of recent factory fires in Pakistan and Bangladesh: a call to protect and respect garment workers' lives. Retrieved from http://www.cleanclothes.org/resources/publications/fatal-fashion.pdf.

Crocker, D.A. (2008). Ethics of global development. Agency, capability, and deliberative democracy. Cambridge, UK: Cambridge University Press.

Frynas, J.G. (2005). The false developmental promise of corporate social responsibility: evidence from multinational oil companies. *International Affairs*, 81(3), 581-598.

Garriga, E., & Melé, D. (2004). Corporate social responsibility theories: mapping the territory. *Journal of Business Ethics*, 53(1/2), 51-71.

Gearhart, J. (Industry All Global Union) (2013). Executive Summary of the Accord on Fire and Building Safety in Bangladesh. Retrieved from http://www.industriall-union.org/sites/default/files/uploads/documents/executive_summary_accord_1.pdf.

Gilbert, D.U., & Rasche, A. (2008). Opportunities and problems of standardized ethics initiatives—a stakeholder theory perspective. *Journal of Business Ethics*, 82(3), 755-773.

Habermas, J. (1996). *Between Facts and Norms. Contributions to a Discourse Theory of Law and Democracy*. Cambridge, MA: MIT Press.

Habermas, J. (1998). *The Inclusion of the Other. Studies in Political Theory*. Cambridge, MA: MIT Press).

Habermas, J. (1999). Introduction. *Ratio Juris*, 12(4), 329-335.

Habermas, J. (2001). *The Postnational Constellation. Political Essays*. Cambridge, MA: MIT Press).

ILO (International Labour Organization) (2009). Women's participation in trade unions in Bangladesh: Status, barriers and overcoming strategies. Retrieved from http://www.ilo.org/wcmsp5/groups/public/@asia/@ro-bangkok/@ilo-dhaka/documents/publication/wcms_125374.pdf.

ILRF (International Labour Rights Forum) (2013). Comparison: the Accord on fire and building safety in Bangladesh and the Gap/Walmart scheme. Retrieved from http://www.laborrights.org/sites/default/files/docs/Matrix%20Comparison%20of%20Accord%20and%20Walmart-Gap%20Plan_0.pdf.

Jenkins, R. (2005). Globalization, corporate social responsibility and poverty. *International Affairs*, 81(3), 525-540.

Jeppesen, S., & Lund-Thomsen, P. (2010). Special issue on new perspectives on business, development, and society research. *Journal of Business Ethics*, 93(S2), 139-142.

Kolk, A., & Van den Buuse, D. (2012). In search of viable business models for development: sustainable energy in developing countries. *Corporate Governance*, 12(4), 551-567.

Kolk, A., & Van Tulder, R. (2006). Poverty alleviation as business strategy? Evaluating commitments of front-runner multinational corporations. *World Development*, 34(5), 789-801.

Kolk, A., & Van Tulder, R. (2010). International business, corporate social responsibility and sustainable development. *International Business Review*, 19(2), 119-125.

Kolk, A., van Tulder, R., & Kostwinder, E. (2008). Business and partnerships for development. *European Management Journal*, 26(4), 262-273.

Labowitz, S., & Baumann-Pauly, D. (2014). Business as Usual is Not an Option. Retrieved from http://www.stern.nyu.edu/sites/default/files/assets/documents/con_047408.pdf.

Lenssen, J.J., & Van Wassenhove, L.N. (2012). A new era of development: the changing role and responsibility of business in developing countries. *Corporate Governance*, 12(4), 403-413.

Lund-Thomsen, P. (2005). Corporate accountability in South Africa: the role of community mobilizing in environmental governance. *International Affairs*, 81(3), 619-633.

Lund-Thomsen, P. (2009). Assessing the impact of public–private partnerships in the global south: the case of the Kasur Tanneries pollution control project. *Journal of Business Ethics*, 90(S1), 57-78.

Marques. J.C., & Utting, P. (2010). Introduction: Understanding business power and public policy in a development context. In J.C. Marques and P. Utting (Eds.), *Business, Politics and Public Policy. Implications for inclusive Development* (pp. 1-29). Basingstoke, UK/New York, NY: Palgrave-Macmillan.

Matten, D., & Crane, A. (2005). Corporate citizenship: toward an extended theoretical conceptualization. *Academy of Management Review*, 30(1), 166-179.

Mena, S., & Palazzo, G. (2012). Input and output legitimacy of multi-stakeholder initiatives. *Business Ethics Quarterly*, 22(3), 527-556.

Merino, A., & Valor, C. (2011). The potential of corporate social responsibility to eradicate poverty: an ongoing debate. *Development in Practice*, 21(2), 157-167.

Muller, N. (Deutsche Welle) (2014). Small signs of progress in Bangladesh's textile sector. Retrieved from http://www.dw.de/small-signs-of-progress-in-bangladeshs-textile-sector/a-17512173.

Newell, P., & Frynas, J.G. (2007). Beyond CSR? Business, poverty and social justice: an introduction. *Third World Quarterly*, 28(4), 669-681.

Nussbaum, M.C. (2000). Women and human development: The capabilities approach. Cambridge, UK: Cambridge University Press.

O'Rourke, D. (2006). Multi-stakeholder regulation: privatizing or socializing global labor standards? *World Development*, 34(5), 899-918.

Palazzo, G., & Scherer, A.G. (2006). Corporate legitimacy as deliberation: a communicative framework. *Journal of Business Ethics*, 66(1), 71-88.

Passariello, C., & Banjo, S. (2013, September 11). Retailers Meet to Set Reparations for Bangladesh Factory Deaths. *Wall Street Journal*. Retrieved from http://online.wsj.com/news/articles/SB10001424127887323864604579069510817914556.

Pieterse, J.N. (2010). *Development Theory*. London: Sage.

Prahalad, C.K., & Hart, S.L. (2002). The fortune at the bottom of the pyramid. *Strategy and Business*, 26(1), 2-14.

Reed, A.M., & Reed, D. (2009). Partnerships for development: four models of business involvement. *Journal of Business Ethics*, 90(S1), 3-37.

Reed A.M., Reed, D., & Utting, P. (Eds.). (2012). *Business Regulation and Non-State Actors: Whose Standards? Whose Development?* London: Routledge.

Risse, T. (1999). International norms and domestic change: arguing and communicative behavior in the human rights area. *Politics & Society*, 27(4), 529-559.

Risse, T. (2011). Governance in areas of limited statehood: introduction and overview. In T. Risse (Ed.), *Governance Without a State? Policies and Politics in Areas of Limited Statehood* (pp. 1-35). New York: Columbia University Press.

Scharpf, F.W. (1997). Economic integration, democracy and the welfare state. *Journal of European Public Policy*, 4(1), 18-36.

Scharpf, F.W. (1999). *Governing in Europe. Effective and Democratic?* Oxford, New York: Oxford University Press.

Scherer, A.G., & Palazzo, G. (2007). Toward a political conception of corporate responsibility: business and society seen from a Habermasian perspective. *Academy of Management Review*, 32(4), 1096-1120.

Scherer, A.G., & Palazzo, G. (2011). The new political role of business in a globalized world: a review of a new perspective on CSR and its implications for the firm, governance, and democracy. *Journal of Management Studies*, 48(4), 899-931.

Scherer, A.G., Palazzo, G., & Baumann, D. (2006). Global rules and private actors: toward a new role of the transnational corporation in global governance. *Business Ethics Quarterly*, 16(4), 505-532.

Sumner, A., & Tribe, M.A. (2008). *International Development Studies. Theories and Methods in Research and Practice*. London, Thousand Oaks, CA: Sage.

UNCTAD (United Nations Conference on Trade and Investment) (2013). World Investment Report 2013. Retrieved from http://unctad.org/42D7D24E-FBCA-41A6-9039-47A2B-D8EF8E7/FinalDownload/DownloadId-19AECC1D1A6BBCF0487642BBE702CA1A/42D7D24E-FBCA-41A6-9039-47A2BD8EF8E7/en/publicationslibrary/wir2013_en.pdf.

UNDP (United Nations Development Programme) (2014). UNDP in Bangladesh. Retrieved from http://www.bd.undp.org/content/bangladesh/en/home/countryinfo.

United Nations (2002). Resolution Adopted by the General Assembly. Implementation of the outcome of the World Summit for Social Development and of the twenty-fourth special session of the General Assembly. Retrieved from http://www.un.org/ga/search/view_doc.asp?symbol=A/RES/56/177.

United Nations (2014). Millennium development goals. Retrieved from http://www.un.org/millenniumgoals.

Utting, P. (2002). Regulating business via multistakeholder initiatives: a preliminary assessment. In UNRISD (Ed.), *Voluntary Approaches to Corporate Responsibility: Readings and a Resource Guide* (pp. 61-130). UN Non-Governmental Liaison Service.

Utting, P. (2012). Introduction: multistakeholder regulation from a development perspective. In A.M. Reed, D. Reed & P. Utting (Eds.), *Business Regulation and Non-State Actors: Whose Standards? Whose Development?* (pp. 1-18). London: Routledge.

Utting, P., & Zammit, A. (2009). United Nations-business partnerships: good intentions and contradictory agendas. *Journal of Business Ethics*, 90(S1), 39-56.

Utting, P., Marques, J.C. (Eds.). (2009). *Corporate Social Responsibility and Regulatory Governance*. Basingstoke: Palgrave Macmillan.

Van Huijstee, M.M., Francken, M., & Leroy, P. (2007). Partnerships for sustainable development: a review of current literature. *Environmental Sciences*, 4(2), 75-89.

Vogel, D. (2008). Private global business regulation. *Annual Review of Political Science*, 11(1), 261-282.

About the editors

Dima Jamali is Professor in the Olayan School of Business (OSB), American University of Beirut (AUB) and currently serving as the Kamal Shair Endowed Chair in Responsible Leadership. She holds a PhD in Social Policy and Administration, from the University of Kent at Canterbury, UK. Her research/teaching revolve primarily around corporate social responsibility (CSR). She is the author/editor of three books (*CSR in the Middle East; Social Entrepreneurship in the Middle East;* and *CSR in Developing Countries: A Development Oriented Approach*) and over 50 international publications focusing on different aspects of CSR in developing countries, all appearing in highly reputable journals. Dr Jamali is winner of Abdul Hameed Shoman Award for Best Young Arab Researcher for the year 2011 and a member of the Eisenhower Fellows, a global network of leading professionals committed to collaborate for a more prosperous, just and peaceful world.

Charlotte M. Karam is an Assistant Professor of Organizational Behavior at the Olayan School of Business, American University of Beirut (AUB), Lebanon. She holds a PhD in Applied Social Psychology with a focus on organizations from the University of Windsor, Canada. Her research broadly examines Responsible Engagement at the intersection between Gender, Corporate Responsibility and Employee Extra-Role Behaviour within developing and emerging economies. Most of her research is examined within a multi-level contextual framework which considers factors relating to societal culture, socio-economic development, as well as political stability. Her work has been published in *Business & Society, Asia-Pacific Journal of Management, Business Ethics Quarterly, Career Development International, International Journal of Human Resource Management*, and *Journal of International Management*, among others. Charlotte's teaching and research has received local and international recognition through excellence awards and research grants. Charlotte is an activist and serves on the board of the Arab Foundation for Freedoms and Equality.

Michael "Mick" Blowfield FRSA is Professor of Corporate Responsibility at the University of Wolverhampton (UK) as well as holding fellowships at the University of Oxford and London Business School. His work on development-oriented CSR dates back to his time with companies, unions and government agencies during the 1980s and 1990s when he carried out work on labour conditions in export-oriented factories, oil palm cultivation, forestry, agriculture and health. He has worked in over 30 countries including living for long spells in Indonesia. He has written more than 20 academic articles on the business–development relationship, and as well as books on business and sustainability and the relationship between business and global crises, is co-author of *Corporate Responsibility* (OUP) which is now in its third edition.

About the contributors

Ismail Adelopo is an Associate Professor in Accounting and Finance, University of the West of England. His research interests cover corporate social responsibility and governance. He is a chartered certified accountant with a doctorate in Accounting and Finance.

Chiara Amini is Lecturer in Economics at London Metropolitan University. She has completed a PhD in Economics at University College London in 2013. Her research currently focuses on corporate social responsibility, FDI and the economics of education in low- and middle-income countries. Chiara has also worked as research consultant for the European Bank of Reconstruction and Development, the Department for International Development and the World Bank.

Ralf Barkemeyer is Associate Professor of Corporate Social Responsibility at Kedge Business School, Bordeaux, France.

Ataur Belal is a reader [Associate Professor] and Head of Accounting Department at the Aston Business School, Aston University, Birmingham, UK. Currently he is joint editor of *Advances in Environmental Accounting and Management* and an Associate Editor of *Accounting Forum*. Ataur obtained his PhD from the University of Sheffield, UK.

Daniela Bolzani holds a PhD in General Management and is a Postdoctoral Fellow at the Department of Management, University of Bologna. Her research interests are in entrepreneurial processes, in particular in the context of immigrant, international and high-tech entrepreneurship.

Silvia Dal Bianco (BSc Bocconi; MSc Oxford; PhD Pavia) has extensively researched in the fields of development economics and growth empirics. She has published in national and international journals, such as *La Rivista Italiana degli Economisti* and *Economic Systems*. Her current research is focused on CSR and development as well as development accounting.

Vimala Dejvongsa is a community relations and development practitioner. She is currently a Senior Social Advisor for Insitu Development Consulting, a small consulting firm specializing in the areas of social performance, development and mining. Vimala has worked in the mining and international development sectors for over a decade, predominately in South East Asia.

Frank Figge is Professor of Sustainable Development and Corporate Social Responsibility at Kedge Business School, Marseille, France.

Dirk Ulrich Gilbert is a professor of business ethics at the University of Hamburg in Germany. He received his PhD from Johann Wolfgang Goethe-University in Frankfurt, Germany. His research focuses on trust in business networks, international business ethics, deliberative democracy, and strategy process management.

Kristin Huber is pursuing a PhD in Business Ethics at the University of Hamburg, Germany. Her research interests include deliberative democracy, the role of business in global governance, political corporate social responsibility, corporate social responsibility and the role of business in developing countries.

Sara Husain is a public health specialist with an interest in developing sustainable models for health systems improvements within the local public healthcare system and effective translation of scientific research to influence policy and decision-making.

Deanna Kemp is an Associate Professor at the Centre for Social Responsibility in Mining (CSRM) at the University of Queensland where she leads an international program of research focused on the social dimensions of mining. Deanna engages with industry, government, civil society groups and mine-affected communities through applied research, advisory work and education.

David Littlewood is a lecturer at Henley Business School, the University of Reading. David's research interests include CSR and social entrepreneurship, with an emphasis on the developing world and particularly sub-Saharan Africa. David is a frequent speaker at international conferences and has published in international peer-reviewed journals, as well as contributing to various books.

Peter Lund-Thomsen is Visiting Full Professor at Nottingham Business School, Nottingham Trent University, and Associate Professor at the Copenhagen Business School in Denmark. His research focuses on the linkages between global value chains, industrial upgrading, and corporate social and environmental responsibility (CSR) in developing countries.

Selenia Marabello, anthropologist, MSc Anthropology and Development at London School of Economics and Political Science, PhD in International Cooperation and Sustainable Development Policies at the University of Bologna. She is currently enrolled as Post-Doc Researcher in Cultural Anthropology at the University of Bologna. Her main research interests are migration and development, Ghanaian migration to Italy, discrimination, and medical anthropology.

John Owen is an Honorary Senior Fellow at the Centre for Social Responsibility in Mining, the University of Queensland. His current work focuses on social knowledge and professional integration in the resources sector. Recent research projects have seen this interest applied to the planning, implementation and evaluation of involuntary resettlement programs throughout the Asia Pacific region.

Lutz Preuss is Reader in Corporate Social Responsibility at the School of Management of Royal Holloway University of London, United Kingdom.

Lukman Raimi holds BSc (Hons) in Economics, Obafemi Awolowo University, Nigeria; MSc in Economics, University of Lagos; MSc in Industrial Relations & Personnel Management,

University of Lagos and is presently PhD Finalist in entrepreneurship & CSR at De Montfort University. His teaching and research interests include: entrepreneurship, development economics, corporate governance and corporate social responsibility.

Jacobo Ramirez holds a doctorate in Business Administration at Newcastle upon Tyne University. He is a multidisciplinary researcher with a career that combines the humanities with the social sciences and business. His main areas of focus are business development in emerging markets, human resource management, small and medium-sized enterprises, institutions and social cohesion.

Jo-Anna Russon completed her PhD at Queen's University Management School, Queen's University Belfast in December, 2014. Her PhD research critically examines the activities of UK multinational companies in sub-Saharan Africa, in the context of poverty alleviation and the UK government's agenda on working with the UK private sector in the delivery of overseas aid.

Asli Tuncay-Celikel completed her PhD at Işık University, Department of Management and post-doc at University of Sussex, SPRU. She is now an Assistant Professor at Işık University. Her main area of focus is innovation management. Specifically, her research interests are R&D management, emerging markets and strategies of MNCs.

Bilge Uyan-Atay completed her PhD at the University of Bath, School of Management. She is now a researcher, lecturer and consultant. Her research focuses on the overall relationship between business and society. Stakeholder management, corporate social responsibility, corporate philanthropy, corporate community involvement, and behavioural theory of the firm all fall within her research interest.

Duane Windsor, PhD, is Lynette S. Autrey Professor of Management in the Jones Graduate School of Business, Rice University. His work focuses on CSR and stakeholder theory. His articles appear in *Business & Society, Business Ethics Quarterly, Journal of Business Ethics, Journal of Business Research*, and *Journal of Management Studies*.

Nonita T. Yap is Professor at the School of Environmental Design and Rural Development, University of Guelph Ontario Canada. She holds a PhD in chemistry and a Master's degree in Environmental Studies. She has worked in nearly twenty developing countries on waste management, cleaner production and environmental impact assessment.

Kemi Yekini is a Senior Lecturer in Accounting and Finance, De Montfort University, Leicester UK. She is an Associate Chartered Accountant and an Association Certified Fraud Examiner (ACFE). Her research interests include corporate disclosure practices, CSR communication, corporate governance and fraud examination.

Index